# Early Greek Philosophies of Nature

Also available from Bloomsbury

*Anaximander: A Re-Assessment,* by Andrew Gregory
*The Presocratics and the Supernatural,* by Andrew Gregory
*Ancient Greek Cosmogony,* by Andrew Gregory
*Plato's Philosophy of Science,* by Andrew Gregory

# Early Greek Philosophies of Nature

Andrew Gregory

BLOOMSBURY ACADEMIC
LONDON • NEW YORK • OXFORD • NEW DELHI • SYDNEY

BLOOMSBURY ACADEMIC
Bloomsbury Publishing Plc
50 Bedford Square, London, WC1B 3DP, UK
1385 Broadway, New York, NY 10018, USA
29 Earlsfort Terrace, Dublin 2, Ireland

BLOOMSBURY, BLOOMSBURY ACADEMIC and the Diana logo are trademarks
of Bloomsbury Publishing Plc

First published in Great Britain 2020
This paperback edition published in 2022

Copyright © Andrew Gregory, 2020

Andrew Gregory has asserted his right under the Copyright, Designs and
Patents Act, 1988, to be identified as Author of this work.

Cover design: Terry Woodley
Cover image © Robert Sharen

All rights reserved. No part of this publication may be reproduced or transmitted in any form or by any
means, electronic or mechanical, including photocopying, recording,
or any information storage or retrieval system, without prior permission in writing
from the publishers.

Bloomsbury Publishing Plc does not have any control over, or responsibility for, any third-party websites
referred to or in this book. All internet addresses given in this
book were correct at the time of going to press. The author and publisher regret
any inconvenience caused if addresses have changed or sites have ceased to
exist, but can accept no responsibility for any such changes.

A catalogue record for this book is available from the British Library.

Library of Congress Cataloging-in-Publication Data

Names: Gregory, Andrew, 1960– author.
Title: Early Greek philosophies of nature / by Andrew Gregory.
Description: London ; New York : Bloomsbury Academic, 2021. | Includes bibliographical references and
index. | Summary: "This book examines the philosophies of nature of the early Greek thinkers and
argues that a significant and thoroughgoing shift is required in our understanding of them. In contrast
with the natural world of the earliest Greek literature, often the result of arbitrary divine causation, in the
work of early Ionian philosophers we see the idea of a cosmos: ordered worlds where there is complete
regularity. How was this order generated and maintained and what underpinned those regularities?
What analogies or models were used for the order of the cosmos? What did they think about causation
and explanatory structure? How did they frame natural laws? Andrew Gregory draws on recent work on
mechanistic philosophy and its history, on the historiography of the relation of science to art, religion and
magic, and on the fragments and doxography of the early Greek thinkers to argue that there has been a
tendency to overestimate the extent to which these early Greek philosophies of nature can be described
as 'mechanistic'. We have underestimated how far they were committed to other modes of explanation
and ontologies, and we have underestimated, underappreciated and indeed underexplored how
plausible and good these philosophies would have been in context"– Provided by publisher.
Identifiers: LCCN 2020022270 (print) | LCCN 2020022271 (ebook) | ISBN 9781350080973 (hb) |
ISBN 9781350080980 (ePDF) | ISBN 9781350080997 (ebook)
Subjects: LCSH: Philosophy, Ancient. | Philosophy of nature.
Classification: LCC B185 .G74 2021  (print) | LCC B185  (ebook) | DDC 113.0938—dc23
LC record available at https://lccn.loc.gov/2020022270
LC ebook record available at https://lccn.loc.gov/2020022271.

| ISBN: | HB: | 978-1-3500-8097-3 |
|---|---|---|
| | PB: | 978-1-3501-9491-5 |
| | ePDF: | 978-1-3500-8098-0 |
| | eBook: | 978-1-3500-8099-7 |

Typeset by RefineCatch Limited, Bungay, Suffolk

To find out more about our authors and books visit www.bloomsbury.com
and sign up for our Newsletters

*For Sheelagh, with love.*

# Contents

|   |   |   |
|---|---|---|
|   | Introduction | 1 |
| 1 | Methodological Issues | 3 |
| 2 | Order in Homer and Hesiod | 25 |
| 3 | Early Ideas on Knowledge and Enquiry | 45 |
| 4 | Anaximander and the *Kubernan* Tradition | 69 |
| 5 | New Explanations, New Philosophies of Nature | 93 |
| 6 | Anaximenes and the *Kratein* Tradition | 113 |
| 7 | Leucippus and Democritus | 137 |
| 8 | The Hippocratic Authors | 161 |
|   | Conclusion | 185 |
| Notes | | 191 |
| Bibliography | | 221 |
| Index | | 237 |

# Introduction

This book is about early Greek conceptions of nature and in particular how the early Greeks thought about order, both in terms of how that order came about and how that order was maintained. What analogies or models were used for the order of the cosmos? What analogies or models were used for natural regularities and what modalities could they generate for phenomena? What did they think about causation and explanatory structure? Is it proper to talk of natural laws at this stage, and if so, how were they framed? The title is deliberately phrased in two senses. First, I believe 'Early Greek' to be better than the currently contentious and possibly misleading 'presocratic',[1] especially as I want to take this study beyond the usual canon of 'presocratic philosophy'. I will pay serious attention to the poets Homer, Hesiod, Terpander, Pindar and Bacchylides, the historians Herodotus and Thucydides, the lawgiver Solon, the playwrights Aeschylus, Aristophanes, Euripides and Sophocles, the Hippocratic corpus and the Derveni papyrus. Second, I believe the plural 'philosophies' to be appropriate, in that I do not believe there to be a single early Greek philosophy of nature, and that it is important to investigate the commonalities and differences between the many attempts to understand order and regularity in this period.[2]

It is often said that there was an important change between the poets and the early Greek philosophies of nature. In Homer and Hesiod there are general regularities of meteorology, the heavens and agriculture, but these can be breached on the caprice or anger of the gods. So Zeus can generate a thunderbolt, Poseidon causes earthquakes, Athena is capable of holding back the dawn, and all of the gods interfere in battles between humans.[3] With the Ionian thinkers, however, we see ordered worlds where there is complete regularity. This contrast has been to some extent overdrawn but is worth examining in detail, not least for the light it can shed on early philosophies of nature. In the first chapters of this book I argue that ideas of order, and the language those ideas were expressed in, did not spring forth *ex nihilo* but came about in interesting ways from engagement with the thought of Homer and Hesiod.

Central to this book will be the claim that there was an important tradition in early Greek thought that expressed the order of the cosmos in terms of the verbs *kubernan*, to steer, and *kratein*, to control, which we have so far under-valued or even ignored. What exercises this steering or control over the cosmos and how it does so, and the roots of this tradition in Homer and Hesiod, will all be issues for this book.

This book will reject what I see as some binary and unnecessarily divisive views. It will reject the idea that early Greek thought was either a precursor of modern science or primitive, and argue that there was important intellectual space between these poles to develop sophisticated ideas on the order of the world, which have subsequently been superseded. It rejects a binary division of poets and philosophers so it can investigate interesting links and influences between them on the question of order. It will attempt to apply similar historiographical principles to both, and more broadly to avoid the idea that Greek philosophy came *ex nihilo* and so constituted a 'Greek Miracle'. It also rejects any binary division between science and religion and any simple conflict thesis between the two.

This book will doubtless be controversial to some for its claim that no one in early Greek thought can in any meaningful sense be described as a mechanist, including the early atomists, Leucippus and Democritus. I do not seek to deride or downgrade early Greek thought on nature here as I think there are a multiplicity of interesting, original and powerful ideas. I argue that because some historiographies see being a mechanical thinker as a good thing, we have benevolently attempted to make many early Greek thinkers into mechanists, but often to the detriment of the coherence of their thought. Drop that drive, and the coherence returns. I was surprised in writing this book at so many attempts to mechanize early Greek thinkers.[4] So I question why we focus on the idea of mechanism, how we have done that and ultimately what the evidence is. Paradoxically, for an investigation that tries to look for 'as it was' rather than 'as we would like it to have been', 'as it was' turns out to be better than 'as we would like it to have been'. Ultimately this book is about how we do the history of early Greek thinking on nature, what we value in the early Greeks and why we value that. Methodology is critical to this, so the first chapter deals with historiography, methods and definitions.

I would like to thank the anonymous referees for their comments on the proposal and draft of this book, my PhD students, Jon Griffiths and Hugh MacKenzie, for their comments on various drafts, the audiences at innumerable papers and conferences where ideas for this book were tried out and finally Chiara D'Agostino, who proofread the transliterations of the Greek with great acumen, accuracy and efficiency.

# 1

# Methodological Issues

As methodological issues will be crucial for this book, I want to discuss some of the key aspects in this first chapter. In particular I want to start with historiography, that is, how we approach doing the history of early Greek ideas on nature. As I will challenge the idea that any early Greek thinker was a mechanist, what assumptions are therefore in play and why have some scholars seen mechanism in early Greek thought? I also want to argue for some important intellectual space between what has direct affinity with modern science and what has been termed 'the primitive'.[1] I will look at how terms such as mechanist have been defined, and argue there is no one agreed definition; rather there is a wide range of views. Some Greek terms need examination as well, most notably the standard term for nature, *phusis*, but also *kubernan*, to steer, and *kratein*, to control. I will also question why scholars have taken supposed affinities between ancient science and seventeenth-century mechanical philosophy to be so important. Finally, I have something significant to say about Plato and early Greek thought. I argue that too stereotypical an approach to Plato in general and the *Phaedo* passage known as Socrates' autobiography in particular gives an account of thought prior to Plato that is too binary and inflexible. A less rigid account of Plato's reactions to his predecessors, which is supported by other passages in Plato, reveals interesting information about early Greek thought on nature.

## Early Greek mechanistic thought?

One important argument of this book will be that there has been a tendency to overestimate the extent to which early Greek philosophies of nature can be described as 'mechanistic', along with an overestimate of how plausible and effective the 'mechanistic' interpretations would have been in context. I take 'mechanistic' quite broadly here, encompassing views on ontology, causation, explanation, analogies and natural laws. The corollary is that we have underestimated the extent to which these philosophies of nature were committed to other modes of explanation and ontologies, and that we have underestimated, and indeed underexplored, how plausible and good these philosophies would have been in context.

It is important here not to privilege mechanistic interpretations in three senses. First, one approach to early Greek philosophies of nature has been to seek affinities with modern science. The view, largely tacit, is that the deeper or more wide-ranging these affinities are, the higher our evaluation of early Greek science will be. Hence there has been a drive to find affinities between early Greek thinkers and either the mechanical philosophy of the seventeenth century and after, or modern mechanistic views. Second, some aspects of the mechanistic view, particularly relating to how we frame natural laws, have become widely and generally accepted. It is important that we do not treat key assumptions here as atemporally evident, or in some sense natural, and everything else as inferior to or as a deviation from these supposed atemporal truths. Third, we must recognize that the mechanistic view has undergone development and has had periodic crises of plausibility. So, in the eighteenth century the mechanical philosophy struggled for plausible explanations of biological phenomena recently discovered with the microscope until more sophisticated modelling techniques were developed. It is critical to recognize that ancient mechanistic views lacked sophisticated modelling, and opposition to them was not wholly based on issues of teleology or theology but could be based on issues of plausibility as well.

This book will argue that there is an important sense in which the early atomists, Leucippus and Democritus, often taken to be mechanists, were in fact not mechanists. Materialists, certainly, with an ontology of atoms and void, what is and what is not. However, there is a difference between materialism and a mechanical interpretation of materialism. If we look at the analogies the early atomists used, they did not use mechanical analogies, they did not liken the world to a machine, but used biological, human, agricultural and maritime analogues instead.

Two arguments against early mechanistic ideas do not interest me.[2] One is that there was some form of disdain for the practical in the early Greek thought. Whether there was such a disdain or not, I would contend that a move to a mechanistic view of the world is not a simple, natural and straightforward consequence of a practical engagement with the world. The other argument is that the early Greeks saw mechanics as in some way contrary to nature or in some sense not part of what they conceived of as the investigation of nature. Recent work has debunked this view.[3]

## Modernization?

I take this issue about affinities and mechanistic thought to be one within a broader phenomenon. In the history of science seeking affinities occurs more broadly, and one can see this process at work in the history of philosophy and in the history of literature too. The problem is not so much seeking affinities on their own but, as von Staden has argued, seeking affinities and eliding differences, or privileging any perceived affinities.[4] There are several considerations to be balanced here. One is historical generosity towards the subject, which will lead us to look at possible affinities. On the other hand, we must be conscious of the fact that ideas do have a history and it is possible to attribute them anachronistically. Even if one is a strong realist about those ideas (so they always exist), human realization of them is a separate issue. I have argued elsewhere that the pursuit of scientific affinities can be misleading and indeed counter-productive.[5] So with Anaximander, trying to make him 'the first Darwinist' conceals the interesting work he was doing in zoogony,[6] recognition of which makes him a less 'modern' thinker, but paradoxically much more coherent and interesting, and one more in tune with the ideas of his time.

I bring up these issues because I have some things to say about Homer and Hesiod that may be controversial. I will argue that there is an important sense in which neither Homer nor Hesiod had philosophies of nature. By this I mean that they had no term for nature, nor did they have any conception of or any term for what is beyond or contrary to nature. Homer's Circe has been hailed as the first witch in the Western literary tradition. However, neither narrator nor characters in the *Odyssey* treat her as a witch, and she does nothing different in kind to other gods and goddesses. This issue is important as it relates to Homer and nature. Is there a conception of beyond the natural to support the assertion of witchcraft? I argue there is not. The idea of Circe as a witch is an anachronistic imposition on Homer. There are other aspects of this phenomenon as well. I am concerned that translating *moira* (lot) as 'fate' can import inappropriate modern ideas to Homer. It is also unfortunate that debates about epistemology in Homer have centred on scepticism, a later idea for which Homer has no recognizable motivation, rather than looking at much more interesting issues of the Muses and the authority of the account given and what humans can know about the gods and *moira*. Finally, I argue that the idea of a *historia*, an investigation or enquiry, is alien to both Homer and Hesiod. If we are going to talk in terms of *peri phuseōs historia*, an 'enquiry concerning nature', we need to understand that later thinkers generated both the notion of *phusis* and the notion of *historia*. Less controversial will be my rejection of the idea that the self-moving equipment of Hephaestus' workshop (*Iliad* XVIII, 414 ff.) and the self-steering ships of the Phaeacians (*Odyssey* VIII/ 555) were mechanical automata. This is a point worth mentioning to show that there can be interpretations of Homer that are too modern and too mechanistic, and a line needs to be drawn somewhere. The result of this process, applied to both poets and early philosophers and medical thinkers, is that we find an interesting engagement with the poets on issues of the generation and maintenance of order and on issues of epistemology as well.

## Reflexivity

As I will point to some affinities between later developments and early Greek thought, there is an issue of reflexivity to account for. Indeed, if we think there is any continuity between the ancient investigation of nature and science, there must be such affinities and we need some affinities in order to be able to demarcate our subject matter from other ancient endeavours. It is not seeking affinities as such that is the problem, but doing so to the exclusion of dissimilarities, doing so within a Whiggish account of the history of philosophy or science, and doing so in a way which over-estimates the modernity of those affinities. I hope, being conscious of those pitfalls, to avoid them and to have a meta-level discussion of the nature and value of any supposed affinities, and as I have suggested above in relation to Anaximander, the depth of those affinities. It is also important to be conscious of attempting to be even-handed here. So one could produce an account that emphasizes the affinities between Homer/Hesiod and modern ideas (or the Babylonians/Egyptians etc.), without doing so for the Ionians, thus downplaying the significance of the Ionians and questioning any specific early Greek contribution to the conception of nature. Vice versa, and we have a huge gap between the Ionians and their predecessors and are forced to invoke a 'Greek Miracle' (see below) to explain such a rapid and significant change. While I will deny aspects of affinity to Homer and Hesiod (no conception of *phusis* or *historia*), I will also deny mechanism and evolution for Anaximander and will question other supposed or assumed affinities in Anaximander and other early Greek thinkers as well.

## Parallels

I want to draw a parallel here with another episode in the history of science, which may help to illuminate some of the aims of this book. William Harvey (1578–1657) discovered the circulation of the blood around 1619. It used to be thought that Harvey did so because he advocated the 'progressive' new methods of the seventeenth century, the mechanization of nature and the mathematization of nature. This has now been shown to be conclusively false.[7] Harvey was an Aristotelian influenced by Renaissance trends in anatomy and philosophy and was an ardent anti-mechanist. He did one experiment that quantified blood flow, but if we look more closely the quantities were all significant underestimates and the argument was a qualitative one that no Aristotelian would have had any issue with.[8] Indeed, a parallel for this sort of experiment and reasoning can be found in Aristotle.[9] Importantly for this book, what might appear at first glance to be mechanical models of the heart and circulation turn out on closer examination to be no such thing. Harvey did not liken the heart to a pump, as has often been said, but to a pair of water bellows, and did so only in his lecture notes, while Aristotle had likened the lungs to a forge bellows. Much more prominent in Harvey is a macrocosm/microcosm analogy between the heart and the weather cycle. So as the sun heats and evaporates water, which subsequently cools and falls as rain, so the heart heats the blood and it is cooled in the extremities before returning to the heart. Aristotle had drawn a microcosm/macrocosm analogy between this weather cycle and the motions of the heavens. Harvey did liken the heart to a musket, perhaps a more promising mechanical analogy, but only in the sense that both heart and musket move too quickly to be observed properly by the naked eye, and not in the sense that the heart was a mechanical entity. It is important to look closely at what might appear to be a mechanical analogy and to examine exactly what was being got out of that analogy.[10]

The result of this re-appraisal of Harvey has been a richer, more interesting account of Harvey and one that gives us a much better understanding of his relation to the science of his time.[11] It allows us to understand why he chose a certain path of research, why he chose to express himself in certain terms, and why he chose a specific means of explaining the nature of the heart and the circulation of the blood. So with the early Greek thinkers, I hope that by giving up the attempt to impose mechanization (and to a lesser extent mathematization) on them we generate a richer account of them, that we can locate them better in their context and we can at least to some extent explain why their fragments chose these particular examples and sought to explain them in this particular way.

I would also draw a parallel here with Unguru's seminal paper on the history of Greek mathematics, where he argues against the view that:

> Greek mathematics, especially after the discovery of the 'irrational' by the Pythagorean school, is algebra dressed up, primarily for the sake of rigor, in geometrical garb.[12]

Unguru also opposes the view that:

> There is nothing unique and (ontologically) idiosyncratic concerning the way in which ancient Greek mathematicians went about their proofs, which might be lost in the process of translation from the geometrical to the algebraic language; the main reason for this being that the ancient mathematical reasonings and structures *are* indeed substantially algebraic.[13]

Unguru's work has resulted in a much richer and contextually plausible account of Greek mathematics. I do not claim the parallels here are exact, but I would caution against taking analogies used by early Greek thinkers as mechanical analogies or mechanical analogies dressed up as something else and believe that something is lost if we do. The analogies used by Harvey, a strident anti-mechanist, were not mechanical, nor were they mechanical analogies disguised in the language of the time for whatever reason. It is also important to recognize that analogies used by the early Greeks had real work to do in their systems if we recognize the questions they were addressing. So returning to Harvey, the macrocosm/microcosm analogy was not just a fashionable, Renaissance means of describing the heart and circulation. Harvey faced two real and critical issues in relation to Galen's conception of blood flow. There are two types of blood in the body, in modern terms oxygenated and deoxygenated, or arterial and venous. If they are in one circulatory system, how do they rapidly and efficiently convert into each other? Secondly, if there is a rapid blood flow around the body, and major organs such as the lungs are part of the circuit, how can so much blood flow across major organs? Harvey resolved those issues using the macrocosm/microcosm analogy of the circulation and the weather cycle. Just as the sun heats water and turns it to vapour, so the heart heats the blood and changes it, and it is changed back by cooling in the extremities. Just as rain can fall on a hill and emerge as springs and streams on its way to the sea, so too can blood pass through the lungs. It is important that we recognize that the importance of the macrocosm/microcosm analogy for Harvey was marginalized in some accounts, and why that marginalization took place.[14]

## Use of *kubernan* and *kratein*

One aspect of early Greek thought that has been marginalized is the use of the terms *kubernan*, to steer or to govern, and *kratein*, to rule, to have power over or to control. The Greek word *kubernan* primarily means to steer, as in being the helmsman, with other senses of to drive, guide or govern. The modern English 'govern' derives from *kubernan* via the Latin *gubernare*. I will take 'to steer' as my primary translation of *kubernan*, although as we will see in Chapter 4, that may underdo the full import of *kubernan*. In Greek sea practice, on larger ships the *kubernētēs* was the captain with someone subordinate to him actually doing the steering, and the *kubernētēs* had responsibility for the ship's safety. I will take 'to control' as my primary translation of *kratein* in cosmological contexts, without forgetting it may have other connotations. Typically, *kubernan* and *kratein* are used for the relationship that the *archē*, the primary or originating substance, has to the cosmos or to everything else. So, in Anaximander the *apeiron* steers all, in Heraclitus and in the Hippocratic *On Regimen* fire steers all, in Parmenides a goddess steers and in Diogenes of Apollonia air steers all. Plato's *Philebus* attests to a tradition of *kubernan* being used in such contexts. In Anaximenes air controls, in the Hippocratic *On Regimen* fire controls, in Heraclitus the divine law controls, in Xenophanes god controls, in Parmenides necessity controls, in the Derveni papyrus air controls, in Empedocles Love and Strife control, and the four elements take turns to control, in Diogenes of Apollonia air controls and in Anaxagoras mind controls. One reason that we can tie *kubernan* and *kratein* together is that some authors (a Hippocratic, Diogenes) use them in the same passage and use them virtually interchangeably.

It is worth doing a short version of this list – Anaximander, Anaximenes, Xenophanes, Heraclitus, the Hippocratics, the Derveni author, Parmenides, Diogenes, Empedocles and Anaxagoras – just to emphasize the large proportion of early Greek thinkers who used either *kubernan* or *kratein* or both. We need an enhanced understanding of what was meant by steering and control and how they related to the regularity and order of the cosmos. It is significant that ideas of steering and control are not even mentioned in important books such as Hankinson's *Cause and Explanation in Ancient Greek Thought*, Burnet's *Early Greek Philosophy* and Barnes' *The Presocratic Philosophers*.[15]

I will also be interested in the origins of the use of *kubernan* and *kratein*, as there are some interesting precursors in Homer and Hesiod. Homer in *Odyssey* and *Iliad* uses *kubernan* and its cognates but only ever in the sense of steering a ship. It is not used by Hesiod. The Phaeacian ships, which do not have human helmsmen, but are capable of steering themselves may provide a model for how the cosmos can steer itself. Homer does use *agein*, to lead, for the gods leading like to like and both Homer and Hesiod use *ithunein*, to guide, for some actions of the gods. More critically, both Homer and Hesiod use the phrase *moira krataiē*, controlling *moira*. What I will argue here is that in Homer, the gods generate and maintain *moira*, and *moira* regulates the affairs of gods and humans. In early Greek thought, the attributes and roles of the gods can be seen to be transferred to the *archai*, the originating or principle substances. So the *archai* are, for example, 'deathless and unaging', and I argue they also take on the role of steering or controlling. I will also be interested in the move from *kata moiran* and *kata aisan* in Homer to the phrase *kata phusin*, according to nature. This transition has an interesting and important intermediate step in that both Anaximander and Heraclitus use the phrase *kata (to) chreōn*, which I will argue should be translated as 'according to what is proper' rather than 'according to necessity'. There are some further interesting *kata* ... phrases in Anaximander and Heraclitus as well.

## Intellectual space

One important theme for this book will be an attempt to escape binary assessments of ancient thought. By binary assessment here, I have in mind a bifurcation between assessing something as either modern or primitive, with little or nothing in between. It is critical to recognize that between modern views and what might be termed primitive or unreflective views of nature, there were many plausible alternatives that have subsequently been superseded. There is a need to investigate why these views were adopted and in particular what it was thought could be gained from these views. Take as a parallel here the centrality and stability of the earth for the early Greeks. This is not the modern view, but to focus on Philolaus' cosmology, the only one with a mobile earth, would seriously distort the history of early Greek cosmology. Nor is early Greek geocentrism reducible to the unreflective anthropocentrism/geocentrism of earlier cultures or the early Greek poets either. It was argued for in interesting and sophisticated ways and was thought to be supported by empirical evidence. It was only superseded, with considerable effort, by the Copernican revolution of the sixteenth and seventeenth centuries.

There were ways in which the early Greeks thought about order that are similarly neither modern nor primitive, and were plausible possibilities for thinking about nature down to the more general scientific revolution of the seventeenth century. So I disagree with Hesse's comment that:

> In a sense the Ionians return to the primitive view in which supernatural powers are not distinguished from their revelation in nature itself.[16]

I disagree that the Ionians thought of any powers as supernatural, as there can be powers beyond inanimate matter that are entirely natural. They also clearly attempt to do something sophisticated and interesting that is beyond any simple, primitive view of the world.

An organic conception of nature was only displaced by the rise of the mechanical philosophy in the seventeenth century. A civil conception of natural law, rather than a mathematical one was common until the time of Descartes. Natural laws have only consistently been expressed in terms of equations from the time of Galileo. An interesting and important example is Plato on the heavens. Plato believed that the heavens moved in a regular and orderly manner because each of the heavenly bodies had a soul and intelligence and thus chose the best (so regular and orderly) path. Here I fundamentally disagree with Burkert, who has commented that:

> Plato thought it an inescapable conclusion that the orderly motion of the stars is due to their having souls; it is a voluntary, chosen order. Here sophisticated Greek science harks back to the pre-scientific way of thinking and comes to rest in it.[17]

As these celestial intelligences will always choose the best, and will always exist in this manner as the demiurge chooses to keep the cosmos in existence, here we in fact have an immensely strong underpinning of the regular behaviour of the heavens. It is very different from the caprice of the gods, which may or may not keep order. It is also significant for this book that while Plato looked at how an ideal intelligence can generate absolute regularity, there was no consideration in early Greek thought of how an ideal machine might generate regularity.

I take it as both meaningful and interesting to investigate this intellectual space between the modern and the primitive. Some criteria of meaning, such as verificationist or experimentalist theories of meaning would render such an investigation meaningless. I contend that we are not looking at fine distinctions between varieties of meaningless or primitive ideas, but investigating how a significant proportion of early Greek thinkers thought about order in ways that were plausible in their context and significantly different from primitive notions.

I take the content of this intellectual space to be rational ideas, which we have later come to have reason to reject. Critical for this book will be the idea of some form of cosmic intelligence that steers or controls. I hold that idea to be rational in an early Greek context, at least in that it can be coherently expressed in words, reasons for that idea can be given and coherent replies to objections made. I do not consider such an intelligence to be beyond or contrary to nature, or to use the modern term, supernatural. It is part of *phusis*, and behaves in a law-like manner, *kata phusin*, according to nature as some of the early Greeks said.[18]

## Analogies

We are familiar with the phrase 'regular as clockwork' but the Greeks were not. This is important as clockwork was the key analogy for expressing the regularity of nature for the mechanical philosophy of the seventeenth century. Instead, we find the early Greeks using a variety of analogies for regularity based on contrasts. So there was civil versus rural living, ordered city versus anarchic city, ordered armies versus rabble, intelligent versus unintelligent behaviour, steered versus unsteered, controlled versus uncontrolled. That the early Greeks used political or commercial analogies to model the cosmos (e.g. Anaximander, Heraclitus) and its regularities is well known, as is the fact that Plato ascribed intelligence to the heavenly bodies and that the early Greeks used organic analogies for the structure of the cosmos. I argue that there has been an interesting reversal in expectations in relation to analogues for order. We take clockwork (or another suitable mechanism) as a paradigm for regular behaviour, and contrast that with the irregularity of humans, and have done since around the seventeenth century and the rise of the mechanical philosophy. The early Greeks though, contrasted the regularity of intelligence, particularly a pure or divine intelligence, with the irregularity of unguided processes. The early Greeks did not use 'weak analogies' as some commentators have asserted.[19] Those they used may be weak for a mechanical or modern conception of the world, but often they were good for the conceptions of nature the early Greeks actually had and gave a surprisingly strong underpinning for their views on order. Conversely, if the early Greeks had used mechanical analogues, these would have been weak, as their machines were not paradigms of regularity and order but were prone to rapid wear and breakdown. It is important here not to refer to non-mechanical analogies as 'alternative' analogies for the early Greeks. That would be to accept a historiography where mechanical analogies are always the primary analogies.

I will be interested in how the macrocosm/microcosm analogy was deployed and what was got out of this in terms of explanation and how it was thought of in terms of causation. I will be interested in the fact (again downplayed in mechanical interpretations) that some early Greek thinkers (e.g. Anaximander, the Hippocratics) believed nature to be divine. What did this help to explain? Was this a form of pantheism and could it avoid the accusation that pantheism is vacuous? I will be interested in a series of analogies used by the Greeks, biological, agricultural, human, meteorological, botanical, culinary, pyrotechnical, commercial and parenting analogies to see what work they did in their particular context.

The 'like to like' principle of the early atomists, and Love and Strife in Empedocles have both been treated as forces. One can see why commentators have pursued this view, pursuing affinities with modern science, but these were not forces. Like particles are sorted together in the vortex but not elsewhere, and there is no force acting between particles. The elements associate or dissociate in Empedocles but again no universally acting force operates between these elements. We also need to generate a history of how the like to like principle changes, from Homer where the gods lead things like to like, through the early atomists to Plato where like knows like, like causes like, and like is drawn to like.

## Early Greek history

There is a benefit here in that this settles the early atomists into the mainstream of Greek thought, rather than generating a mechanist approach out of nothing, which would raise the spectre of a 'Greek Miracle'. One intention of this book is to undermine the idea of a 'Greek Miracle', by demonstrating that we have a strong context in Homer and Hesiod for ideas concerning order, which can help explain the specific examples and the language used to express them. These ideas were not generated *ex nihilo*, and while brilliant, seminal and innovative they were not miraculous. It is also the intention of this book to undermine the idea of an 'Ionian Enlightenment'. The European Enlightenment of the eighteenth century is supposed to entail the spread of mechanical and secular thought, so some see it as good if we can attribute such an Enlightenment to the Ionians as well. There was no such spread of mechanical thought in the early Greeks. Science in the European Enlightenment was done predominantly by Christians who believed they were investigating the glories of the world that their god created and maintained and there was no noticeable secularization. It is more accurate to say that during both the European Enlightenment and the early Greek periods there was a significant and important rethinking of the relation of god/gods with nature and the investigation of nature. Finally, this book will also undermine any simple *muthos* to *logos*, myth to reason account of early Greek thought. There are important differences between Homer, Hesiod and early investigators of nature, but *muthos* to *logos* puts these changes in far too binary a form, and invites ideas of rapid and wholesale change and discontinuity that are simply not there in the evidence.

## Mechanists and *mēchanē*

As I will oppose the idea that the early atomists, and indeed any early Greek thinkers were mechanists, I will say something to clarify what I mean by 'mechanists'. As Berryman comments,

> The term 'mechanical' is freely used in current scholarship in sometimes anachronistic or ill-defined – and certainly various – ways, as though it were a self-evident concept available to all.[20]

The Greek term *mēchanē* is much better translated as 'contrivance' than 'machine' for the period we are looking at. In Homer, *amēchania* signifies human helplessness in relation to the gods, while Odysseus is frequently described as *polumēchanos*, which is usually rendered resourceful but literally 'of many devices', those devices being human attributes or stratagems.[21] Aristotle also tells us that 'Anaxagoras makes use of mind as a device (*mēchanē*) in cosmos generation', whenever he is at a loss to explain (*Metaphysics* I/4, 985a8). Anaxagoras' cosmic mind can hardly be thought to be mechanical. In line with my approach to *phusis*, it is revealing to look at the negations of *mēchanē* to help determine meaning and use.

As a first differentiation, I would say there are two broad senses in which a thinker or an explanation might be thought to be mechanical. Here I follow Lonie's definitions:

> A mechanistic explanation is one which involves the mathematical application of the science of mechanics to bodies in motion.[22]

> We label 'mechanistic' an explanation which is modelled upon the workings of machines or automata.[23]

One critical point here is that one can be a materialist without being a mechanist. During the seventeenth and eighteenth centuries there was a close association of materialism and mechanism but that has not been so for all periods. As a modern example, we have a material account of the brain. Is that though a mechanical account? We have far more sophisticated accounts and analogies for what is happening with the brain and many would deny the merit, benefit or possibility of reducing those accounts or analogies to something underlying that is mechanical.[24] Prior to the seventeenth century it was possible to be a materialist without being a mechanist. The key case for this book will clearly be the early atomists, Leucippus and Democritus, and I am happy that they have an ontology of atoms and void. The intuitive view, which has been expressed to me several times at conferences, is that Leucippus and Democritus were mechanists because of their ontology and because they explained everything in terms of the interactions of particles. I will argue though that they made no use of mathematical mechanics and they did not conceive of nature as working like a machine. Yes, they explained in terms of the interactions of particles but not the mechanical interactions of particles. It is also important not to assume that the early atomists shared some of the ideas developed by later mechanical philosophers. It is by no means clear that they share ideas about the mathematization of nature, about the vacuum or about the conservation of energy. I will also argue something stronger, which is that they could not have made use of mathematical mechanics because of their use of *ou mallon*, indifference arguments, in reply to Parmenides. Attempts to 'retrofit' a mathematical mechanics to them, which is effectively to say that a basis was there for them to have applied such mathematical mechanics, ignore this crucial context. Such attempts are also prone to attributing anachronistic assumptions to make such a mechanics work.[25] I will also argue that it is both philosophically and historically highly implausible that they would have used mechanical analogies and in fact they did not, using meteorological, maritime, biological and agricultural analogies instead as well as the macrocosm/microcosm analogy.

## Unitary definition of mechanical?

It is important to recognize that there is no single 'correct' mechanical philosophy and definitions of what it is to be a mechanist vary widely.[26] Pyle gives perhaps the narrowest definition,[27] the mechanical philosophy being defined following Thomas Hobbes as the denial of action at a distance, the denial of the spontaneous initiation of motion and the denial that incorporeal agents are capable of moving bodies. The denial of action at a distance would exclude much of the mechanical philosophy following Newton and his theory of gravity. The recently published *Routledge Handbook of Mechanisms and Mechanical Philosophy* on the other hand gives this definition of mechanism:

> A mechanism for a phenomenon consists of entities (or parts) whose activities and interactions are organized so as to be responsible for the phenomenon.[28]

The authors of this definition are aware that this is 'one by which a great number of things will count as mechanisms'. That is deliberate, as they recognize debate between many mechanistic approaches (ontological, metaphysical, methodological, epistemological) spread of many disciplines, beyond the usual mechanical physics (biology, medicine, cognitive science, neuroscience, sociology, political science, economics and history). It is notable here that neither the application of mathematical mechanics to particles nor the machine analogy are fundamental tenets of this new view that is essentially about mechanisms, which can be biological or social. There is no necessary commitment that biological or social mechanisms ought or can be reduced to material ones, or that 'entities (or parts)' such as 'people, families, political parties' can be so reduced. In terms of direction of explanation, instead of the relentless downward-looking reductionist approach, the new mechanism looks to locate mechanisms in complex situations so must look 'down, around and up'.

One thing that should be clear about this modern view of mechanisms is that if applied to the ancients, it will not cleave the early Greeks along the same lines as the teleology versus materialism or a supposed teleology versus older mechanistic view will. Indeed, Popu has argued that the arch-teleologist Aristotle makes significant use of mechanisms in this modern sense.[29] I would argue that he could be joined by several, if not all, of the early Greek thinkers beyond Leucippus and Democritus on this definition.[30] I raise these issues because it is important to challenge the linear progressive history narrative for the mechanical philosophy. It is also important to show that there have been many variations of the mechanical philosophy or mechanical or mechanistic approaches, influenced by the current state of science.[31] The nineteenth century emphasized point matter and forces, strict mechanical modelling, and avoidance of debates about the nature of matter or the issue of action at a distance in a way not seen before or since. There is no simple, atemporal, Platonic form of the mechanical philosophy. The idea of thinking about nature in a mechanistic manner is not atemporally evident, nor is it something that arises naturally in all situations. The early Greeks used analogies for natural processes that were to hand: maritime, architectural, agricultural, meteorological, craft, commercial and a host of other analogies. They did not use machine analogies as these were not there to be used. It was only with the rise of the machine, in particular the mechanical clock and to a lesser extent more sophisticated pneumatics, that the mechanical philosophy of the seventeenth century came about.[32] We need to be careful not to project key ideas from that mechanical philosophy back onto the early Greeks, nor project back the basis that led to some of those ideas. So I radically disagree with Heidel, who has commented that for the early Greek investigation of nature:

> Even where it considered biological and intellectual processes, it started with mechanical notions and arrived in the end at materialistic conclusions.[33]

Equally I disagree that:

> When the pre-Socratic asked what a thing was, the answer he desired, if given with ideal completeness, would have presented its chemical formula.[34]

I deal with the key case of Leucippus and Democritus in Chapter 7. Other important cases of early Greeks who have had mechanistic views incorrectly attributed to them, are Anaximander (Chapter 4), Anaximenes, Empedocles and Anaxagoras (Chapter 6) and the Hippocratics (Chapter 8).

## Why not or why?

I want to introduce one important historiographical nuance that will run through this book, borrowed from analyses of why a scientific revolution occurred in Europe and not elsewhere in the seventeenth century. It is possible to generate a very positive account of the history of the introduction of mechanistic ideas, and Dijksterhuis has said that:

> Among the numerous modifications that scientific thought about nature has undergone in the course of the centuries, it would be difficult to point to one that has had a more profound and far-reaching effect than the emergence of the conception of the world usually called mechanical or mechanistic.[35]

Given that the title of his book is *The Mechanization of the World Picture*, that is perhaps not surprising and is a good example of privileging mechanistic explanations. If we treat progress towards a mechanical world view as part of a linear and progressive history, the tendency is to ask where someone fits in this history, and if they do not fit, why they do not fit. Often there is an accompanying assumption that mechanical ideas are somehow natural or evident, again prompting us to ask why someone did not fit in this history. Berryman has commented that:

> A number of classic explanations have been offered as to why ancient Greek thinkers might not have seen the applicability of ideas from mechanics to the understanding of the natural world.[36]

That is a fair assessment of how the issue has been approached. Just prior to the seventeenth century, in addition to Western Europe, both the Chinese and the Arabic/Islamic cultures had good technology and sophisticated social systems. Why then did this revolution occur only in Western Europe? If we take this scientific revolution to be a natural progression from a certain state of technological and social development, then the tendency is to ask why did it not happen elsewhere, and what other factors inhibited it. However, it is also possible to take the converse view. If this scientific revolution was not an evident, natural progression, then one might ask why did it happen in Western Europe instead. These different approaches will generate significantly different answers. This book will take the view that 'mechanization of the world picture' is not something natural or evident and will be interested in looking at questions of why anyone in early Greece would be attracted to it, especially in the absence of machines or a developed science of mechanics. Whether we phrase the question as 'why?' or 'why not?' will be applicable to several other issues this book will address.

## Modern and seventeenth-century mechanical philosophy?

As someone who teaches some aspects of History and Philosophy of Science from the ancients through to the moderns, it has always puzzled me that debates about mechanistic thought in the ancient world use the mechanical philosophy of the seventeenth century as a reference point. There have been significant developments both in the nature of the mechanical philosophy and its status since then. This can be masked by linear progressive histories of mechanization, especially if those histories stop soon after the seventeenth century, as Dijksterhuis' does. So too referring to the science of the seventeenth century as 'early modern science' (in contrast to the ancient/medieval science that it allegedly abruptly replaced) can also give the sense that the fundamentals of modern science are in place with the mechanization and mathematization of the seventeenth century, so there is continuity with modern science. This is not so.

The mechanical philosophy in its classical form of particles interacting by contact action only failed to account for gravity.[37] Gravity after Newton was thought of as a force acting at a distance, not reducible to the collisions of atoms as in Descartes' vortex theory of gravity. One can reformulate a new mechanical philosophy to include such forces, but it is a significant change. General Relativity treats gravity in an entirely different manner, which cannot be thought of as mechanical in any meaningful sense.

Mechanical chemistry failed. Treating chemistry as the interactions of the philosophically smallest particles proved unproductive. Only when Lavoisier defined a chemical element as something that could not be broken down further *by chemical means* did chemistry arrive at a useful theoretical foundation. Mechanical biology failed, quite spectacularly. The use of the new microscopes in the eighteenth century generated many novel discoveries in morphology, embryology, reproduction and cytology, which the mechanical philosophy of the time was unable to cope with in any plausible manner.[38]

The rise of quantum mechanics has also been problematic for the mechanical philosophy. One key issue is that it is clear that the micro, quantum world does not behave like the macro world, so any analogy from the macro world, let alone a machine analogy, is likely to be inappropriate. Sub-atomic particles simply do not behave like miniature snooker or pool balls. Quantum indeterminacy, quantum tunnelling, wave/particle duality, and a fundamentally probabilistic interpretation of nature all run counter to the mechanical philosophy. One might argue that although the initial mechanical chemistry failed, the later solid atom or the electron/proton/neutron atom with solid sub-atomic particles reinstated a mechanical view. However, modern chemistry has long passed beyond this simple model and is underpinned by quantum mechanics, which gives such a good account of electron orbits, energies and bonding characteristics that chemistry is in one sense considered theoretically closed. I agree with Garber and Roux that:

> However mechanical philosophy is defined, its ambition was greater than its real successes.[39]

Newtonian science is still taught to a certain level on science courses as it is a reasonable description of slow-moving macro objects and is a good way of introducing many scientific ideas, but for proper science it has long been superseded. So too the idea of the mechanical modelling of phenomena in terms of 'levers, springs, pulleys, wheels, gears, deformable jelly, etc.'[40] or the favourite seventeenth- and eighteenth-century analogy of clockwork has long been superseded in favour of more sophisticated, flexible, layered and interactive ways of understanding phenomena. The *Routledge Handbook of Mechanisms and Mechanical Philosophy* comments that:

> Although mechanical philosophy receded for much of the twentieth century, it is again resurgent.[41]

One can see why the first part of this comment is true from the development of scientific ideas in the twentieth century. It is also true that mechanical explanations are having something of a revival, but in a very different form. As we saw above, the new conception is that 'mechanism for a phenomenon consists of entities (or parts) whose activities and interactions are organized so as to be responsible for the phenomenon' and that is a much broader conception of what constitutes a mechanical explanation,[42] which would have been rejected out of hand by seventeenth-century mechanical philosophers.

## Nature and *phusis*

The standard Greek term for nature was *phusis*. It can mean the nature of something, whether that is of an object or a person, and can also mean nature in the broader sense as one might talk of the nature of the universe. Aristotle gives several definitions of *phusis* in *Metaphysics* V/4. The term *phusis* also has connotations that are not fully captured by the translation 'nature'. First, it has a sense of giving the origins, development and current constitution of something, as LSJ have it '*origin . . . the natural form* or *constitution* of a person or thing *as the result of growth.*' Second, *phusis* derives from *phuein*, 'to grow', and so can carry a strong organic sense to it. Third, as Mourelatos has recently argued, the verb *phuein* can have a sense of dynamic being, of coming into being, where the verb *einai* (to be) expresses a more static sense of being.[43]

The first use of *phusis* is in Homer, where Hermes shows Odysseus the *phusis* of the Moly plant. It is common here to undermine this use of *phusis* by saying that the Moly is magical.[44] I disagree, for a reason outlined above. Homer had no conception of or term for nature or anything contrary to nature in the broader sense, so had no conception of, or indeed term for, magic. He may have ascribed more powers to plants than we would, but could not and did not distinguish between magical and non-magical plants. No doubt we, from a modern perspective, consider the Moly to be magical, but that is not the point – Homer did not. This is though the only use of *phusis* in Homer or Hesiod and did not give a general notion of *phusis*.[45]

On the issue of whether the early Greeks invented a conception of nature or not, I hold a position between that of Grant,[46] who argues it was not, but was a given for all humans, and Lloyd who argues it was invented.[47] I hold that the Greeks discovered the idea of a domain of nature that can be contrasted to a domain of non-nature, which does not exist, but had to generate the contents of that domain.[48] Some of that generation was discovery, some invention.

## Plato and *peri phuseōs historia*

At Plato's *Phaedo* 96a8, we find the phrase *peri phuseōs historia*, 'enquiry concerning nature'. It is important that we are clear about the meaning of this phrase, especially as it has been used for some early Greek thought. The term *historia* is relatively unproblematic, though I prefer 'enquiry' to 'investigation' as it gives a looser, less methodologically rigid and more philosophical sense to the project, which I believe to be appropriate.[49] The real issue is with the Greek term *phusis* and more generally with the cognate terms *phusikoi* and *phusiologoi*, literally 'naturalists' and 'those who talk about nature'. It is highly misleading here to translate *phusis* as 'physics' or something similar, or to translate *phusikoi* or *phusiologoi* as 'physicists'.

The early Greek enquiry into nature was much broader than any modern conception of physics. This is clear from any inspection of what is included in works titled '*Peri Phuseōs*'. It is also clear that Plato recognized this, from *Phaedo* 96a5, where the questions Socrates first mentions in relation to *peri phuseōs historia* are to do with coming to be, existing and perishing, zoogony, psychology, epistemology and cosmology. So too in the *Timaeus* where Plato gives an account of *phusis*, giving the origins, development and current constitution of the cosmos and living things. The cosmos itself is a living thing and there is of course great emphasis on coming into being. This may seem relatively evident, but it is alarming how often terms such as physics, physicist and materialist are used in this context even in relatively modern work.[50] Physics/physicist also has connotations of physicalism or materialism, which are inappropriate for many thinkers before Plato. Only Leucippus and Democritus qualify as physicalists or materialists. Anaxagoras and *nous* would be a key example here, not least because Plato recognized Anaxagoras and *nous* as part of this enquiry concerning nature. We also need to be careful about the phrase 'physical explanation'. If what is meant by this is that some early Greek thinkers explained in terms of *phusis*, rather than in terms of the gods,[51] then that is generally, though not exclusively, true.[52] If what is meant is that explanation was in terms solely of physical entities, then that is quite false. A better phrase would be natural explanation. Grant has defined natural philosophy as 'all enquiries about the physical world', where I would insist on 'all enquiries about the natural world', especially for the early Greeks who believed there to be natural non-physical entities.[53] It is of course important to bring our understanding of *peri phuseōs historia* into line with modern discussions of the full connotations of meaning of *phusis*.

## Plato and *peri phuseōs skopein*

Plato did not reject all of *peri phuseōs historia* either in the *Phaedo* or elsewhere, or consider *peri phuseōs historia* to be entirely physical or mechanical in ontology or explanation.[54] In the *Phaedo*, he accepted an explanation of the earth's stability in terms of equipoise and also accepted a like to like principle. In the *Philebus* Plato says that:

> Well, Protarchus, should we say that the whole universe is ruled by unreason, irregularity and chance, or on the contrary, as some of those who came before us said, say that *nous* and a marvellous organizing intelligence steer (*diakubernan*) it.[55]

So Plato recognized and approved of a tradition of thinking in terms of *kubernan* in his predecessors.[56] Another significant passage is *Gorgias* 508a1–5:

> The wise (*hoi sophoi*) said this, Callicles, that heavens and earth and gods and humans hold together by partnership, friendship, propriety, self-control and justice. This is why they call this whole a cosmos, O friend, and not disorder or intemperance.

Again, Plato recognized a tradition of explanation in cosmology that went beyond the physical or mechanical. One reason for the overestimation of the extent to which early Greek thinkers were mechanists stems from a too stereotypical approach to Socrates' autobiography whereby Plato is supposed to reject all of *peri phuseōs historia* as physical or mechanical. I also reject the idea that Plato had only one typology or taxonomy for earlier natural philosophy.[57] So, for example, the 'gods and giants' distinction of the *Sophist* is different from that employed in Socrates' autobiography in the *Phaedo*, as is the contrast between those who believed in an 'indefinite plurality of things' and those who did not,[58] those who employ *tuchē* (chance) and those who do not or those who employed *ou mallon* arguments and those who do not. Plato did not have a simple teleology versus physical/mechanical views bifurcation for earlier natural philosophy.[59]

This is important as it gives us more flexibility in understanding earlier natural philosophy and gives us some further insights into some debates. It is also important evidence that it would be wrong to see early Greek thought simply as telelologists versus mechanists, or even teleologists versus materialists. In conjunction with the proliferation of uses of *kubernan* and *kratein* listed above, these passages from the *Philebus* and the *Gorgias* give us justification for the investigation of other possibilities.

It is also critical to recognize that Socrates' biography is not the only source of information in Plato on the *peri phuseōs* tradition. At *Phaedrus* 270cd, Plato has Socrates say:

> So see what Hippocrates and true reason (*ho alēthēs logos*) say concerning nature (*peri phuseōs skopei*).

This passage is interesting for Plato scholarship, as Plato clearly thinks that there is a proper method for conducting some form of enquiry *peri phuseōs*,[60] and this is at least part of it.[61] This discussion of method is prompted by Socrates' question of whether it is possible to gain any worthwhile knowledge of the nature of the soul (*psuchēs oun phusin*, 270c1) without the nature of the whole man (*tēs tou holou phuseōs*, 270c2). Phaedrus replies that if Hippocrates is to be trusted, we cannot know the body either except by this means of pursuing the enquiry (*Phaedrus* 270c).[62] It is also worth noting here that Plato and Hippocrates had a dynamic conception of *phusis*, as at *Phaedrus* 270d we ought to investigate its power to act (*skopein tēn dunamin autou*).

With the multiple uses of *skopein* in this passage, we could just as easily use *peri phuseōs skopein* as we could *peri phuseōs historia*. Here *skopein* means to contemplate/consider/examine/observe, so perhaps the simplest English translation would be 'the contemplation of nature'.[63] It is important that we do not fixate on Socrates' autobiography as the supposed primary source of information on Plato and early Greek thought, and it is also important that we do not have too stereotypical an account of Socrates' autobiography. There are of course agendas in play here in relation to Plato, so I will make my own clear. I take Plato to be serious and sophisticated in discussing his own natural philosophy and also sophisticated in discussing or alluding to earlier Greek thought on nature.

## Conclusion

This book then will argue for the importance of a tradition of *kubernan* and *kratein* as key ideas in early Greek thought on nature and will argue that no early Greek was a mechanist in any meaningful sense. I emphasize again that this is not to deride or downgrade the early Greeks who had interesting ideas on how the cosmos gained and maintained order. It does though raise questions of what we value and why in their thought. Some, especially those who are sceptical or opposed to this line of thought, might like to read the chapter on Leucippus and Democritus first, as these are the best candidates for mechanists in early Greek thought. I will proceed chronologically though, as I think there is much to be gained from a fresh and more flexible look at Homer and Hesiod on issues of order and how the Ionian thinkers may have been influenced by and transformed their ideas.

# 2

# Order in Homer and Hesiod

There is a great deal of order and regularity in the worlds described by the epic poetry of Homer and Hesiod. That is so both in a social/political sense, in that there is an order to the affairs of gods and humans and also in the sense that what we would think of as natural phenomena occur in a reasonably regular manner. It is clear that for both Homer and Hesiod this social/political order is generated and maintained by the gods. This is the focus for both of them, though both have important things to say about the relation of the gods to what we would consider to be natural phenomena as well. This is interesting for its own sake, since it is part of Greek thinking about the order of the world, but is also important in relation to the enquiry concerning nature. One aspect of the differences here is the transfer of the attributes of the gods to the new *archai* such as the unlimited, air, fire or mind. A simple lead example is that while in Homer and Hesiod the gods are *athanatos*, undying, in Anaximander it is the *apeiron* that is *athanatos*.[1] What I want to investigate are possible ways in which the gods generate and maintain social/political order in Homer and Hesiod and how that may be transferred to the *archai* of those conducting the enquiry into nature. Of particular interest will be Homer and Hesiod's use of *kubernan* and *kratein* along with their cognates and related verbs and the fact that nothing happens by chance in the worlds of Homer and Hesiod. This is part of a broader strategy on my part to attempt to understand why the early enquiry concerning nature had a particular content and shape. This cannot be explained on simple 'Greek Miracle', 'Greek Enlightenment' or '*muthos* to *logos*' (myth to reason) accounts, or by supposing that for some reason abstract philosophical issues were suddenly engaged with. Such considerations do not generate the specific content we find in the fragments. I will develop this theme in Chapter 5. If we are to understand early Greek philosophies of nature properly, we must understand them in context as a reaction to and development of what we find in Homer and Hesiod. Here I will argue that there is an important sense in which Homer and Hesiod did not have a conception or philosophy of nature in that they did not have a term for nature in the general sense nor did they have any contraries for it. There is one and only one use of the term *phusis* in Homer and none in Hesiod. This singular instance needs to be looked at carefully to see what sense Homer has used it in and to see what it tells us about Homer's world. I argue that what provides the link to later thinking about order is Homer and Hesiod's notion of *moira*, 'lot' or 'fate' where we do find an interesting range of contrasts and contraries, we find *kata moiran* (according to *moira*), significant in relation to the later *kata phusin* (according to nature) and an interesting use of *kratein* in relation to *moira*.

## Homer, Hesiod and *phusis*

There is a reasonable sense in which neither Homer nor Hesiod had a philosophy of or indeed a conception of nature. This is not a criticism of Homer and Hesiod, merely recognition that these were epic poets who worked before the *peri phuseōs historia* tradition and had other major concerns. This is true of other early cultures too, and in an important recent book, 'Before Nature', Rochberg has argued that the Babylonians, while they did important work in astronomy and medicine, had no concept of nature.[2] They had 'no articulated sense of nature in our terms, no reference or word for it.'[3] There is no general term for nature in either Homer or Hesiod. It is significant that when at *Iliad* XVIII 468 ff. Hephaestus makes a great shield that has the earth, heavens, sea, sun, moon and stars on it, which is generally thought to be a representation of Homer's world, we do not find the words *phusis* or *cosmos* at all. It is also significant that in the Babylonian culture, and in Homer and Hesiod, all diseases ultimately derive from the gods.[4] There is no sense, as there importantly was in the Hippocratic writers, that diseases are natural. In Babylonia, you would be first seen by a Baru who would interpret omens and diagnose how you had offended the gods, then by an Ashipu who would help you make recompense to the gods, and only then receive what we would recognize as medical treatment from a third person known as an Asu. The beginning of the *Iliad* has the Greek army at Troy afflicted by a plague sent by the gods because Atreides had dishonoured Chryses the priest. The plague is to be dealt with by assuaging the gods, not by medical means.[5]

Most importantly in Homer and Hesiod, there are no contraries or contrasts to a term for nature. So nowhere do we find a contrast between the natural and the unnatural or the non-natural or the supernatural or other such terms. Again, that is not unusual and to quote Rochberg's *Before Nature*:

None of the categories defined in relation to nature ... the supernatural, preternatural, artificial and unnatural serve in any but an anachronistic way to describe what the Assyrian and Babylonian scribes observed and predicted in their conceptual and experiential world.[6]

In Akkadian, there is a contrast between *kitti* and *la kitti*, in some contexts 'true' and 'untrue', in astronomical contexts 'regular' and 'irregular', but no contrasts for nature.[7] In the mythologies of many early cultures, what we would consider to be natural and supernatural were mixed together without any distinction between them. I would also agree with Hesse that:

This monism of the Ionians cannot properly be called materialism, since materialism cannot arise until non-material forces or powers have been distinguished from matter.[8]

Here we come to an important methodological issue. My view is that ideas of nature are best investigated through examining local contrasts of what is and what is not nature.[9] Whether we can produce a definitive modern account of what nature is or not, ancient ideas of nature should not be investigated as matching or failing to match such an account, but in terms of how they define themselves, explicitly or implicitly through contrasts. As we do not find such contrasts in Homer and Hesiod, in this sense I argue they had no conception of or philosophy of nature. This is not to deny that they may have had considerable knowledge of nature, in the folk knowledge sense of knowing the heavens, flora and fauna and treatments for diseases.[10] As Grant comments,

The first humans must have been aware of nature, which was all around them and which was involved in everything they did.[11]

I have no doubt that these peoples were aware of what was around them but would contest whether they conceived of all these things as 'nature', would deny that they had a term for 'nature' and would deny that any had a conception of what was contrary to nature. There were things that we might consider to be supernatural or magical in the worlds of Homer and Hesiod. Whether they would consider these things to be supernatural or magical, and whether they treated them differently compared to other phenomena, is another issue. Without a strong conception of or vocabulary for what nature is (and that is hardly Homer or Hesiod's main concern in their poems), it is difficult to develop a strong conception of or vocabulary for what is beyond or contrary to the normal or natural (again, not a major concern for Homer or Hesiod). As we shall see, Homer does have an extensive and interesting vocabulary of contrasts for *moira*, lot or fate.

## Homer and *phusis*

At *Odyssey* X, 303 Hermes gives the Moly plant to Odysseus, who is on his way to meet Circe, and Odysseus says that Hermes showed him its *phusis* (*moi phusin autou edeixe*). I agree with Naddaf that it is interesting that Homer uses *phusis* here, rather than *eidos*, *morphē* or *phuē*, (form, shape or growth), such that we can expect more about the Moly than just its exterior aspects, which would be the case with these other words. As Heubeck has argued, *deiknunai* can mean more than simply 'to show' but can mean to instruct as well.[12] As Odysseus is going to have to use the Moly to counter Circe's attempt to transform him into a pig, perhaps Odysseus needs to know more about the Moly than just its exterior appearance. According to Naddaf, Circe is a witch, with a magic wand, who casts spells, so Odysseus needs knowledge of the full *phusis* of the Moly to ward off her magic.[13] While the use of *phusis* is interesting at *Odyssey* X, 303, I disagree with Naddaf on the nature of Circe. I do not consider Circe to be a witch, and this is important in relation to how Homer conceived of the world. It is also worth noting that Odysseus is a hero who is *polumēchanos, polutropos, polutlas and polumētis* (of many devices, much travelled/turned, much enduring, of many counsels) rather than a rank and file mortal.[14] I have argued in detail elsewhere that Circe was not a witch for Homer and these are the key arguments.[15]

Neither the narrator nor Homer's characters treat Circe as a witch nor refer to her as a witch. This is not surprising as Homer did not have terms for 'witch' or 'magic',[16] nor did he have general terms for nature or natural, nor did he have contraries for them. If we think of a witch as someone who calls on powers outside themselves, Circe was not a witch. Homer's poems gave intrinsic powers to goddesses who need not, did not, and indeed could not call on other powers.[17]

Circe was a Homeric goddess with powers similar to other Homeric divinities.[18] A critical question here is this: when Zeus throws a thunderbolt, is he exercising the powers he has as a Homeric god or is he doing something magical? The former is intuitive and correct. We can then ask: when Circe does something that we consider to be magical, is she exercising her powers as a Homeric goddess or doing something magical? If she does do something magical, how does that differ from Zeus and other Homeric deities exercising their powers? An interesting case to consider here is when Aphrodite breaks Paris' helmet strap to rescue him in his fight with Menelaus and then envelops him in mist and takes him away (*Iliad* III, 369 ff.). Is she exercising her powers as a Homeric goddess or performing magic? Note that she does this 'easily, as a goddess can', *Iliad* III, 381.

Circe has powers that are shared by other Homeric deities. Like other Homeric gods and goddesses, she is capable of weather working,[19] travelling unseen,[20] transformations,[21] foresight,[22] and influence over animals.[23] There is no indication that Circe exercises these powers differently from other gods and goddesses. If Circe is a witch for having or using any one of these powers, there are many other witches in Homer. So too if we define witch in terms of a collection of these powers, there will still be many others, and indeed as the male gods have these powers, there will be warlocks too.[24]

Does Circe do anything morally problematic in exercising her powers such that she should be considered to be a witch? She turns some of Odysseus' crew into pigs, but other deities do worse than this in Homer without being witches or warlocks.[25] Circe does not send a deadly pestilence on the Greek army (*Iliad* I, 10), nor, unlike Athena, does she generate bad winds and huge waves to kill mortals who have offended her (*Odyssey* V, 108 ff.). Circe does advise Odysseus on what we would call necromancy. However, Circe does not perform necromancy though Odysseus, Hermes and Persephone do.[26] Does that make them witches and warlocks? What we call necromancy would have had different resonances for the Greeks of Homer's time. There is no sense in Homer that either the pig transformation or necromancy is something impious or sacrilegious, nor is there any sense that there will be a punishment from the gods.[27]

Circe's *rhabdos* was not a magic wand but was rather a herding stick. It is described as very long, *perimēkēs*, more appropriate for a herding stick. It can also be contrasted with the *rhabdoi* possessed by Hermes and Athena, both of which are gold. There is a further contrast in how these *rhabdoi* are used. Circe drives (*elaunein*), appropriate for a herding stick, while Athena touches. Circe did not use a spell.[28] Here it is important to be clear on the sequence of events. First Circe gets Odysseus' crew to drink, then she drives them with her *rhabdos*, then she pens them in sties. She gets Odysseus to drink, then hits him with her *rhabdos*. What Circe then says, when Odysseus does not move, is 'go now to the sty, and lie with your comrades', *ercheo nun supheonde, met' allōn lexo hetairōn* (*Odyssey* X, 320). That is a herding instruction, backed up by a stroke of the herding stick, rather than a spell. I would expect a spell to be phrased differently, and certainly in later Greek I would expect *katadesmeuein*, 'to bind'. If we look at the reverse sequence, when Circe transforms the pigs back into men, we find further corroboration. First Circe drives them, then she applies the *pharmakon* and there is no mention of any spell. What Circe says at *Odyssey* X, 326-8, after she has attempted to transform Odysseus, is of critical importance:

> I am amazed that you have drunk this *pharmakon* and not been beguiled. No other man at all has resisted this *pharmakon*, once he has drunk it past the barrier of his teeth.

Circe is amazed that the *pharmakon* has not worked, not that the supposed 'magic wand' has failed or that the supposed 'spell' has failed.

## Circe *polupharmakos*

The making and composition of what Circe uses to transform Odysseus' crewmen is also of interest and importance. There is good evidence that *pharmaka* are either naturally occurring plants or are simple preparations of such plants in Homer.[29] I favour translating *pharmaka* consistently as 'herbs' here.[30] That *pharmaka* are natural in this sense is clear in the case of the Moly *pharmakon*, where Hermes simply picks it from the ground.[31] It is also clear for Agamede where *pharmaka* are 'nourished by the broad surface of the earth' (*Iliad* XI, 741), and for Helen and Polydamna where Egypt produces the most *pharmaka* from the grain giving earth, with no differentiation between grain and *pharmaka* (*Odyssey* IV, 228). Circe's *pharmaka* might be thought to be different in that they are *kaka* (X, 213) and *lugra* (X, 236), but such *pharmaka* are also naturally occurring in Homer.[32] When Circe makes her *kukeōn* (X, 290, 317), presumably a simple mix of barley, cheese and wine,[33] the verb is *teuchein*, a standard verb of manufacturing, handiwork or cooking in Homer, rather than anything more sinister. Circe throws, *balein*, the *pharmaka* into the *kukeōn*.[34] So Circe does not enchant her *pharmaka*. She has no need to. Homer's poems may credit plants with more powers than we would, but these are natural powers in the sense that they are inherent to the plants and are not induced by any magical action of gods or humans.

There are some issues in relation to the Moly given by Hermes to Odysseus.[35] It is not clear what Odysseus is supposed to do with the Moly (possess it, eat it, put it in Circe's *kukeōn*, or something else) in order to be proof against Circe's *pharmaka*.[36] Nor is it entirely clear why, if Odysseus has the Moly, he makes Circe swear an oath to do him no further harm. Odysseus may be meant to eat it raw, or perhaps consume some simple preparation of it. If that makes him proof against one administration of Circe's *pharmaka*, that would make reasonable sense of the narrative.[37]

Circe then was not a witch, did not have a magic wand and did not cast spells. So contra Naddaf, the hero Odysseus did not need a thorough knowledge of the

Moly in order to combat Circe. In fact, all we are actually told about the Moly is that it has a black root and a milky flower, and that while it is hard for mortals to dig, the gods can do anything. To the modern eye, this is a little disappointing as we see the Moly as magical and would like to know more about it.[38] The reason we get so little about it is that the *pharmaka* of Hermes and Circe are naturally occurring and Homer sees nothing magical here. Odysseus simply consumes the Moly. It is also important here that Hermes tells Odysseus 'all of the cunning plans of Circe' (*panta de toi ereō olophōia dēnea Kirkēs*, X, 289), but says no more than that Circe will mix and *kukeōn* and throw *pharmaka* in it (X, 290). There is nothing here for Homer to make a great fuss about, especially as this is marginal to the drama of the interaction between Circe and Odysseus. Homer is more interested in what Odysseus must do to show bravery and leadership.

This sort of knowledge of the *phusis* of *pharmaka* may be quite widespread in Homer, at least in the sense that Circe is *polupharmakos*, 'of many herbs' (*Odyssey* X, 276). There are also the *ietroi polupharmakoi*, healers/doctors of many herbs, at *Iliad* XVI, 28.[39] Agamede, who knew all the *pharmaka* nourished by the earth (*Iliad* XI, 741), and quite possibly Helen and Polydamna had such knowledge of *pharmaka* too, especially as every Egyptian was an *iētros*, healer (*Odyssey* IV, 231).[40] The *phusis* we get of the Moly is form, use and property. In order to be immune to Circe's *pharmaka*, you must use, probably eat, this *pharmakon*, which has the property of making you immune to the *pharmaka* Circe will use. Circe is not a witch, the Moly is not magical and Odysseus the hero does not need to know why the gods created it or to know its full origins, growth and current constitution.

It is no surprise that we do not find terms for witch or the idea of a witch until we have articulated ideas about nature and contraries to nature. We find none of these in Homer or Hesiod. I would draw a parallel here with my treatment of the early enquirers into nature. It is of course tempting to say that Homer's Circe is the first witch in the Western literary tradition, just as it is tempting to say that Anaximander was the first Darwinist.[41] One can see the motivation for these statements but both are incorrect and seriously misleading.

## *Kubernan* and *kratein*

Let me now address the question of order in Homer and Hesiod and how ideas of divine control of that order were transferred to the *archai* of the early Greek enquirers. This is in effect an extension of a view of Jaeger, that:

What happens in Anaximander's argument (and that of his successors in line) is that the predicate God, or rather the Divine, is transformed from the traditional deities to the first principle of Being (at which they arrived by rational investigations), on the ground that the predicates usually attributed to the gods of Homer and Hesiod are inherent in that principle to a higher degree or can be assigned to it with greater certainty.[42]

The predicates that Jaeger refers to are ungenerated, incorruptible, undying, indestructible. Anaximander's *apeiron* was undying and we find this in other places too, so Euripides Frag. 910:

> Blessed is the person who practices enquiry, he will neither harm nor wrong his fellow citizens, but looking at the ageless order of immortal nature (*all' athanatou kathorōn phuseōs kosmon agērōn*), will ask where, from what and in what way it was put together.

The contention is that ideas of divine control of the affairs of gods and humans and the cosmos more generally are transferred to the *archai* of the early enquirers into nature and this is the source for the use of the verbs *kubernan* and *kratein* for control and the source of *kata*... expressions like *kata phusin*, which becomes the common expression for 'according to nature', and other expressions such as *kata to chreōn* and *kata tou chronou taxin* 'according to what is proper' and 'according to the ordering of time', which we find in Anaximander's extant fragment, and *kata chreōn* and *kata erin* 'according to strife' and *kata ton logon* 'according to the logos', which we find in Heraclitus.

With *kubernan* and its cognates, we do not find their use other than in the nautical sense of steering in Homer and Hesiod. However, at *Odyssey* VIII, 555 ff. Alcinous says to Odysseus:

> Tell me your country, people and city, so that our ships may discern the course with their minds. The Phaeacians have no helmsmen (*kubernēteres*) nor any rudders, but the ships themselves know the thoughts and hearts of men.

This is significant as it suggests that the steering of a physical entity can be accomplished by a non-human entity that has a mind of its own. There are two other interesting verbs used in relation to the gods that have a sense of steering or guiding. Firstly, at *Odyssey* XVII, 218 we find that:

> As always, the god leads like to like (*hōs aiei ton homoion agei theos hōs ton homoion*).

This is the first known instance of a like to like principle in the Greek tradition. It is not explicitly a physical like to like principle, and is part of an insult to

Odysseus, who is told that he is the 'vile leading the vile' as he is working with animals. However, it is a god who 'leads' (*agei*) like to like and this principle could be used more broadly. Nor was like to like later thought of as a force acting between like things but it was thought of more as a principle by which like things were sorted together.[43] We can also look outside Homer and Hesiod here as Terpander,[44] Fragment 2 runs: *Zeu pantōn archa, pantōn agētor*, 'Zeus is *archē* of all, leader of all'. Our second verb is *ithunein*, to guide or to straighten, which is used in both senses. Certainly *ithunein* in Homer can mean to straighten, usually in relation to woodwork or military fortifications.[45] However at *Odyssey* V, 270; XI, 10; XII, 82; XII, 152 and *Iliad* XXIII, 317 *ithunein* is what a *kubernētēs*, a helmsman does, that is guides a ship.[46] The gods can guide as well, not in cosmological contexts, but they can and do guide projectiles to their target. Athena guided (*ithunen*) the arrow that strikes Menelaus on the belt (*Iliad* IV, 132) and Zeus guides all of the missiles (*pant' ithunei*) of the Trojans (*Iliad* XVII, 632).[47]

In Hesiod *Works and Days*, *ithunein* is used three times. Twice, at *Works and Days* 7 and 263, it means to straighten or rectify, as it is used in contrast to *skolios*, curved or crooked, and in relation to judgements. However, at *Works and Days* 9 it may mean 'guide' or it may mean 'straighten'. Hesiod begins by invoking the Muses, then invoking Zeus, asking him to *ithunein*, to guide or perhaps straighten the judgements. There are some interesting epistemological issues about the nature of Hesiod's account that are sensitive to the translation here, which I will come back to in the next chapter.

We do find *kratein* and its cognates used in Homer and Hesiod. Most uses of *kratein* are to express power over in circumstances that are not of great interest. However, we do find use of the adjective *krataiē* in the phrase *moira krataiē* nine times in Homer and once in a fragment of Hesiod. This phrase is usually translated as 'strong' or 'powerful' *moira* but without losing those connotations I will translate *krataiē* here as 'controlling'.[48] This phrase is interesting for several reasons. First, there is a sense in which *moira* expresses an order to the affairs of gods and humans in Homer and Hesiod. The gods (principally Zeus) set *moira* for humans and this structures much of what happens in their worlds. Second, we find a rich vocabulary of terms around *moira* and a rich vocabulary of contraries and contrasts. Third, we find the phrases *kata moiran* and *ou kata moiran*, 'according to *moira*' and 'not according to *moira*', which I find interesting in relation to the later phrase *kata phusin*, 'according to nature', found in the early enquirers into nature.

## Hephaestus, Phaeacian ships and mechanism

Hephaestus had bellows, tripods and golden maidens that could move themselves.[49] Some of the literature has treated these as precursors to or anticipations of later automata, not least because they were generated by the craftsman/blacksmith Hephaestus, who used simple tools.[50] Clearly the technology for fully mechanical beings did not exist yet, but the literature of the nineteenth century imagined automata and the literature of the twentieth century imagined robots/mechanoids/androids far in advance of their technology.[51] However, there is nothing to indicate that Hephaestus' works were mechanical entities. There is not even the simplest mechanical construction for their internal workings to explain how they might move themselves. The handmaidens have minds, understanding and speech,[52] while both the tripods and the bellows move at the willing of Hephaestus.[53] There is no need here for a dichotomy of magic and mechanism. The magic option I reject for the reasons given above. There is no magic in Homer, just deities exercising their powers.[54] Rather, we should consider Hephaestus' devices to be ensouled entities.[55] An interesting parallel here is Hesiod *Works and Days* 60 ff., where his Hephaestus, on the orders of Zeus, mixes earth and water, puts voice and strength into it and fashions it into a beautiful maiden. Athena then gives her knowledge of craft and Hermes gives her character. What is important here, as with Homer's Hephaestus, is that the gods use their powers to animate and ensoul these entities. Similar considerations apply to the Phaeacian ships. These are neither mechanical nor magical entities. They are capable of discerning the required course with their minds and know the hearts and thoughts of men. We are not told the provenance of the Phaeacian ships, but it may be significant that the Phaeacians are described as godlike (*antitheoisi*) at *Odyssey* VI, 238.

## The *moira* vocabulary

The Greek word *moira*, can mean share, portion or lot, or one's portion or lot in life, and so in some contexts, especially relating to the death of mortals, it has been translated as 'fate'. I am going to leave *moira* untranslated, as I think 'fate' can be misleading and may impose inappropriate modern conceptions of fate and determinism on Homer. There is also a goddess Moira. There are two other important related words here, *aisa*, which functions very much like *moira*, and again there is a goddess, Aisa. There is also *kēra*, which has more of a sense of death but can also mean doom, and yet again there is Kēr, the goddess of death or doom, although with *kēra* we do not get the interesting contrasts that we do with *moira* and *aisa*. Finally, there is *potmos* and its cognates, meaning 'lot' or 'destiny'.

We do get the sort of contrasts with *moira* and *aisa* that we get with *phusis* in later writers. So we can frequently find *kata moiran* or *ou kata moiran*, there is an instance of *para moira* (*Odyssey* XIV, 509) and several instances of *huper moiran* (*Odyssey* I, 34, 35; V, 46; *Iliad* XX, 30, 336; XXI, 517). We even find at *Odyssey* XX, 76 that Zeus knows the *moira* and *ammoira* for all mortals, where I would translate that Zeus knows what is and what is not the *moira* of all mortals. Similarly, we find *kat' aisan* at *Iliad* X, 445 and XVII, 716, and we find *kat' aisan . . . oud' huper aisan* at *Iliad* III, 59 and VI, 333. There is also a vocabulary of *kata kosmon* and *ou kata kosmon*, but this is never used in connection with the cosmos or the regular behaviour of natural phenomena. It is used in relation to things that are well said or not, or orderly horses or armies.[56]

In many instances *kata moiran/aisan* and *ou kata moiran/aisan* simply mean 'well/properly said' or 'not well/properly said', or have a sense of proper, duly or fitly.[57] There are other instances where *kata moiran* means 'in good order' or 'in their proper turn'.[58] However, there are passages where *kata moiran* certainly does relate to something like lot/fate. This might seem rather thin to base a transition from *kata moiran* to *kata phusin* on, but there is an important intermediate step. The extant fragment of Anaximander claims that things happen *kata to chreon*, and later I will argue that this should be translated 'according to what is proper' rather than the usual 'according to necessity'. So it is possible to trace a path from *kata moiran* to *kata phusin* via Anaximander's *kata to chreon*.

There are nine uses of *moira krataiē* in the *Iliad*.[59] In six instances *moira krataiē* is part of a larger phrase, *thanatos kai moira krataiē* 'death and controlling *moira*', sometimes said in the sense of 'death and controlling *moira* took him' as someone dies, at *Iliad* V, 83, XVI, 334 and XX, 477.[60] In other places it is said when it is thought that death is near to someone, so *Iliad* XVI, 853, XXI, 110 and XXIV, 132, with a sense of 'death and controlling *moira* will take you'. At *Iliad* XIX, 410 Achilles' horses speak to him, given human voice by Hera, saying that his day of doom is close, but 'we are not to blame, but a mighty god and controlling *moira* (*moira krataiē*)'. At *Iliad* V, 629 Heracles is 'urged on by controlling *moira* (*moira krataiē*) against godlike Sarpedon'. Finally, and perhaps most interestingly, at *Iliad* XXIV, 209 we find Hecabe saying to Priam about their son Hector, 'In this way controlling *moira* (*moira krataiē*) spun with thread for him at birth'. That is important because it gives *moira krataiē* an influence from birth to death.

## Setting *moira*

Who or what sets order in Homer and how is it regulated and maintained? There are three clear instances where *moira* is spun for humans at birth:

> In this way controlling (*krataiē*) *moira* spun with thread for him at birth, when I myself gave birth to him, that swift footed dogs would satiate themselves on him far from his parents.
>
> *Iliad* XXIV, 209

> We have all come down from Olympus to join this battle, in order that he (Achilles) will suffer no harm today. After this he will suffer whatever *aisa* spun with thread for him at his birth.
>
> *Iliad* XX, 127

> Nor in the meantime will he suffer any evil or harm, until he sets foot on his own land. After that he will suffer whatever *aisa* according to grave Klothes spun with their thread for him, when his mother bore him.
>
> *Odyssey* VII, 195

We might add to those Hector's comments to his wife at *Iliad* VI, 488:

> No man has ever escaped *moira*, whether he is worthless or noble, when once he is born.

We might also add Agamemnon's comment at *Iliad* X, 71 that:

> I suppose Zeus sent heavy misery to us at birth.

It is also clear that the gods spin *moira* for humans. There are five passages where spinning is attributed to the gods, one where it is attributed to Zeus and one where it is attributed to some daemon, all using the verb *epiklōthein*, to spin.[61] Primarily it is Zeus among the gods who sets *moira*, as *Iliad* XXIV, 525 ff. makes clear, with Zeus giving out gifts of evil and good things to humans. This should be clear from the setup of the *Iliad*, as in *Iliad* I, 1ff. where the Muses sing of the accomplishment of the will of Zeus. I am not overly concerned here about the relationship of personified Fates and standard gods. There is a debate in Homer scholarship as to whether Zeus is superior to fate or not and whether fate in Homer is equivalent to the will of Zeus. My own view is that Zeus is not independent of *moira*. If the *moira* of mortals is spun for them at birth, and Zeus is in complete control of that spinning, why would Zeus spin death in battle at the hands of Patroclus for his son Sarpedon? This is clearly something he does not want (he mourns Sarpedon, *Iliad* XVI, 456) and which he seriously considers changing. I will not press this point as my main concern here is that someone, whether that is Zeus, the gods more generally or the personified 'Fates' of Moira, Aisa and Kēra, or some mix of those, set *moira* for mortals and so generate an order for gods and humans in Homer. There is also an interesting passage in the Derveni papyrus that gives us a link between spinning fate, Zeus and Zeus exercising his power by means of *kratein* and a transfer of the attributes of the gods to a substance. Derveni papyrus Col. 19 runs:

> Existing things have each been called a single name on account of what controls (*epikratountos*) them, all things being called Zeus for this reason. Air controls (*epikratei*) all as far as it wants to. When they say that Moira span (*epiklōsai*) they say that the understanding of Zeus sanctions how the things that are, that have been generated and the things that will be must come to be and cease.

We will look at this passage more closely in Chapter 6. There is also an interesting passage at Euripides *Iphegenia in Tauris* 1486 where Athena says:

> What is proper controls you and the gods (*to gar chreōn sou te kai theōn kratein*).

That is significant as a key steppingstone in the development of ideas about control and in the move from *kata moiran* to *kata phusin* via Anaximander on *kata to chreōn* and Heraclitus Fr. 80 on *kat' erin kai chreōn*. We will look at this more closely in Chapter 5.

## Maintenance of *moira*

How is *moira* maintained? There are many passages where it is clear that in order for *moira* to be maintained there must be the intervention of the gods, otherwise something would happen *huper moira*, beyond *moira*. So for example:

> Then the Argives would have achieved their return home *hupermora*, if Athena had not spoken to Hera.
>
> *Iliad* II, 155

> The Argives would have grasped glory *huper Dios aisan* due to their power and strength, but Apollo urged on the Aeneans.
>
> *Iliad* XVII, 321

> Then would unhappy Odysseus have died *huper moron* if flashing eyed Athena had not given him wisdom.
>
> *Odyssey* V, 436

A further important passage here is *Odyssey* V, 113 ff., where Zeus bids Calypso to send Odysseus on his way, as it is not his *moira* to die far from his home and friends. Do humans also act to maintain *moira*? This is more controversial, as it begins to touch on issues of *moira* as fate and its relation to human choice and action, but at *Iliad* XX, 332 ff., Aeneas is advised that Achilles is better and is loved by the immortals, so he should withdraw rather than fight him, in order that he does not beyond his *moira* (*mē kai huper moiran*) go to the house of Hades.

## Inevitable *moira*?

Is *moira* inevitable or inescapable in Homer? This is a complex and contested question and it is more than can be done here to decide this matter. Whatever the ultimate decision on that issue, it must be stressed that *moira* is very strong. The reason I am interested in this issue is the transfer thesis. The language of *kratein* for how the *archai* control the cosmos comes directly from Homer and Hesiod on *moira*, the language of *kubernan* less directly but the influences are still perceptible. Where do the early enquirers into nature get the idea of what we would call inviolable laws of nature? If *moira* in Homer is inviolable, then we have a good precursor; if it is not inviolable but very strong, then it is only a small step to inviolable laws of nature. There is no *ex nihilo* generation of this sort of thinking, no 'Greek Miracle'.

It is important to make a distinction between types of *moira* statement in Homer. To say that 'all mortals are fated to die' is clearly a different sort of statement from 'tomorrow you die in battle at the hands of X'. So, in the first context one might translate *moira* as fate, but there are other contexts where *moira* is less inevitable. Is it straightforward that all mortals must die though? This may not be quite so clear as one might think. Could Odysseus become immortal? At *Odyssey* V, 136 and 209 Calypso makes the following offer when attempting to persuade Odysseus to stay with her, by saying 'You would be immortal (*athanatos t' eiēs*)'. Odysseus recalls this promise twice, at *Odyssey* VII, 256 and XXIII, 336, which are duplicate lines:

> She nourished me and promised she would make me immortal and ageless for all my days (*athanaton kai aghraon ēmata panta*).

One can argue that Calypso is lying here in order to persuade Odysseus to stay and she has no power to make Odysseus immortal; indeed, it is beyond the power of any of the gods to make a human immortal in the strong sense.

However, there is also another possibility. Circe and Athena have the ability to make humans younger, so it might be the case that Calypso could periodically rejuvenate Odysseus so that he would not die and would not age while he was with her. Against that, it is clear at *Odyssey* V, 113, where Zeus instructs Calypso to let Odysseus go, that Odysseus' *moira* is to return home, so anything Calypso offers can only be temporary.

There is also the case of Zeus' son, Sarpedon, who is fated (*moir*) to be killed by Patroclus (*Iliad* XVI, 433 ff.). Zeus tells Hera that he is unsure whether to save Sarpedon or not. Hera's reply is:

> Most dread son of Kronos, what a tale you have told! A man who is mortal, long so destined by *moira*, and you wish to free him entirely (*exanalusai*) from dolorous death? Do it (*herd*). The other gods will entirely disagree with it though.
> 
> *Iliad* XVI, 440[62]

It is clear that Zeus can do what he has in mind here and it is also clear that other gods have this ability too as Hera is concerned that if Zeus does this, other gods will do it for their children as well. Precisely what Zeus has in mind is less clear. Does he wish to save Sarpedon from death in this instance or to save him from death permanently? In favour of the latter option, *exanalusai* looks rather strong for one instance of danger. It may also be that Hera's reply is a little more subtle than has been appreciated. If she does mean 'free him entirely from death' the point may be that Zeus cannot do this but can only save him from this particular death. Zeus will have to save Sarpedon again and again if he does not want him to die. As with Calypso, that may be a possibility. If Athena and Circe can rejuvenate humans one would expect Zeus can too, and certainly he seems to have the power to remove Sarpedon from any external danger. In relation to this passage it should be noted that Zeus does save Sarpedon from imminent death twice, at *Iliad* V, 662, when he is struck in the thigh by a spear but his father 'wards off his destruction', and at *Iliad* XII, 400, when Sarpedon is struck by an arrow but Zeus 'wards off the *kēras*'.[63] Other divinities save their favourites too, for example, Aphrodite saving Paris at *Iliad* III, 369 ff., and Athena saving Menelaus at *Iliad* V, 290, so too Poseidon at *Iliad* XX, 291 and Apollo at *Iliad* XX, 321, 443. However, in each case one might argue that is the maintenance of *moira* (these characters were not fated to die then), and the issue at *Iliad* XVI, 433 ff. is whether Zeus should change the *moira* of Sarpedon.

We have looked at some counter-factual passages where something would have happened beyond *moira* if a god had not intervened. There are usually held to be two passages that state that things actually happened beyond *moira*. Our first passage is significant as being part of the opening of the *Odyssey*.

> Mortals blame (*aitiōntai*) the gods. It is from us, they say, that evils come, but by themselves, due to their own recklessness, they have pain beyond that which was allotted (*kai ... huper moron*), like now, when Aegisthus (*kai ... huper moron*) beyond that which was allotted took the wife of the son of Atreus and slew him.
>
> *Odyssey* I, 35

I agree with commentators here who have said that we need to give the *kai* its full force of something in addition to something else.[64] Humans have pain beyond their *moira* and that is due to their own recklessness. I take this passage to be critical as it occurs early in the *Odyssey* and sets the tone, and also because we see instances of it played out in the *Odyssey*. If you do stupid or reckless things, the result is worse for you than if you do not. Odysseus' crew are clearly warned several times not to eat the cattle, but in *Odyssey* XII stupidly and recklessly they do so. Importantly, it is not presented as their fate that they have to eat the cattle, but their poor choice that they do so. So too at Odyssey X, 45 ff. Odysseus' crew stupidly open the bag of winds, to their detriment. The second passage for something happening beyond *moira* is at *Iliad* XVI, 780:

> Then beyond what was fated (*huper aisan*) the Achaeans were the better.

If one wants to argue for inevitable fate in Homer, then one can isolate these passages by arguing that they deal with 'lot' while other passages deal with fate, or by arguing that these passages are phrased in this manner for dramatic or poetic effect and Homer does not intend to say that anything *huper moira* could actually happen.

I am not convinced that these are the only passages that generate problems for the idea of inviolable fate in Homer though. At *Iliad* XX, 30 Zeus says that:

> I fear (*deidō*) the wall will be taken *huper moron*.

Why would Zeus fear that something would happen *huper moron*? Especially if Zeus knows what is and what is not the *moira* of all mortals? So too this is problematic if Zeus is in control of and sets the *moira* of all humans. There is a similar passage at *Iliad* XXI, 517, where Apollo enters Troy because he is concerned that the Greeks may breach the walls *huper moron*. Problems are also posed by the passage at *Iliad* XVII, 327, where Apollo says:

> I have seen other men trusting in their strength, their might, their manhood and their numbers hold their country against Zeus (*kai huper Dia*).

One might argue for a pattern here. If one does something exceptional (in trusting strength, might, manhood, etc.) then it is possible to get slightly better than your lot. If one does something, reckless, cowardly or stupid it is possible to get slightly worse than your lot. On the issue of whether it is someone's *moira* to die on a specific day, here it would seem that the gods can, and do, intervene.[65] As we have seen, Zeus (for Sarpedon), Aphrodite (for Paris) and Athena (for Menelaus) all intervene to delay death. It is also possible for the gods to bring forward the day of death. So for example:

> Pallas Athena was hurrying on (*epornue*) his day of doom (*morsimon ēmar*) under mighty Peleus.
>
> *Iliad* XV, 613

A further consideration here is whether Achilles, who is said to have two fates, has a genuine choice between those fates. So at *Iliad* IX, 411 Achilles says that:

> My mother, the silver footed goddess Thetis, tells me that twofold dooms (*kēras*) are carrying me towards death (*thanatoio*).[66]

So either Achilles stays and fights, when he will win glory but not return home, or he can return home without glory and as at *Iliad* IX, 416 'my end of death will not reach me swiftly'. Does he have a genuinely free choice in this matter? Elsewhere in the *Iliad* mortals are depicted as making genuine choices, sometimes with the intervention of a god helping to decide, sometimes not. We have seen passages where it is said something would happen beyond *moira* if someone had not intervened. One could take the view that nothing could happen beyond fate. Does that mean that the intervention was fated as well? I would say that imposes an anachronistic, unwarranted later determinism on Homer. Homer as literature is much more interesting if his characters can make genuine choices. Mortals may not be able ultimately to escape death, but can possibly better their lot by choosing to act in ways that Homer approves of.

I do not claim to have any definitive solution to these issues here, just to have raised some of the problems in what is a highly complex matter. On whether there is a definitive solution, I would ask two questions. First, with around 30,000 lines of oral poetry to co-ordinate, which quite possibly synthesize previous oral traditions, can we expect Homer to give an entirely consistent account of *moira*? Second, can we expect Homer, whose main concerns may have been poetic/literary/dramatic to produce a philosophically sound and entirely consistent account of *moira* in an age before any formal philosophy?[67] Without doubt *moira* is very strong but whether it is in the fullest sense inescapable is not entirely clear and I very much doubt that it would have been entirely clear either to the early enquirers into nature.

## The gods of the poets

The gods of Homer and Hesiod are clearly not omnibenevolent and are not omniscient nor omnipotent either. I have two concerns here. First, I think it is inappropriate to try to impose later theological ideas on Homer and Hesiod, just as it is inappropriate to impose later philosophical or scientific ideas on the early enquirers into nature. Second, while I am aware there are passages that might suggest omnipotence or omniscience, particularly on the part of Zeus (all powerful, knows all) there are also passages where it is clear that Zeus' power or knowledge are limited. So at *Iliad* XIII, 5 Zeus is wrong about immortals, at *Works and Days* 50 and *Theogony* 535 Zeus is deceived by Prometheus, and in Homer Zeus is routinely deceived by Hera. We must remember here that this is poetry prior to any organized philosophy. So Homer and Hesiod may say things for poetic/dramatic effect (Zeus is all powerful, Zeus knows all) and not be overly concerned as to how that sits philosophically with other things they say. *Works and Days* 662 says that:

> The Muses taught me to delight in this 'not to be said even by a god' (*athesphaton*) hymn.

That is a marvellous piece of poetry extolling this hymn, but can we take it literally? How have the Muses taught it to Hesiod other than orally? Can Hesiod say this to himself or anyone else and so delight in it? We may see something similar with *moira*. Yes, there are strong expressions of *moira*, with great poetic and dramatic effect, but it may not be appropriate to interpret these in terms of later notions of fate, and they do not fully fit with what is said about *moira* in other places. One might also question whether the will of Zeus is always carried out. The *Iliad* opens with an impressive statement of giving an account of how Zeus' will was carried out concerning Troy, at *Iliad* I, 5 ff., and perhaps in a broad sweep sense that is true, but it is also clear that Zeus does not impose his will at all times, whether he is being deceived by Hera, having walls built against his will (*Iliad* XII, 5) or men holding their country against him (*Iliad* XVII, 327).

## Hesiod and *moira*

With Hesiod, there are some interesting similarities and dissimilarities with Homer. Although *moira* still has a role, Hesiod lays more emphasis on Zeus' *noos*, his mind or perhaps his will. Moira and Kēra are personified in Hesiod,[68] and we do not find the *kata moiran* phrase at all. As with Homer, there is no role for chance in Hesiod.[69] We do find the phrase *moira krataiē*, but only in one of the fragments, 212b line 1, with no context.

It is clear from the opening passage of *Works and Days* that Zeus is the key figure in the arrangement of the world. Through Zeus mortals are famed or unfamed, named or not named, and easily Zeus can strengthen, or crush the strong, easily he diminishes the conspicuous or increases the inconspicuous, easily he straightens the crooked or withers the proud. All this is done by the will of Zeus (here *ekēti*, so unambiguously 'will'). In both *Works and Days* and in the *Theogony* it is also clear that the mind/will of Zeus is inescapable. So at *Theogony* 613 we find that:

> It is not possible to cheat nor to elude the mind (*noon*) of Zeus.[70]

So too at *Works and Days* 105, where it is not possible to escape the diseases that Zeus has visited on humans, and Zeus has made those diseases silent:

> So it is not in any way possible to evade the mind (*noon*) of Zeus.

The verb used to describe Zeus' reign is *kratein*. So at *Theogony* 403, we find that:

> He himself has great power and reigns (*autos de mega kratei ēde anassei*).

At *Works and Days* 252 ff. Zeus also has 30,000 spirits keeping watch on the judgements and deeds of humans.[71] Furthermore, in what follows Zeus has a daughter, Justice (*Dikē*), who knows of any wrongdoing and passes that on to Zeus, and at *Works and Days* 268 Zeus' eye sees all things and knows all things. There is also a strong sense of Zeus setting out justice in Hesiod. So at *Works and Days* 239 we find that 'far seeing Zeus marks out justice', while at *Works and Days* 275, Zeus has drawn up (*dietaxe*) this law (*nomon*) for men (animals devour each other but men know what is right).

## Conclusion

There is an important sense in which Homer and Hesiod did not have a conception or philosophy of nature. They had no term for nature and did not have any contrasts or contraries for it. This was not unusual for the ancient world, as Rochberg has argued in relation to the Babylonians.[72] There is no term for magic in Homer and no sense of magic being apart from nature. Circe certainly should not be considered to be a witch, as she does nothing other deities do not do and there is no term for witch in Homer. It was up to the early inquirers into *phusis* to develop a conception of what is and is not included in that term. In the next chapter I will argue that *historia* (enquiry) and *skopein* (to examine) are also absent from Homer and Hesiod and this is no accident as humans therein largely depended on the gods for anything of consequence that they knew. The early enquires into nature had to generate a notion of enquiry and seeking for themselves as well as a notion of nature. The Homeric gods generated order and exercised their control of affairs by 'leading' (*agein*) or by 'guiding' (*ithunein*), and through 'controlling *moira*' (*kratein* with *moira*), which they set up and actively maintained. As we shall see in the next chapter, later poets (Pindar, Bacchylides) use *kubernan* for the activities of their gods. With *moira* (and *aisa*) we do find a range of contrasts analogous to those for *phusis* in later writers. If these attributes of the gods are transferred to the *archai* of the early enquirers into nature, we can see where their usage of *kubernan* and *kratein* came from. As we shall see, *kata moiran* undergoes an interesting transformation into *kata phusin*. Whether *moira* was inevitable or not in Homer, it was certainly very strong and gave a good basis for thinking about exceptionless steering or control of nature. The intelligent, knowledgeable Phaeacian ships that steer themselves and do so successfully whatever the conditions may also form an important background to the *archai* of the early enquirers into nature, where those *archai* are said to steer.

# 3

# Early Ideas on Knowledge and Enquiry

I have avoided calling this chapter 'early epistemology', as approaching the material in that way can import later philosophical concerns and I am not convinced that Homer and Hesiod, although having some interesting things to say, had anything that would amount to a formal epistemology. The previous chapter looked at how the gods generate and maintain a form of order in Homer and Hesiod through *moira*. We saw that it required the actions of the gods to set up and maintain *moira* for mortals. In this chapter I want to look at what can be known about the gods and *moira* and how it can be known. I will argue there are significant differences with the early enquirers into nature and the idea of *historia* had to be generated as well as the idea of *phusis* in order for there to be *peri phuseōs historia*. Neither Homer nor Hesiod use *historia* or *skopein*. I will begin by looking at how the gods intervene in the world for Homer and Hesiod, as this is important for whether there can be general laws. This is a little more complex than it is usually portrayed, as I do not think that the term 'supernatural' properly captures what is going on. I will also argue that there are more problems in formulating laws in Homer and Hesiod than is generally recognized. The idea of a general law too had to be generated. The usual debate about Homer and knowledge is whether the ships and leaders catalogue of *Iliad* II, 484 ff. commits Homer to a form of scepticism. I argue it does not and try to broaden the approach by considering the status of the narrator and of the poem. How is it that the narrator is able to give this privileged account? This is important because it shows that in Homer if we want to know, we must appeal to the Muses rather than mount a *historia*. I argue this is typical of Homer and Hesiod. If humans wish to learn about *moira*, or about many other things, then they must turn to the gods.

## Actions of the gods

While there is a good deal of order for Homer and Hesiod, it is also well known that the gods actively interfere in events in their worlds. It is worth cataloguing how they do so. Some epithets of the gods indicate what they are able to do with meteorological phenomena. So Zeus is the cloud gatherer, Poseidon is the earth shaker and Zeus hurls thunderbolts. Other deities are also able to alter the weather. Athena, when offended (*Odyssey* V, 108) generates *anemone te kakon kai kumata makra*, an evil wind and huge waves, though she is also able to give a favourable wind, *Odyssey* II, 420, XV, 292. Athena can also generate mist to hide Odysseus at *Odyssey* VII, 140, XIII, 90. Circe and Calypso both give Odysseus favourable winds when he leaves their islands. The gods can and do intervene in the world on their own caprice, manipulating the weather to help or hinder Odysseus. It is also very important that it is possible for Athena to hold back the dawn, breaching the regularities of time and the heavens (*Odyssey* XXIII, 242). Zeus sends stars as portents to sailors (*Iliad* IV, 74). At *Iliad* XIX, 115 Hera can and does advance birth, causing a child to be born after a seven-month pregnancy. Diseases are also caused by the gods in both Homer and Hesiod.[1] The opening passage of the *Iliad* is:

> Sing, goddess, the wrath of Achilles Peleus' son, the ruinous wrath that brought on the Achaians woes innumerable, and hurled down into Hades many strong souls of heroes, and gave their bodies to be a prey to dogs and all winged fowls; and so the counsel of Zeus wrought out its accomplishment from the day when first strife parted Atreides king of men and noble Achilles. Who among the gods set the twain at strife and variance? Apollo, the son of Leto and of Zeus; for he in anger at the king sent a sore plague upon the host, so that the folk began to perish, because Atreides had done dishonour to Chryses the priest.[2]

To relieve the plague, there is no question of any cure, except trying to assuage the anger of the gods, by returning the daughter of the priest.[3] In Hesiod's *Works and Days* 85 ff., we have the tale of Pandora's jar carrying diseases, sent by Zeus as a punishment. We also have:

> But for those who practise violence and cruel deeds far-seeing Zeus, the son of Kronos, ordains a punishment. Often even a whole city suffers for a bad man who sins and devises presumptuous deeds, and the son of Kronos lays great trouble upon the people, famine and plague together, so that the men perish away, and their women do not bear children, and their houses become few, through the contriving of Olympian Zeus.[4]

The gods are also capable of interfering with human minds and indeed do so. Perhaps the most famous example of this in the *Iliad* is where Agamemnon, robbed of his lover by Achilles, steals Achilles' lover and then states that the cause of his behaviour was Zeus, Moira and the Erinyes taking away his understanding.[5] It is common in Homer for the gods to send bewilderment, infatuation, blindness or delusion to humans. This can work in a positive manner too, as at *Odyssey* V, 436 where Athena gives Odysseus wisdom (*epiphrosunē*) so that he does not perish.

There are several important instances of the gods interfering in battle between humans. At *Iliad* III, 369 ff. Paris is being choked by his helmet strap and would have been dragged away by Menelaus if Aphrodite had not intervened to break the helmet strap. Aphrodite then shrouds Paris in mist, snatches him up and then deposits him in a chamber. At *Iliad* V, 853 Athena catches a spear with her hands and diverts it before driving home a spear at V, 856, while at *Iliad* XI, 438 Athena prevents a spear strike on Odysseus from being fatal. At *Iliad* VIII, 311 Apollo causes an arrow to swerve, while Zeus twice saves his son Sarpedon from wounds being fatal at *Iliad* V, 662 and XII, 400. At *Iliad* XXIII, 859 ff. Teucer does not vow a sacrifice to Apollo and misses a bird with his arrow shot; Meriones does vow a sacrifice to Apollo and hits the bird. At *Iliad* XV, 458 ff. Teucer has his bowstring broken by Zeus, who is protecting Hector.

## Chance

It is an important fact about the worlds of Homer and Hesiod that nothing occurs by chance. Is it luck that at *Iliad* IV, 132 Menelaus is hit by an arrow on his belt where his corselet was doubled, and so was only scratched? No, Athena guided the arrow (*ithunen*) there. Is it by luck at *Iliad* V, 290 that a spear enters the nose by the eye and cuts through tongue and teeth? No, Athena guided it (*ithunen*). At *Iliad* XVII, 632 is it by luck that all the missiles of the Trojans hit home, whether shot by good men or bad? No, Zeus guides them all (*pant' ithunei*). When at *Odyssey* X, 551 the young and not very bright Elpenor wakes up having been very drunk, trips over a ladder on the roof of Circe's house and falls to his death, this is not a matter of chance but an evil *aisa* of some daemon (*Odyssey* XI, 61). The drawing of lots from a helmet might be thought to be a matter of chance, but is in fact *moira* working through what may appear to be chance for humans. It reveals the *moira* that has been set at birth for humans. It is important that at *Iliad* VIII, 70 ff. when lots are cast, a prayer is offered to Zeus concerning the outcome, which strongly suggests that the outcome is in Zeus' hands. The best way to phrase this may be that humans discover their lot through the drawing from the helmet. This is parallel to Zeus' scales at *Iliad* VIII, 70 ff. and XXII, 208 ff. where Zeus does not so much determine *moira* by raising the balance arm as reveal what has already been set. So too Menelaus is aware that 'death and *moira*' have already been prepared (*tetuktai, Iliad* III, 101).[6] There is one further passage in relation to *tuchē*, which is at *Iliad* VIII, 429ff. where Hera and Athena tire of battling Zeus for the sake of mortals, and say of two humans 'Of them let one die and the other live, as *tuchē* will have it.' Here I would read that the humans will live or die as their lot has it, rather than the goddesses scheming. Nothing random will happen to them but the goddesses will no longer seek to manipulate the *moira* of these men.[7] So chance plays no role in the social or political order of the world in Homer or Hesiod and certainly has no role to play in how their physical worlds come to be or are organized.

## Intervention?

I take it that the gods of Homer and Hesiod are real independent entities and effective. One might argue that the gods are a personification of weather phenomena so do not so much interfere with the weather, but rather are the weather. So every thunderbolt comes from Zeus and all earthquakes are due to Poseidon. However, some weather phenomena (for example, mists, storms at sea) can be generated by many gods so no one god can be their personification. Is it also the case that all weather phenomena, however minor (routine showers or mists) are due to the gods? In Hesiod that does not seem to be the case. *Works and Days* 663 ff. is important here, where sailing in the period of fifty days after the solstice is recommended, as the breezes are regular and the sea harmless. However, there is a significant conditional. If Poseidon or Zeus want to destroy you, the outcome of all ventures, good or bad, is in their hands and their actions can override the normal behaviour of the winds. At *Iliad* XIX, 21 ff. Thetis, at Achilles' prompting, says she will ward off flies from the body of Patroclus so that it is not consumed by maggots. Unless one wants to argue that the behaviour of flies and maggots is due to a god or is personified by a god, then there is a routine process of the world that is being overridden by the intervention of a god. This is not the only instance of this sort of phenomenon. At *Iliad* XXIII, 184 ff. Aphrodite keeps the dogs away from Hector's body, *Iliad* XXIV, 18 Apollo protects Hector's dead body from injury even when he is dragged by Achilles, and *Iliad* XXIV where the gods close his battle wounds as well. One reason that I have brought together all these instances of the actions of the gods is that it then becomes clear that the personification argument will not work over all of these instances. We can try Zeus as personification of the thunderbolt, but what of gods guiding projectiles, or warding off flies from the dead?

There is a more subtle reply to the view that the gods interfere in the world for Homer and Hesiod, which is to say that the gods are simply part of the world for them and we should not impose later ideas of transcendent gods.[8] The gods do what is within their powers, whether that is Zeus hurling a thunderbolt or any of Circe's actions. In a sense that is right and that it would be wrong to think of the actions of the gods in Homer and Hesiod as supernatural interventions. Having said that, it is clear that certain things would happen in Homer (Hector's body deteriorating) if the gods did not exert their powers. Indeed, one could try to formulate plausible general laws in Homer, such as 'all dead bodies will X in circumstances Y' (all dead bodies will be eaten by maggots/eaten by dogs/deteriorate/not have their wounds heal in the presence of flies/dogs/etc.) when the actions of the gods would violate those general laws. What I want to look at next is whether the gods can be brought into a general scheme of laws and explanations and what we as human beings can know about the gods.

## Formulating laws in Homer?

One might also try to formulate general laws for the gods along the lines suggested by Barnes and discussed by Hankinson.[9] So:

Whenever Poseidon is angry to degree d with inhabitants of place p and time t, he shakes p at t + n to degree F(d).

As Hankinson points out, such formulations do not lend themselves to empirical testing unless 'some independent, non-question begging way can be found to determine the degree of Poseidon's wrath'.[10] There are some further problems with such formulations though.

Firstly, the weather is perhaps the most plausible case for attempting to bring the actions of the gods under general laws. However, it would be very difficult to specify general conditions for when the gods send *atē* to a mortal. So too it would be difficult to specify conditions under which a god is going to interfere in battle between mortals or refrain from doing so, or to specify how they are going to interfere.

The t + n formulation might work if justice were genuinely reciprocal in Homer and Hesiod, in the sense that a wrongdoing was immediately followed by retribution. That is not the case though, either in the sense that retribution always follows transgression or that there is a predictable amount of time between transgression and retribution. At *Works and Days* 270 ff. Hesiod tells us that while there is injustice now Zeus will not let things end that way, but does not specify any time period for Zeus' retribution.

The F(d) formulation is also problematic in that there is no evidence at all that there is any relation between the degree of anger Poseidon has and the amount or intensity of shaking that he does. Anger does not always produce shaking from Poseidon. There is also no way for humans to tell what will make Poseidon angry. The following passage at *Odyssey* I, 19–20 is also problematic for the Barnes' formulation:

> All of the gods pitied him except Poseidon. He raged unceasingly (*asperches menainen*) against godlike Odysseus until he reached his own land.

If Poseidon is unceasingly angry, then we should get either one continuous shaking of the earth or one massive shaking of the earth. What we in fact get are random acts of spite against Odysseus, where Poseidon's rage does not happen at a specific (t + n) and the degree of shaking is not a function of the greatness of his anger. It is also not at all clear that every time Zeus is angry he hurls a thunderbolt (he has other options) or that every time he hurls a thunderbolt he is angry (sometimes he is quite calm and deliberate in doing so).[11]

Finally, I return to Hankinson's initial concern about whether it is possible to determine the degree of Poseidon's anger. What can humans know about the gods from their own investigations in Homer and Hesiod? The concern here is that humans cannot know about the minds of the gods unless gods choose to tell them and there are significant problems with that too.[12] I am aware that Barnes' formulation is a suggestion of how one might try to formulate laws for the behaviour of the gods. I have looked at it in detail not to be critical of Barnes, but to bring out the problems of formulating laws for the behaviour of the gods in Homer and Hesiod beyond issues of verification.

## Knowing gods

What can humans know of the gods, and in particular of the minds of the gods? Solon says that:

The mind of the immortals is entirely unseen by humans (*pantēi d'athanatōn aphanēs noos anthrōpoisin*).

Clement of Alexandria, *Miscellanies*

As Guthrie once said, for the poets 'Mankind had no sure knowledge unless the gods chose to reveal it.'[13] I will begin with a passage from Hesiod that puts one of the issues clearly. *Works and Days* 483 says that:

> Different at different times is the mind (*noos*) of Zeus who holds the aegis, and it is difficult (*argaleos*) for men who are mortal to comprehend.

We could ask here whether the gods are genuinely, intrinsically capricious or not, or just appear so to humans. By capricious I mean prone to sudden and unaccountable changes of mood or behaviour, changing according to no discernible rules or, in short, unpredictable. At *Theogony* 307 Typhoeus is referred to as *anomos*, lawless, which may indicate he is indeed capricious. So too at *Theogony* 441 ff. Hesiod tells us that:

> Hecate can easily give a large catch of fish and can easily take it away if she wishes in her spirit (*ethelousa ge thumō*), and she is good at increasing livestock if in her spirit she wishes (*thumō g' ethelousa*).

At *Works and Days* 5 ff. Hesiod tells us that Zeus can easily strengthen or crush the strong, easily diminish the conspicuous or increase the inconspicuous and easily straighten the crooked and wither the proud. So as Most has noted, the gods have the capacity do one thing or its opposite without humans being able to determine the outcome.[14] We can find similar passages in Homer where at *Iliad* XX, 242 Zeus increases or decreases valour in men, just as he wishes (*hoppōs ken ethelēsin*) or at *Iliad* XVII, 175 where always the mind of Zeus is strong, as he puts brave men to flight and easily takes away victory, or rouses men to fight. So too at *Odyssey* VIII, 567 ff. Poseidon could smite a ship and hide a city, but these things he will bring about or not, as he is inclined. The gods then are difficult to know for mortals. If they are intrinsically capricious, mortals cannot formulate general laws about them, but that will also be so if the gods appear to be capricious to humans and humans have no way of knowing the gods better.[15]

It may also be the case that even the gods cannot fully comprehend the mind of Zeus. At *Iliad* I, 545 ff., Zeus says that:

> Hera, do not hope to understand all of my words. They will be difficult (*chalepoi*) for you, even though you are my wife. Whatever it is fitting to hear, no other, whether they be god or human will know first. However, what I myself wish to think, apart from the gods, on this do not question me or ask closely.

Hera replies:

> Most awesome son of Kronos, what a tale you have told! Never before have I questioned you or interrogated you closely.

One way of reading this is as a matrimonial dispute, with Zeus taking the patriarchal role and effectively saying to Hera 'do not question my authority, woman'. However, there is a more interesting reading of this passage, which is that the questioning is not an affront to Zeus' authority or manhood, but is futile as none of the other gods, not even Hera his wife, will be able to comprehend his mind. They will all be told what is fitting for them, but that is Zeus' decision. The gods may know some things about Zeus with certainty, but only with Zeus' consent. It is perhaps significant that just before this exchange, at *Iliad* I, 526, Zeus tells Thetis that he will bow his head to her, so she knows that what Zeus has said is irrevocable, not deceitful and will come to pass, though there are issues with that as well, as we shall see in a moment.

## Reliable gods?

Humans do receive information from the gods in various ways. How reliable is that information? Hussey has said that in Homer the gods:

> Supply reliable information to the human race through the medium of dreams, omens, portents and oracles.[16]

In one sense this is true. A good example here would be the information that Hermes supplies to Odysseus in order for him to succeed against Circe, or indeed the information that Circe supplies to Odysseus to aid his homecoming. The problem is that the gods, if they wish, can deceive humans, and humans, when first supplied with the information, have no means of deciding whether the gods are being deceptive or not. The classic instance here is the dream that Zeus sends to Agamemnon at the beginning of *Iliad* II. The dream is described at *Iliad* II, 6 as an *oulon oneiron*, a 'destructive dream'. It tells Agamemnon that he may now take Troy, that the immortals are now all agreed, having been persuaded by Hera, and that this is the will of Zeus. All these things are in fact false, and at *Iliad* II, 38 the narrator states that Agamemnon did not know what Zeus was planning. At *Iliad* II, 109 ff. and IX, 17 ff. a bitter Agamemnon says that Zeus the Great ensnared him with a grievous *atē*, was merciless (*schetlios*) in doing so and that now he plans a cruel deceit (*kakēn apatēn bouleusato*). If we read *hos prin men moi hupescheto kai kateneusen* at II, 112 and IX, 19 as 'who at one time promised me and nodded his head to it' then there is a serious problem with Zeus' reliability, for as we saw in the last section, when Zeus nods his head that is supposedly an assurance that what he has said is irrevocable, not deceitful and will come to pass.[17] This would appear to undermine all three. Whether or not Zeus in fact nodded his head to Agamemnon, Agamemnon believed that he did. Also relevant here is the concern in Nestor's prayer to Zeus at *Iliad* XV, 372 ff. Nestor asks Zeus if he nodded his head to sacrifices and entreaties by the Achaeans for a safe return home, then to think of this and not give a victory to the Trojans. One might also note that at *Iliad* XII, 164 Zeus is openly called a 'lover of lies' in a speech addressing him. Again, whether Zeus in fact lied is not the important issue, that a mortal can believe that Zeus lied undermines the reliability of the gods.[18] Is there a privileging of some people in relation to whose dreams will be believed? Nestor says that if anyone other than Agamemnon, the best of the Achaeans, had told of this dream they might consider it to be false and rather turn away from it. So Nestor does not think dreams are *per se* veridical, but is willing to believe this one because Agamemnon, best of the Achaeans relates it. Even then, Agamemnon's dream proves to be false. My concern is not whether such dreams are damaging or whether the effects of them are long-lasting,[19] but that there is a sense in which such dreams render all other dreams unreliable because humans cannot tell a deceptive dream from a non-deceptive dream, so all dreams must be to some extent suspect.

There is a related issue here, which is that the gods can interfere with human mental states and indeed can send *atē* to a human. With dreams humans cannot judge that a dream is deceptive while they have that dream or in the immediate aftermath. So too humans cannot tell that they are subject to an attack of *atē* during the attack or in the immediate aftermath. So it is only much later that Agamemnon claims that his actions were not his fault but due to *atē*.[20] The focus on *atē* has been largely moral, not epistemological and of course one can see why the moral dimensions of *atē* are important in relation to culpability. The epistemological implications for humans are significant as well though. How can we know that we are not being deceived by a god, either by means of dreams, lies or an attack of *atē*?

That mortals can be deluded by gods or be subject to attacks of *ate* is not surprising, as the gods, including Zeus can be subject as well. So in Homer, Hera's ongoing deception of Zeus is well known, at *Iliad* XIV, 157 ff., early in XV and recurring at XIX, 97. Zeus is blinded by an attack of *atē* from his daughter Atē at *Iliad* XIX, 95. In Hesiod Zeus is deceived by Prometheus at *Works and Days* 50.

That other gods delude or are deluded is also in Homer, for example, *Odyssey* VIII, 272 ff. where Hephaestus deceives Ares and the deluding of gods by each other is part of Xenophanes' well-known critique.[21]

## Knowledge of *moira*?

As I have argued that *moira* is important in how the worlds of Homer and Hesiod work, what knowledge can there be of *moira* for humans and how is that gained? There is an interesting contrast in that Zeus knows (*oiden*) the *moira* and *ammoira* of all mortals (*ho gar t' eu oiden hapanta, moiran t' ammoriēn te katathnētōn anthrōpōn, Odyssey* XX, 75–6). When humans speak about Zeus, in relation to his will or about *moira*, they express their view in terms of *pou*, I suppose. There are examples of this at *Iliad* II, 116, III, 308, X, 71, XIV, 120 and *Odyssey* IX/ 262. Humans do not know their own, or anyone else's *moira* unless that information comes from the gods. There seems to be no way in Homer for humans to investigate *moira* other than through the gods. A good example here is *Iliad* VII, 50, where Hector's brother says to him:

> It is not your *moira* yet to die and meet your doom. For so I have heard the gods who are for ever.

So too we might look at *Iliad* XVIII, 95 where Thetis tells Achilles that he will die soon after Hector, or *Iliad* XIV, 120 ff. where Thetis tells Achilles his life will not be long and that she is a messenger from the gods. It is interesting that emphasis is laid here in both passages on Thetis being the mother of Achilles and there is a theme in Homer of mothers having privileged knowledge of their children. We might also look at *Odyssey* V, 203 ff. where Calypso knows the *aisa* that will befall Odysseus, but he does not.

Is it possible for a human to be wrong about *moira*? It is, and the following case is interesting in that Hecabe, wife of Priam and mother of Hector, says that:

> In this way controlling fate (*moira krataiē*) span a thread for him at birth, when I myself gave birth to him, that swift footed dogs would satiate themselves on him far from his parents.
>
> *Iliad* XXIV 209

However, Hecabe is wrong because Priam does manage to secure the release of Hector's body and that body has been preserved by the gods. It is possible, though unlikely, that Hecabe is lying to prevent Priam from going. Already she has prophesized that she will never put Hector on a funeral bier at *Iliad* XX, 83 ff. Priam's reply is also interesting. He is not persuaded by Hecabe and recognizes that even given her status as Hector's mother, she could be wrong. So too Priam says he would reject such advice if given him by seers who sacrifice or by priests, so again, despite their position, he recognizes that they could be wrong. He goes to ransom the body of Hector because he has been visited by the goddess Iris, who is acting as the messenger of Zeus. So knowledge of *moira* is problematic for humans and how we acquire that knowledge shows something important about Homer and Hesiod.[22] If we want to mount an investigation of *moira*, then we must look to the unreliable gods for our information. There is no question of bringing together argument and evidence, no question of observation, our knowledge of *moira* only comes from the gods.

## Divine knowledge and language

The Moly passage of the *Odyssey* is very interesting in that it suggest that there is a divine language, unknown to humans unless revealed by a god, as the plant that Hermes gives to Odysseus 'is called Moly by the gods' (*Odyssey* X, 305) and seems to have no human name. There is one other passage where there is a divine name, *planktai*, (*Odyssey* XII, 61) but no human name, and four others where there are both human and divine names for things (*Iliad* I, 403, II, 813, XIV, 291 and XX, 74). I agree with Clay here that where there are divine and human names, it is likely that the divine names are more natural and appropriate and signify greater knowledge on the part of the gods.[23] Where there is no human name, knowledge of name and nature of the entity only comes by the grace of the gods.[24] The *planktai* are rocks through which only one human ship has ever sailed, and that only with the grace of Hera, so in normal circumstances they would be beyond the knowledge of mortals. In contrast the goddess Circe has full knowledge of them (*Odyssey* XII, 59-72), which she then passes on to Odysseus, the only way that Odysseus will find out about this peril. The Moly is then an interesting case, as it is *chalepon*, hard, difficult or dangerous to dig for mortals (*Odyssey* X, 305), but 'the gods can do all things' so Hermes can uproot it. Hermes can then tell Odysseus the nature (*phusis*) of this plant as both the white flower and black root are now visible to Odysseus. I take this as highly significant as in the one passage in Homer where *phusis* is mentioned, the only way in which a human comes to know about that *phusis* is through the actions and benevolence of a god. So too the only way in which humans will learn about divine words that have no human counterparts is through the gods. No enquiry will help in either case and humans historically have not learnt about Moly or the *planktai*.

## Human knowledge generally

I now wish to shift focus a little from the characters in Homer and Hesiod to the narrators and the nature of the account they recite. This too can tell us something interesting about the nature of investigation for humans in Homer and Hesiod. What can mortals know more generally in Homer and Hesiod? One passage which has been much discussed is the catalogue of ships and captains that begins at *Iliad* II, 484. The debate has centred on whether Homer can be said to have advocated a form of scepticism and, in particular, on *Iliad* II, 485–6:

> You are goddesses, and are present, and know all things
> We hear only rumour and know nothing.

With Zellner, I am wary of reading an epistemology straight out of this passage.[25] In fuller context, the narrator invokes the Muses and the passage follows a typical Homeric pattern of ascribing some property to the gods and denying it to human beings.[26] The important point for Homer is the gulf between gods and mortals and, as I argued in the last chapter, it would be unwise to read divine omniscience or omnipotence into such comparisons, especially as this passage is a prayer asking the Muses for something.[27] Just as the gods are not omniscient, humans do know some things, but of a different nature and not nearly as many as the gods.[28] One might also note that at *Iliad* II, 594 Thamyris offends the Muses by saying he would win a singing competition even against them, so they take away his voice and his playing ability. It is prudent to praise the Muses.

I am also concerned about taking these two lines out of their context. Here is the passage in full, and note that these lines come from the narrator:

> 484 Tell me now, Muses who have your homes on Olympus –
> 485 you are goddesses, and are present, and know all things,
> 486 we hear only rumour and know nothing –
> 487 who the leaders and commanders of the Danaans were,
> 488 of this multitude I could not tell or name,
> 489 not if I had ten tongues and ten mouths
> 490 a voice unbreakable and I had a heart of bronze
> 491 unless the Olympian Muses, Aegis-bearing Zeus'

492 daughters, bring to mind those who came from Ilios.
493 The leaders of the ships I will now tell.[29]

An important point here is the contrast between the first person singular referring to the narrator and the first person plural of 486 referring presumably to all mortals.[30] A critical decision must be made here about the status of the narrator as it is clear that the narrator has moved from a state of ignorance to a state of knowledge. Lines 486–90 express the narrators ignorance, 491–2 give the means of gaining knowledge, 493 shows the narrator is now in possession of the required knowledge, presumably under the influence of the Muses, and will share it. He proceeds to give the catalogue of leaders and ships at length and with no hint that this is not knowledge, not a fully reliable account of ships and leader. Does that count as human learning in Homer and so dispose of the attribution of scepticism?

There is a broader point here about the authority and nature of the *Iliad* and *Odyssey*. The narrator was not present at all the events that they describe. Are these poems then only rumour devoid of knowledge? Presumably not as both poems open by invoking the Muses. The Muses are invoked twice more, once during the catalogue of ships and leaders (*Iliad* II, 594, 761) and again at XI, 218, XIV, 508 and XVI, 112. At *Odyssey* VIII, 488 the minstrel Demodocus is praised for having spoken *kata kosmon* (according to good order, i.e. well) of the Achaens, having been taught by a Muse or Apollo. While the human characters in *Iliad* and *Odyssey* may have difficulty in acquiring knowledge and sometimes say so, there is no sense that the narrator has any doubts about the tale that he puts forward. It is also worth remembering that this was originally an oral tradition, so the human narrator would need to give some authority to his account, some reason why you should listen to them telling this tale, hence the contrasts of 'I' who invoke the Muses and 'we' who know nothing.[31] Hussey has argued that:

> The bare possibility of deception by the Muses is allowed to disqualify claims to knowledge.[32]

Here I would separate two things. Can the gods deceive humans? Yes, they can as I have argued above. Is it right to import Hesiod *Theogony* 27–8 where the Muses know how to say false things that are similar to true things? I would at least question that as there is no indication of this in Homer. Do the Muses ever deceive in Homer? It would seem that they do not. Does the narrator ever question the status of the account they give? Not at all. If Homer wanted to establish some form of scepticism about knowledge, I would expect something more about why we should be cautious of what the Muses tell us, as they are pivotal, but we find nothing. One interesting point here is whether a bard can pass on their knowledge. If one could repeat the poem having heard it from the bard, would that count as knowledge? Or does what the narrator says only count as knowledge because the Muses help him bring it to mind as in lines 491–2? Lines 488–90 would seem to preclude the former possibility. One can only give this account of ships and leaders with the aid of the Muses. A modern philosopher, trained in ideas about generalization and reflexivity, might well have concerns that an appeal to the Muses will not generate a philosophically sound route to knowledge in Homer. Whether such concerns would occur to Homer is another matter and he shows no signs that the account that the narrator gives is anything less than knowledge.

This preamble to the leaders and ships catalogue is not about epistemology as such, and while I would agree that the passage has religious dimensions (praise of Muses, deprecation of mortals) the real intent of this passage is to establish the privilege and authority of the person telling the tale and the veracity of the tale itself, even if there are knowledge issues for characters in the tale. It is significant that the content here is a catalogue, one of the most difficult things to remember or to justify the memory of.

## Knowledge in Homer

I am conscious of having bypassed a debate about knowledge in Homer here. There is the Snell-Frankel thesis, which is that in Homer to know is to know by direct personal experience and there is no general concept of knowledge at all, just knowledge by personal experience.[33] This is now generally discredited on the grounds that gods and seers may know the future and that ordinary mortals make claims to knowledge of the future and of events they have no personal experience of.[34] This is motivated at least in part by line 485 'you are goddesses, and are present, and know all things' where the 'are present' is taken as critical to knowing. One can then go into detail about verbs of knowing in Homer and how they are used and what events humans may or may not be present at in the required sense. All this is in some ways important, but in another misses the point of the preamble to the leaders and ships passage, which is the justification of the account the narrator is going to give. No doubt there are problems which beset knowing and learning for humans in Homer, but the key here is: How does the narrator exempt themself from this state? The answer is clear - it is by appeal to the Muses.

What I want to bring to the fore here is that, for the poetry of Homer and Hesiod, if humans want to know more about our world, they do not mount an investigation in the sense that the early enquirers into nature will enquire, but they appeal to the gods. The provenance of human skills is also significant here. As Jouanna has questioned, are they gifts from the gods, or are they something that humans have discovered for themselves?[35] A simple example here is knowledge of medicinal herbs. A specific case is that Hermes instructs Odysseus on the Moly plant, more generally at *Iliad* XI, 831 knowledge of medicinal herbs and the healing of wounds are said to have descended from Cheiron the Centaur via Achilles. In Chapter 2, we found that there was no conception of *phusis* in Homer and Hesiod and only one very specific use of the term. Here it is important that the terms *historia* and *skopein* are absent from Homer and Hesiod and there is no conception of enquiry for humans, other than appeal to the gods. In order to have *peri phuseōs historia* or *peri phuseōs skopein*, there was a need to generate conceptions of *historia* and *skopein* as well as of *phusis*. This is not to deny that humans have both some knowledge and skills in Homer and Hesiod. They can acquire knowledge, and be said to know, if they have witnessed something. Humans have skills, particularly in war and are said to know how to do things.[36] As Lesher has argued though, humans do not always recognize the full significance of what they witness and they tend to be creatures of the moment, incapable of looking before or after.[37] They may occasionally test something to determine the truth, usually in relation to someone's identity, though even then the test may be competitive rather than about evidence.[38] There is no sense of a proper investigation of the world.

## Historians and *historia*

It is notable that the two great early historians, Herodotus and Thucydides, do not privilege their accounts by any appeal to the Muses. Herodotus famously comments at II, 99 that his writing previous to this is the result of his own observation (*opsis*) knowledge (*gnōmē*) and investigation (*historiē*).[39] It is also significant that at VII, 89 ff. Herodotus gives us a ship catalogue, which follows a catalogue of the nations and troops on the Persian side at VII, 61 ff., neither of which have any invocation of a Muse. So too in Thucydides we have no mention of any Muse at any stage, but we do have the famous section on method, Thucydides 1, 22:

> With regard to my factual reporting of the events of the war I have made it a principle not to write down the first story that came my way, and not even to be guided by my own general impressions; either I was present myself at the events which I have described or else I heard from eye-witnesses whose reports I have checked with as much thoroughness as possible.

An important shift takes place from Homer and Hesiod not only in philosophical works but in historical works as well. One might also note here how the writers of the Hippocratic corpus base their accounts in observation and practice. Indeed, they reject the idea *mantikē*, the art of prophesy or foresight and base their prognoses on what they can observe. They privilege their accounts in this manner and privilege themselves as the proper doctors to choose from in a wide range of supposed healers all competing for patients.[40]

## Hesiod and revision?

There is an interesting further aspect of this in Hesiod, as *Works and Days* may revise something said under the inspiration of the Muses in *Theogony*. As we have seen, Homer invokes the Muses at the very beginning of both *Iliad* and *Odyssey*. Hesiod also invokes the Muses at the beginning of the *Theogony* and at the beginning of *Works and Days*. At *Theogony* 22ff. we get a contrast between humans, shepherds in the fields, things of shame and mere bellies, and the Muses who can speak false things as if they were true, but also know how to speak the truth at *Theogony* 26–8. Although it is possible for the Muses to be deceptive, again I see no sign here that the narrator is concerned about that in reciting the *Theogony*. At 36 the narrator says 'Let us begin from the Muses', at 38 the Muses will tell what was, what is and what will be and at 39 they will do this with an untiring (*akamatos*) voice, and there is an interesting comparison here with Homer *Iliad* II, 490 (one would need an unbreakable voice). The Muses are referred to throughout the *Theogony* and at 916 we learn they are the daughters of memory.[41] At *Works and Days* 658 ff. the narrator disclaims any personal knowledge of boats or seafaring, but claims the Muses taught him to sing of what follows about when it is best to set to sea. At 662 we find that:

> The Muses taught me to delight in this 'not to be said even by a god' (*athesphaton*) hymn.

This takes *athesphaton* in its literal sense of 'not god speak' (*a – theos – phēmi*) but however we translate this, it is a very strong way of describing the account.

Again, this looks like an attempt by the narrator to privilege and lend authority to their account at a point where they might be challenged. On privileging an account for Hesiod, it is interesting that at *Theogony* 30, the Muses give him a 'staff of luxuriant laurel' when they breathed the divine voice into him, presumably to give him some authority when he recounts what they tell him.

The opening part of *Works and Days* may have an interesting development. *Works and Days* opens with an invocation of the Muses and praise for the power of Zeus. *Works and Days* 11–12 then tells us that:

> There is not only one birth of strife, but upon the earth there are two.

This contradicts *Theogony* 225, where there is only one birth for Strife. This appears to be a self-conscious correction, as Hesiod could easily just have stated that Strife has two births. Hesiod though was under the inspiration of the Muses in the *Theogony*, so how is he going to manage this correction of the previous account? After praising Zeus' powers, *Works and Days* 9–10 says that:

> Give attention as you see and hear, with justice straighten (*ithune*) the judgments.
> I would like to speak truthfully to Perses (*egō de ke Persē etētuma muthēsaimēn*).[42]

Most in the Loeb adds a note here that 'These requests are addressed to Zeus' and I agree.[43] One way of reading this is that the Muse-inspired account of the *Theogony* was not perfect, indeed made an error on Strife, so now there is an appeal to Zeus to make sure that the account is correct. The correction on the birth of Strife follows this directly. This points to something interesting about investigation for Hesiod. If the Muse-inspired account proves to be insufficient, he does not go to evidence or discussion, but appeals to a higher authority in order that the new account will be correct.

Clay has argued that *Theogony* offers an 'Olympian perspective on the cosmos' and deals with what is known to the gods, while *Works and Days* presents a 'human viewpoint'[44] and deals with things within human experience. In her view these differences can explain the differences of invocations in the two works.[45] To some extent I agree, and Clay makes many valid and interesting points. However, the birth of Strife in *Works and Days* is something that is beyond human experience and that is the first issue after the invocation of Zeus, and he has just claimed that he will tell the truth to Perses.[46] The invocation of Zeus cannot then be just due to a difference in content but should also be due to a difference in authority and trust.

One important theme for this book is that the views of the early Greek natural philosophers did not spring out of nothing but were often rooted in their perception of the earlier and contemporary poets. One aspect of that is the shift from a reliance on revelations from the gods to a reliance on human investigation. Was there a debate about knowledge among the poets? There is a good case that Hesiod recognized the problems in Homer with the veracity of the Muses and so raised the issue early in the *Theogony*, with the Muses able to speak the truth and also able to tell falsehoods that seem to be true, so highlighting the difficulty.[47] It may then be that *Works and Days* moves this forward with an appeal to Zeus. Whether that is meant to be a solution or to highlight further problems is open to debate. Zeus, in his dealings with Prometheus, can still be deceitful, as is clear from *Works and Days* 69 ff. and indeed can be deceived (54 ff.). As a solution, we appeal to the higher authority to correct the Muses as appropriate. That may work fully, in that Zeus under this invocation, will 'with justice straighten the judgements' every time, or partially, so even if Zeus is not fully reliable, he will straighten some judgement and this is better than appealing to the Muses alone. As highlighting problems, it may show that even if we appeal to the highest authority we may still be deceived.

## Pindar and Muses

Pindar also makes some interesting references to the Muses. *Olympian Ode* 10, 4 is significant in relation to the opening passage of Hesiod's *Works and Days* and says that:

> Oh Muse, you and Zeus' daughter Truth, with correcting hand, ward off falsehood and any rebuke for sinning against a friend.

So as with Hesiod, there is an invocation to a higher power to help generate a true account. There is also *Incert* Fragment 214, which again emphasizes the wandering nature of human thought and the way in which their judgements might be steered:

> With him lives sweet Hope
> Heart-fostering nurse of old age,
> Which most of all steers (*kuberna*) mortals'
> Much wandering judgements

The *Paean Ode* 6, 51–8 attributes a knowledge of everything to the Muses:

> As to when the strife of the immortals began
> The gods are capable of trusting this to the wise

> But mortals are without the means to find this
> But, virgin Muses, you know everything (*isate panta*), with your father of the dark clouds and Mnemosyne, as you have that privilege, speak to me now.

Pindar is perhaps a little more trusting of the Muses, as at *Pythian Ode* 4, 278 he says that:

> The Muse gains honour by giving correct messages.

That does not rule out the possibility of the Muses deceiving mortals, but maybe has a slightly different tone to Homer. On why his writing is privileged, *Dithyramb* 2, 25 says that:

> The Muse has promoted me as herald of wise tales.[48]

How should humans try to find things out? They should consult the Muses rather than undertake any investigation of their own according to *Paean Ode* 7b, 15 ff.:

> I pray to Uranus' well robed daughter Mnemosyne and her daughters to give good means (*eumachanian*),[49] for blind are the minds of men if anyone searches out the deep road of wisdom without the Heliconians. To me they have given this immortal work.

Again, we have the privileging of Pindar's work. This is quite radical, as the minds of men are blind if they search out the road of wisdom without the aid of the Heliconian Muses. We see similar themes in *Olympian Ode* 12, 6:

> As for the hopes of humans, they often rise, and at other times fall, while making their wandering way with vain untruths. None on the earth has found a trustworthy sign concerning things that will be from the gods, as their knowledge of what they will do is blind. Many things befall humans contrary to their thought.

So Pindar too privileges his work by reference to the Muses, and again there is no sense that humans can find out anything worthwhile without the help of Gods or Muses. Bacchylides also has something interesting on the same theme. *Ode* 12 says that:

> Like a wise steersman (*kubernētas*), Klio queen of song guide (*euthune*) my thoughts now if you ever did before.

The verb *euthunein* is a late form of the Homeric *ithunein*, 'to guide', which we have already seen. Again, as with Hesiod we have an invocation of a higher power to guide one's thoughts. All that is useful in relation to the similar relation between poet, poem and Muse in Homer and Hesiod. Pindar is generally reckoned to have lived *c.* 518–438 BCE. As mentioned in the introduction, I have no intention of trying to impose a linear, ascending narrative on the early Greeks such that Homer is improved upon by Hesiod who is improved upon by Thales who is improved upon by Anaximander and so on. I take Pindar's dates to indicate that there was an interesting live debate between the philosophical tradition grounding their work in debate and access to a *logos* and some of the poetic tradition privileging their work by relation to the Muses.[50]

## Xenophanes

Xenophanes Fr. 18 is also important in this context, as a contrast to Homer, Hesiod and Pindar:

> The gods have not revealed all things to men from the beginning, but by seeking (*zētountes*) in time they find (*epheuriskousin*) what is better.

Here I disagree with Deichgraber (1938) who aligns Xenophanes' contrasts between the capabilities of gods and humans with those of Homer and Hesiod.[51] There are similarities between the two on the current state of humans, but it is what to do about that situation where the radical difference lies. In both Homer and Hesiod, we find out critical things by appeal to the Muses, in Xenophanes we conduct an investigation. I would also extend a point made by Lesher in relation to some of Xenophanes' comments on natural phenomena. That Xenophanes gives a natural explanation and does not give an explanation in terms of the gods would have struck his readers, well versed in Homer, as odd.[52] Here, I suggest to make no mention of the Muses would have struck an audience well versed in Homer, Hesiod and Pindar as something odd, new and exceptional. Xenophanes' critique of contemporary theology is well known. Fragments 11, 14, 15 and 16 are usually cited here:

> Homer and Hesiod have ascribed to the gods all those things which are shameful and reproachful among men: theft, adultery and deceiving each other.[53]

> Mortals believe that the gods are born, and that they have clothes, speech and bodies similar to their own.

> If cattle, horses and lions had hands, and could draw with those hands and accomplish the works of men, horses would draw the forms of gods as like

horses, and cattle like cattle, and each would make their bodies as each had themselves.

> The Ethiopians claim their gods are snub-nosed and black, while the Thracians claim theirs have blue eyes and red hair.

A more implicit criticism of Homer and Hesiod is Xenophanes Fragment 1:

> Do not speak of Titans or Giants or Centaurs, fictions of old, or furious battles. In these there is nothing useful.[54]

Finally, it is interesting that Xenophanes rules out divination as possible means to knowledge. Cicero, *On Divination*, I, 3, 5, says that:

> Certain carefully worked out arguments of the philosophers for the reality of divination have been collected; among these, to speak of the earliest, Xenophanes of Colophon, one who said that the gods existed, repudiated divination in its entirety. The remainder, except really only Epicurus who spoke rather obscurely about the nature of the gods, approved of divination.

So for Xenophanes we do not consult the gods to gain knowledge, nor do we consult the Muses, nor do we write mythology, but we seek knowledge out ourselves. We can see similar themes in Heraclitus. Heraclitus Fr. 78 gives us a contrast between what gods know and what humans know:

> Humans do not have true judgement but gods do.

Heraclitus Fr. 1 then gives us the idea of an independent logos, of humans who either do or do not know of the logos and how we should learn about the logos:

> Concerning the logos, which is as I describe it, humans always to be void of understanding, both prior to and after hearing it. For although all things occur according to this logos (*kata ton logon*) they are like un-experienced people, even when they experience words and deeds and I distinguish in detail how each thing is according to nature (*kata phusin*) and tell what characteristics it has. However other humans fail to notice what they do when they are awake just as they forget what they do when they are asleep.

I do not have the space here to enter into the vexed question of the exact nature of the *logos* for Heraclitus or how we can come to know the *logos*. What I take to be important here is that the *logos* can be engaged with by humans, that it does not deceive and is accessible to humans. Heraclitus can privilege his account on the basis that he is awake and has engaged with the logos, although it is for others to engage with the logos as well. Fragment 30 says:

> Listening not to me but to the *logos* it is wise to agree that all things are one.

I take the importance of being awake in Heraclitus and the importance of the idea of 'what is common' also to be important relative to Homer. The gods in Homer appear to humans in their sleep or send dreams that may be deceitful and knowledge is often particular to an individual rather than common. Finally, it is also important that Heraclitus says in Fragment 101:

> I searched out myself.

I take another important theme in Heraclitus to be that we are responsible for what we do, and I take that to have both an epistemological dimension (we are responsible for finding out about the world on our own, not depending on gods or Muses) and an ethical dimension (we are responsible for our actions, not the gods, *moira* or *atē*). Alcmaeon Fragment 1 may also be important here:

> The gods have certainty about unseen things (*tōn aphaneōn*)[55] but humans conjecture from signs (*tekmairesthai*).

Now *tekmairesthai* could have a variety of meanings, but I follow Lesher's suggestion of a parallel with Thucydides 1, 1, 1, where unable to get clear information, he is able from the evidence (*ek de tekemēriōn*) to push his conclusions further.[56]

## Parmenides' challenge?

There is also an interesting comparison here between Homer and Hesiod on how to gain knowledge and Parmenides Fr. 7, 5, where the goddess says to the boy:

> Judge (*krinai*) by reasoning the contentious argument that I have uttered.

So the goddess asks the human to judge and to do so by reasoning, not to appeal to a god to find out more, quite unlike Homer and Hesiod.[57] Personally I would push this further and see the demand to judge as not only from the goddess to the boy but from Parmenides to his listener/reader as well. You must judge the argument that Parmenides has put forward. Again, this is radically different from Homer and Hesiod invoking the Muses to give authority to their account. I find this conducive as I treat Parmenides as a philosopher of challenge rather than a philosopher of doctrine. That is, I believe Parmenides sets problems for anyone who wants a coherent account of the world rather than states a doctrine.[58] I would say something similar about the frame for the *Timaeus* as well. At *Timaeus* 27c Timaeus invokes the gods, but at *Timaeus* 27c9 he says:

> I who speak and you the judges (*hoi kritai*), we are human in nature.

So again human judgement is key and again I would at least suggest that the 'you the judges' resonates beyond the text to include the reader as a judge as well.

## Conclusion

In the previous chapter we saw that Homer and Hesiod had no conception of *phusis*. They did though have a strong conception of *moira*, generated and maintained by the gods. In this chapter we have seen some of the problems associated with this view. It is difficult to formulate laws about the behaviour of the gods and the only real source of information about *moira* for humans is through the gods. The gods though are unreliable as they can and do practice deception on humans. Even when humans are in a sense privileged, as with Agamemnon as the best of the Greeks or Hecabe as the mother of Hector, they can still be deceived or be wrong about *moira*. There is no real sense of *historia* or *skopein* in Homer and Hesiod and indeed these terms are absent from them. Both Homer and Hesiod have the narrator of their poems appeal to the Muses to give authority to their account. So ideas of *historia* or *skopein* have to be generated as well as an idea of phusis in order for there to be *peri phuseōs historia* or *peri phuseōs skopein*. The contrast between what gods and humans can know continues in early Greek thought, but there is much greater optimism on what humans can learn for themselves.

# 4

# Anaximander and the *Kubernan* Tradition

The reconstruction of Anaximander's views is something of a battleground. As Conche has put it, we can have an 'interprétation mécaniste' or an 'interprétation vitaliste'.[1] Here I will argue for an 'interprétation vitaliste' based on steering, *kubernan*, being an important idea for Anaximander. Firstly, that needs to be established by looking at the evidence in Aristotle and in other early Greek thinkers, particularly in relation to how widespread the phenomenon of steering was. We also need to consider how this steering might work. There are then a range of issues in Anaximander where the merits of a mechanical or an organic model can be debated, such as cosmogony, vortices, number of *cosmoi*, astronomy and cosmology.

## Anaximander and *kubernan*?

As the role of *kubernan* in Anaximander has been downplayed and even ignored by some, it is important to establish the basis of its attribution. Aristotle, *Physics* III/ 4, 203b says:

> This is why we say that this has no *archē* but this seems to be the *archē* of all other things, and **surrounds all and steers all** (*kai periechein hapanta kai panta kubernan*), as with all those who do not suppose other explanations, such as mind or love, beyond the unlimited. This is the divine, for it is immortal and indestructible, as Anaximander and most of the physiologoi say.

It is important here to translate *kai periechein hapanta kai panta kubernan* 'surrounds all and steers all', as 'surrounds and steers all' would mask the double 'all' structure in the Greek. The double 'all' structure is significant as Aristotle's Greek is notoriously terse so this does not seem the sort of phrase Aristotle would come up with if he were not quoting.[2] It is also significant in terms of earlier poetry, as Terpander, Fragment 2 is *Zeu pantōn archa, pantōn agētōr,* Zeus is *archē* of all, leader of all. So an important possibility here is that Anaximander uses the double 'all' structure, alluding to Terpander, but transfers the functions of a god to the *apeiron*, as with the *apeiron* being 'immortal and indestructible', or taking on the regulatory role of the gods. So I take Aristotle's Greek to be indicative that Anaximander did indeed have a steering principle, and I have printed '**surrounds all and steers all**' in bold as I would elevate these words to being a fragment of Anaximander.[3]

## The *kubernan* tradition

Anaximander was far from being the only early Greek thinker to use *kubernan* in a cosmological context. In the *Philebus* Plato has Socrates say:

> Well, Protarchus, should we say that the whole universe is ruled by unreason, irregularity and chance, or on the contrary, just as some of those who came before us said (*hoi prosthen hēmōn elegon*), say that *nous* and a marvellous organizing intelligence steer (*diakubernan*) it.[4]

Plato then recognized that there were people before him who believe that an intelligence steered the whole universe.[5] Whether he would include Homer in that, with the gods 'leading like to like' is difficult to tell, but here are four cases of early Greek thinkers using *kubernan* in cosmological contexts, Heraclitus, a Hippocratic author, Parmenides and Diogenes of Apollonia. With Heraclitus we have Fr. 41:

> All things are steered (*ekubernantai*)[6] through all.

We also have Fr. 64:

> The thunderbolt steers (*oiakizei*) all things.

With Fr. 64, according to LSJ *oiakizein* means to 'steer: hence, govern, guide, manage.' Thus it seems to have roughly the same sorts of meaning as *kubernan*.[7] The Hippocratic author of *On Regimen* tells us that:

> The hottest and strongest fire, which controls (*epikrateitai*) all things, manages everything according to nature (*kata phusin*), it is imperceptible to sight or touch. In this are soul, mind, understanding, growth, change, diminution, separation, sleep, waking. This steers all things though all (*panta dia pantos kuberna*) both here and there and is never still.[8]

Diogenes of Apollonia, Fr. 5 says that:

That which has intelligence is called air by men, and all men are steered by this and it has a power over all things (*kai hupo toutou pantas kai kubernasthia kai pantōn kratein*). This seems to be a God to me and to have permeated everywhere (*kai epi pan aphichthai*), to arrange (*diatithenai*) all things and to be in all things.

Finally, Parmenides Fr. 12 says that:

> The narrower rings are full of unmixed fire, those close by are full of night but with some measure of flame. In the middle of this there is a goddess, who steers all things (*panta kubernai*), ruling the hateful birth and mixture of all things, sending female to have sex with male, and conversely male with female.

## The extent of *kubernan*?

One might question the extent of steering, either in terms of time (perhaps it operates at certain times only) or in terms of space (perhaps it operates in certain places only). As we have only the Aristotle passage attributing steering to Anaximander, it is difficult to tell in his case, though in others the issues are clearer. For the other early Greeks steering is ongoing, that is it operates at all times, and thoroughgoing, that is it operates in all places. Heraclitus says that 'All things are steered through all'.[9] So there can be no question that steering is thoroughgoing for Heraclitus. As there is no cosmogony for Heraclitus, this cannot be only an issue for cosmogony. The key passage for Heraclitus' views on cosmogony is Fragment 30:

> This *cosmos*, the same for all,[10] was not made by gods or men, but has always existed and will always exist. It is an ever-living fire, kindling in measures and going out in measures.[11]

There is no time boundary for steering, and given that the cosmos is an 'ever-living fire, kindling in measures and going out in measures' it is likely that steering is continuous. The Hippocratic author says that 'This steers all things though all (*panta dia pantos kuberna*) both here and there and is never still.'[12] Again, there can be no doubt on the thoroughgoing nature of steering and the 'is never still' would again strongly suggest that steering is continuous. The proliferation of the Greek word *panta* in Diogenes Fr. 5 also makes it clear that the steering influence of air is thoroughgoing and ongoing, as it steers and has power over all things, permeates everywhere, arranges all things and is in all things. As the interpretation of the third part of Parmenides' poem is so contentious, I am reluctant to say a great deal about it. Whether this is Parmenides' own view, is some form of challenge, or some form of critique of previous thinkers is not entirely clear. What I will say though is that Parmenides does use *kubernan* and does so in a manner which indicates an ongoing process and that as the goddess steers all things (*panta*) it is a thoroughgoing process as well. Even if this is not Parmenides' view and is meant as critique or challenge, it gives a useful confirmation of the attitude to *kubernan* of earlier thinkers.

## Plato and Aristotle

In addition to the evidence from the early Greek thinkers, Plato and Aristotle use *kubernan* in interesting cosmological contexts. Aristotle is clearer in his usage. At *Meteorology* I/2 he says that:

> The entire terrestrial realm is composed of these bodies [earth, water, air, fire], and as we have said it is the processes which affect them that concern us here. This realm is of necessity contiguous with the upper motions, which means that all of the motions here are steered (*kubernasthia*) by the upper motions. As the source of all motion, the upper motions must be accounted as the primary cause. These are eternal, unlimited with respect to place but are always complete. In distinction, all of the other bodies comprise separate regions from each other. The result of this is that fire, earth and their kindred must be accounted as the material reason for coming to be, while the ultimate reason for their motion is the motive ability of the eternally moving things.

So for Aristotle steering permeates everything that happens in the terrestrial realm and as there is no cosmogony for Aristotle, does this in an ongoing manner. In the *Politicus* Plato refers to god as the helmsman of the *cosmos*. In the myth there is a contrast between the *cosmos* under the guidance of this helmsman god against the gradual deterioration into chaos when this god releases control of the *cosmos*. So:

> When the time of all these things came to an end and change was to occur, and all of the earth born race had been used up, each soul having given back all of its births, each having fallen into the earth as seed the prescribed number of times, the helmsman (*kubernētēs*) of the universe let go the rudder.[13]

The myth continues, emphasizing god's role as orderer and helmsman of the *cosmos*:

When the world nurtures within itself living things under the guidance of the helmsman (*kubernētou*), it produces little evil and much good. However, when it becomes separated from him, it fares best during the time immediately after the release, but as time proceeds and it grows forgetful, the old condition of disorder gains sway more and more, and towards the conclusion of time little good and much of its opposite flourishes, and there is danger of the destruction of the world and those in it. At this moment God, the orderer of the world, perceives that it is in trouble, and being concerned that it should not be storm driven by confusion and broken up into an endless sea of unlikeness, he takes his old place at the rudder, and reverses the sickness and destruction of the first period when the world moved itself, and he orders and sets it right again, forming it deathless and ageless.[14]

There are of course questions here about how far we should take this myth as expressing Plato's own cosmology, but Plato clearly thinks of steering as thoroughgoing and dependent on an intelligent entity to do the steering. Steering is ongoing in the sense that it is longer than just for cosmogony, though not for the whole cycle.[15]

## How does steering work?

That steering was an important metaphor in early Greek cosmology is then beyond question. How steering worked though is another matter on which we have relatively little information.[16] There are several conceptions of how steering might operate. It might act like what is now known as intelligent design. The best evidence for this is the Plato *Philebus* passage we have already looked at, especially the line 'that *nous* and a marvellous organizing intelligence steer (*diakubernan*) it.'[17] This can be taken in conjunction with Aristotle, *Physics* III/4, 203b7ff, where just after 'surrounds all and steers all', the *apeiron* is referred to by Aristotle as *to theion*, the divine. In Plato, a better translation might be 'govern' rather than 'steer', as govern has greater connotations of rational, conscious control.[18] Plato's evidence needs to be treated carefully though. We cannot be certain that Anaximander is being alluded to here, as several thinkers used *kubernan* in such contexts. It may also be the case that Plato interprets or represents presocratic philosophy in a way conducive to his own views.[19] Having said that, let us look at the Phaeacian ship passage again:

> Tell me your country, people and city, so that our ships may discern the course with their minds (*tituskomenai phresi*).[20] The Phaeacians have no helmsmen

(*kubernēteres*) nor any rudders, but the ships themselves know the thoughts and minds of men (*isasi noēmata kai phrenas andrōn*).²¹

These ships then have some mental function (they discern the course with their minds) and are able to steer themselves. They are able to know the thoughts and minds of men. They also have considerable knowledge (they know the cities and rich fields of all men, *Odyssey* VIII/ 560) and they are capable of crossing the sea quickly, even in adverse weather conditions, without damage or disaster (*Odyssey* VIII/ 561 ff.). So here we have a physical entity, a Phaeacian ship, which is capable of discerning the required course and steering itself, and seems to be conscious to some extent. This seems a good precursor for the *apeiron* being to some extent conscious and being capable of steering itself to a desired goal. Another question to consider here is if the steering of Anaximander's *apeiron* is modelled on the Phaeacian ships, what might the *apeiron* know? The thoughts and minds of men? Full geographical knowledge? Full knowledge of weather conditions? It is significant that for the Hippocratics nature can know. *On Regimen*, I/ says on the physician's art that 'Nature herself knows how to accomplish these things (*ē phusis automatē tauta epistatai*)'.²² So too in the Dervni papyrus air/ Zeus knows everything that was,²³ is and will be and Anaxagoras' nous has similar knowledge as well.²⁴

A second way of thinking about steering is in terms of organic growth. Aristotle tells us that the *apeiron* '*periechein hapanta kai panta kubernan*'. Instead of surrounds, we might translate as to defend, to protect, or guard. In a passage on zoogony Anaximander has the first living creatures enclosed/ protected (*periechomena*) in spine like bark.²⁵ An interesting form of *periechein* is *to periechon*, which in Theophrastus can be the envelope of a seed.²⁶ So the *apeiron* might then function as the envelope of a seed, the *gonimos* being the seed and the earth and rest of the *cosmos* being the product of the seed's growth. So the *apeiron* may steer in a biological fashion as a seed steers the growth of a plant.

It is also worth considering what a *kubernētēs*, usually translated as a helmsman or steersman, did in the ancient world, as this may affect our translation and understanding of both *kubernētēs* and the verb *kubernan*. The first point here is the status of the *kubernētēs*. In modern vessels the helmsman is quite low in the chain of command and their only task is to turn the ship's wheel under command from the bridge officer. This was not the case in the ancient world. Ships typically had three officers, the *kubernētēs* who was the commanding officer, the *keleustes* who was the rowing officer and the *prorates* who was the bow look out, a far more important role when navigating without charts. Plato says that a *kubernētēs* is so called for his leadership of the crew, not for his navigation abilities and Pindar refers to *kubernatēr oiakostrophos*, a 'helm wielding captain'. On larger ships the *kubernētēs* might delegate the actual steering to a subordinate. There was even a term, *pedialiouchos*, for the person who held the steering oar distinguishing them from the *kubernētēs*. Casson's *Ships and Seamanship in the Ancient World* refers to the *kubernētēs* as the 'executive officer'. Aristophanes' *Knights* 544 ff. says that someone must first know how to row, how to keep watch at the bow, then how to gauge winds before he can become the *kubernan*.[27] It is also significant that Plato in the *Republic* treats a *kubernētēs* as an intelligent, multi-skilled person, often paired with doctors and used in comparisons for the philosopher rulers. So *kubernan* should not be restricted simply to steering, but should have a strong sense of governing or leading as well.

## Steering and safety

Homer thought that a *kubernētēs* did his job by skill (*mētis*) when he guided (*ithunein*) a ship being buffeted by winds (*Iliad* XXIII, 313), which brings me to a further point about safety. We can find a strong association of the *kubernētēs* with safety/ salvation. Plato at *Republic* 346a has the main task of the doctor as health and the main task of the *kubernētikē* as safety, *sōtēria*. *Gorgias* 511d ff. has the knowledge of the *kubernētēs* saving souls, bodies and property from danger and the *kubernētēs* deserving pay whether he has brought people and property safely from Aegina, Egypt or the Pontus. We can find this association of the *kubernētēs* with safety throughout Plato and Aristotle, e.g. *Politicus* 273de as we have seen above, *Symposium* 197e, *Laws* 707a, 961e, *Physics* 195a, *Metaphysics* 1013b and *Protrepticus* 69–70 echoes the doctor/ health and *kubernētēs* with safety formula of the *Republic*. We also find this association of the *kubernētēs* with safety/ salvation in Herodotus *Historiae* 8.118, where the Persian king asks the *kubernētēs* if there is any possible salvation from a storm, Xenophon *Cyropaedia* 1.6.6 talks of those who do not know how to steer should not pray to save the ship by taking the helm of the ship. Aeschylus *Supplices* 765 also associates safety and skilled seamanship with the *kubernētēs*. So too in the Hippocratic *Ancient Medicine* IX, a bad *kubernētēs* is like a bad doctor, unnoticed in good conditions, but problematic in a storm when salvation is required.

At Herodotus 118, 11 we have the tale of the Persian nobles throwing themselves off of a stricken ship in order to save the king. The point here is not whether the tale is true or not,[28] but that it is the *kubernētēs* who is held responsible for the ship's safety, which can be seen by the facts that he is consulted in the storm as to what to do, he issues the orders and he is subsequently beheaded.[29] It is also interesting that in some Christian writing, such as Theodoretus, Joannes Chrysostomus and Gregorius Nazienzenus there is a sense that Christ is a *kubernētēs* with the same word, *sōtēria* being used for the salvation of the soul.

There is a cosmological dimension to this issue of safety. Ancient ships used to employ cables called *hupozōmata* to strengthen the hull. These passed under the ship from stem to stern and were deployed prior to storms. The *kubernētēs* had the discretion of when to deploy them. In the Myth of Er in Plato's *Republic*, at 616bc, a light, like a rainbow but purer, acts as the bond of the heavens (*sundesmon tou ouranou*) and is like the *hupozōmata* of triremes (616c3), in the same manner holding together (*sunechon*) the revolving whole.[30] So if we return to Aristotle's report on the *apeiron* for Anaximander, that it *periechein hapanta kai panta kubernan*, surrounds all and steers all, does it also bind everything together like *hupozōmata* do? If the *kubernētēs* has such an important safety function, should we give *periechein* more a sense of 'protects' rather than surrounds? If the *apeiron* acts for the safety of the cosmos, this has some implications for the fate of the cosmos in Anaximander, which I will come to shortly.

In previous discussions of steering in Anaximander, I have marginally favoured the idea of organic growth and steering as a seed guides a plant to grow,[31] but having looked further I now favour steering in Anaximander being modelled to some extent on the Phaeacian ships with a strong sense of an intelligent, knowledgeable and safety conscious steerer, that being adaptable to different uses of *kubernan* in early Greek thought about nature. Whether that works for all instances of *kubernan* in that tradition is another issue. It would possibly work better for Diogenes and the Hippocratic author than Heraclitus, but each might model steering slightly differently.

## Pindar, Bacchylides and *kubernan*

While Homer used guiding verbs for his gods (*agein, ithunein*) he did not specifically use *kubernan*, though *ithunein*, to guide, was what a *kubernētēs* did in Homer. It is also implied the Phaeacian ships steer themselves. We can strengthen the idea that *kubernan* was something done by the gods and get a little more information about *kubernan* from looking at Pindar *c.* 518–438 BCE and Bacchylides *c.* 518–*c.* 451 BCE. Both postdate Anaximander 611/ 610–547/ 546 BCE so there is no simple *muthos* to *logos* move here. What this will show is that poets did use *kubernan* for what their gods did, and there may have been an ongoing dispute between poets and early philosophers/ medics on the use of *kubernan*. So Pindar, *Pythian Ode* 5/ 122 says that:

> The great mind of Zeus steers (*kuberna*) the fortune/souls (*daimon*) of men he loves.

*Pythian Ode* 4/ 274:

> Unless a god becomes a helmsman (*kubernatēr*) for those who lead.

*Pythian Ode* 10/ 72:

> With the good lies the governance (*kubernasies*) of cities.

*Olympian Ode* 12/ 3:

> For you guide (*kubernōntai*) on the sea swift ships, on land quick battles and assemblies which give advice.

*Incert* Fragment 214:

> With him lives sweet Hope
> Heart-fostering nurse of old age,
> Which most of all steers (*kuberna*) mortals'
> Much wandering judgements

We can also look at Bacchylides *Ode* 12:

> Like a wise (*sophos*) steersman (*kubernētas*), Klio queen of song guide (*euthune*) my thoughts now if you ever did before.

It is interesting that the steersman can be wise, also, as we have seen that a god can be described as steering human thoughts. So to we can see this in Sophocles *Ajax*, 35 where it is the hand of Athena which steers (*kubernōmai*) Odysseus. Bacchylides *Ode* 14, 10 talks of:

> When a man has steered (*kubernasen*)[32] what is at hand with a just mind.[33]

Finally, Bacchylides *Ode* 13, 146 says:

> With garland-loving Eucleia she steers (*kuberna*) the state, along with sound-minded Eunomia, possessor of festivities, who guards (*phulassai*) the cities of pious men in peace.

So according to these lyric poets, the gods can steer and in some of these fragments there is also a sense of steering with justice and steering with safety, especially the last passage from Bacchylides, where the steering god guards (*phulassai*) the cities of pious men in peace. There is also, unsurprisingly, a political dimension to *kubernan* in the sense of governing or steering cities yet even here there is an important sense of steering or governing with a sense of safety and with a sense of justice, and as we saw in Chapter 3, the minds, thoughts or judgements of men can be guided as well.

## Anaximander's Cosmogony process

Let us now turn to the debate about whether Anaximander was a mechanist or not. Aristotle tells us that:

> There are those for whom the contraries are in the one and are separated (*enkrinesthai*) out of it, as Anaximander says, along with those who say that the one is many, such as Empedocles and Anaxagoras. They too produce the other things from the mixture by separation (*enkrinousi*).[34]

The verb *enkrinein* may indicate a simple separation,[35] but it can mean to secrete, in the sense that living things secrete.[36] The verb *apokrinein*, found in the doxography derived from Theophrastus, does mean to set apart or to separate without the organic sense of secretion. One might accept Aristotle on the grounds that he is the earlier source, but really our choice here is underdetermined. Clearly *enkrinein* is more suitable for a biological reading of Anaximander while *apokrinein* is more suitable for a mechanical reading. Pseudo-Plutarch gives us something more specifically cosmogonical:

> He says that which is productive (*gonimon*) of the hot and cold was separated at the genesis of this *cosmos*, and that a sphere of flame was formed around the air around the earth like the bark (*phloion*) around a tree. When this was broken off and enclosed in certain circles, the sun, moon and stars were formed... The stars were generated as circles of fire, separated off from cosmic fire, surrounded by air.[37]

Here we have a *gonimos*, 'something productive of the hot and cold.' The term *gonimos* can have organic connotations, meaning productive, fertile or fruitful. The *gonimos* has been interpreted in many different ways. Cornford argued for an association with the Orphic cosmogonical egg.[38] I am sceptical about that, as for Anaximander the *gonimos* is produced from the *apeiron* and has a part in the generation of the opposites and ultimately the *cosmos*. We lack the typical Orphic precursors and successors to the egg. So we have no Kronos, Aether and Chaos as precursors and we certainly do not have gods as successors to the egg.[39] If a sense of fertile production is meant, a seed rather than sexual reproduction might be a better analogue here. It may be significant that *periechein*, which is used of the *apeiron*, can have the sense of a seed case, and here we have the seed itself from which the *cosmos* will grow in an organic manner.

## Vortices in Anaximander?

The supposed evidence for a vortex in Anaximander is at Aristotle, *On the Heavens*, II/13, 295a7 ff:

> If the earth now remains in place by force, it was also assembled in the centre by being carried there because of a vortex. For this is the reason which everyone gives, through what occurs in water and around air. In these the larger and heavier things are always carried to the centre of the vortex. So all those who say that the heavens are generated have the earth being assembled in the middle.[40]

Aristotle could not have had Anaximander in mind here.[41] Aristotle was aware that Anaximander did not use force to explain why the earth remains in place and was also aware that he gave an indifference argument instead.[42] The vortex was a well known idea with a well defined term, *dinē*. If Anaximander did employ a vortex, it is very surprising there is no mention of it in the doxography. Anaximander had no need of or motivation for a vortex, nor did he have the ontology to support vortices. Did Anaximander need a vortex to stop the heavens falling to earth? Simplicius *De Caelo*, 374, 32 ff. tells us that

> Some say that a physical mechanism keeps the sky from falling, namely the action of a vortex which holds it up since the downward pull on the heavens is less than the force exerted by the vortex. Empedocles and Anaxagoras say this.

One can see why that would be so for Empedocles and Anaxagoras, but Anaximander is not named here, quite rightly. For Anaximander the heavenly bodies had a core of fire and a surrounding coating of compressed air. There is no reason why these should fall to earth and so Anaximander had no need of a vortex to keep them in position.

Did Anaximander need a vortex for the heavens to move in a circular fashion? West has argued that 'Such a system patently resembles a vortex.'[43] I disagree, and would cite Plato and Aristotle as two clear contrary cases. Circular motion of the heavens does not entail a vortex. The doxography does refer to an eternal motion of the *apeiron*, though it does not make clear the nature of that motion.[44] West has associated the formation of vortices with random motion, as he says we find in Leucippus and Democritus, and that:

> This motion probably consists of random currents running in no fixed direction. From time to time they result in a vortex which lasts for a while and then slows down and disappears.[45]

There is no evidence to support this supposition though. If the *apeiron* has a steering function, that, on its own, should rule out any random motion in the *apeiron*.

Vlastos has argued that the *gonimos* can be thought of as a process rather than as a thing,[46] and the process is a vortex.[47] Stokes has been critical, arguing that it is unclear how a process can be separated out from the *apeiron*.[48] I agree with Stokes that Democritus Fr. 167 is not a sufficient parallel. With the context from Simplicius, this runs:

> When Democritus says that 'A vortex of all shapes is separated off from the all' (how or by what cause he does not say), it appears that this occurs spontaneously or by chance.[49]

Here it is shapes (i.e. the atoms) that are separated, not a process. An important distinction between Anaximander and Empedocles and Anaxagoras is that Anaximander's *apeiron*, prior to the beginning of cosmos formation, is partless, is homogenous, does not consist of particles (so no shapes) and is not a mixture. As we have seen, Aristotle recognized this at *Physics*, I/ 4, 187a20 where he contrasts those who say that the one is many (Empedocles and Anaxagoras) with Anaximander who says it is one, and Aristotle has contraries being excreted from the *apeiron*, not, shapes, atoms or vortices. The critical point here is that Anaximander is a pre-Parmenidean thinker. Anaximander did not need to think of change in terms of the redistribution of changeless parts of matter, but can have the qualities being generated out of the *apeiron*.[50] Without atoms or other particles of matter, vortices are simply not applicable to Anaximander. So too vortices sort like to like. In Anaximander there are no like or unlike particles to be sorted, and there is no mention of any like to like principle. There is then no evidence that Anaximander employed a vortex or vortices, he had no need for them, they did not fit with his thought and it is hard to see what would have motivated him to suppose them.

## *Cosmoi* for Anaximander

There has been a long running debate about the number of *cosmoi* for Anaximander. The three views are a single, eternal cosmos, successive *cosmoi* with only one cosmos existing at a time or multiple co-existent cosmoi. A more organic view of the cosmos has been associated with the single *cosmos* and the successive *cosmoi* view, while a more mechanical view has been associated with the multiple co-existent *cosmoi* view. I have discussed this issue extensively elsewhere, so I will give summaries of the key points here, though first I wish to add three further considerations in favour of a single, eternally existing cosmos for Anaximander.[51] I take the following passage to be critical for the view of Leucippus and Democritus:

> Democritus holds the same view as Leucippus... There are innumerable *cosmoi*, which differ in size. In some of these there is no sun or moon, in some they are larger than ours and in some more numerous. The spaces between *cosmoi* are not equal, in places there are more and in others less, some are growing, some are in their prime, some declining, some are coming to be and others failing. They are destroyed by falling into each other. There are *cosmoi* bereft of animals and vegetation and all moisture. In our *cosmos* the earth was generated prior to the stars, and the moon is the lowest, followed by the sun and then the stars.[52]

So *cosmoi* are different from each other. There may be some structural similarities as all have been generated from vortices, but there is a different order to each cosmos and we can explain the order of our cosmos as one of an infinite array of differently ordered *cosmoi*. I would argue something similar for Empedocles, as Aristotle, *Physics* II/4, 196a20 ff. tells us that:

> Empedocles says that air is not always separated out upwards but according to chance – He says in his cosmogony 'Thus at one time it ran by chance, but many times it was otherwise' – and he says that the parts of animals are for the most part generated by chance.[53]

In Anaximander we find a precise account of the cosmos with a great deal of symmetry and *taxis*, order, but no sense whatever of what different *cosmoi*, either co-existent or successive, might be like, why they would be different, or what their supposed existence would explain.[54]

The second new consideration is based on the safety and captaincy role of the *kubernētēs*. The myth of Plato's *Politicus* is important here. At *Politicus* 273e the god is specially a *kubernētēs* who steers the cosmos with a *pēdalion*, a steering oar. All is fine with the cosmos while the god performs this function. When the appointed time of change comes though, the *kubernētēs* drops the oar and the cosmos begins to deteriorate and over time this deterioration becomes serious. However,

> Then god, the orderer of the cosmos, perceived that it was in trouble, and concerned that it should not be storm driven by confusion and broken up into an endless sea of unlikeness, again took seat at the oar, and whatever had become diseased or dissolved in the first period he ordered, restored and made perfect making it immortal and ageless (*athanaton auton kai agērōn apergazetai*).

The maritime imagery is interesting and important here, the *kubernētēs* god having to save the cosmos from the storm. It is also significant that the *kubernētēs* god has the power to make the cosmos immortal and ageless (*athanaton kai agēron*), and clearly has a strong cosmogonical role in ordering the cosmos in the first instance. Whether this myth is Plato's actual cosmology is debateable, though the imagery stands whether it is or not and I would note that although expressed in different terms, in the *Timaeus* the demiurge certainly has what would in modern terminology be called a 'duty of care' for his cosmos.

The critical question then is this. Given that the *apeiron* surrounds (protects?) all and steers all for Anaximander, does it perform a divine safety role for his cosmos as well? If so one would very much expect there to be a single eternal cosmos in Anaximander. Even in adverse weather conditions, the Phaeacian were capable of steering a course to the desired goal without damage or disaster (*Odyssey* VIII/ 563) and if we transfer that capability to the *apeiron* we would have a single indestructible cosmos.

Thirdly, has the sort of historiography which has led us to overestimate the role of mechanism in early Greek thought also led us to suppose that there were more successive *cosmoi* and more multiple existent *cosmoi* theories than there actually were? I do not have the space to discuss this in depth here, but one can certainly see how that might have come about with multiple world theories currently being popular in modern cosmology.

## Supporting infrastructure?

I will divide the points in favour of a single cosmos in Anaximander into four sections, lack of supporting philosophical infrastructure, lack of motivation, the nature of the doxography and the question of cosmic decay. The ideas of chance or of *ou mallon* considerations are critical for multiple *cosmoi* view in generating the differences between *cosmoi* that make these multiple *cosmoi* views. However, there is no mention of any element of chance in Anaximander and no mention of any *ou mallon* considerations. In early Greek theories of successive or co-existent *cosmoi*, we find boundary and individuation criteria for *cosmoi* which allow us to identify successive *cosmoi* or multiple co-existent *cosmoi* and say that there is a plurality of them. In Leucippus and Democritus there is a membrane that surrounds, and effectively individuates each cosmos and there are clear descriptions of the growth, decline and death of *cosmoi*. In Empedocles, there are clear states (total association of the elements, total dissociation of the elements) that mark key parts in the cycle and allow the differentiation of one cosmos from the successive or preceding one. We find no such criteria in Anaximander. As argued above, we do not find particulate matter nor do we find vortices in Anaximander. I would also question whether there is sufficient similarity between Anaximander's *apeiron* and the early atomists' notion of space to support infinite *cosmoi* in Anaximander.[55]

## Motivation

What would be Anaximander's motivation for postulating multiple *cosmoi*? This is not a 'no precedent' objection, as Anaximander was an original thinker capable of interesting new ideas. Rather, if we take the steering principle seriously then Anaximander can explain the order of our cosmos without recourse to multiple *cosmoi*. This is also an issue of explanation. Where Leucippus, Democritus and Empedocles explain aspects of the order of our cosmos, whether physical or biological, in terms of chance happening among many accidents (cosmos formation, species formation) we find no trace of this sort of explanation in Anaximander.[56] One might also ask about the motivation for some of the ideas needed to underpin multiple *cosmoi*, especially for a pre-Parmenidean thinker. There is nothing that motivated a particulate account of matter prior to Parmenides, nothing which motivates an infinite rather than an unlimited conception of space, nothing which motivates cosmic vortices. A specific account of history which sees those all as positive moves towards some mechanistic *telos* may have a strong motivation to suppose such ideas in Anaximander, but in context there is no evidence of these ideas and no motivation for them. As argued in the introduction to this book, it is sometimes just as important to ask why as to ask why not.

## Positive Doxography

While the doxography is usually thought to support successive or multiple co-existent *cosmoi* in Anaximander, there are some passages which support the single eternal cosmos view. Diogenes Laertius, *Lives of the Philosophers*, 2, 1–2 says that:

> kai ta me merē metaballein, to de pan ametablēton einai.
> The parts change, but the whole is changeless.

That is correct for Anaximander.[57] The constituents of the *cosmos* may change but the *cosmos* itself does not.[58] So the formula 'generated out of x... dissolved into x' does not imply the dissolution of the cosmos for Anaximander. There are two passages from Aristotle which are also important. Aristotle *On the Heavens*, I/10, 279b13ff say that:

> Everyone believes it to have been generated, but some believe it to be eternal once generated, others believe that it is destructible like any other formation in nature, while others believe that it alternates, at one time being as it now is, and at another time changing and going to ruin, such as Empedocles of Acragas and Heraclitus of Ephesus.

Anaximander is here conspicuous by his absence. Who are those who believe in eternal once generated, other than Plato? Aristotle later says:

> They say that nothing is ungenerated, and that everything is generated. Once generated, some things remain deathless while others again perish. Hesiod and his followers take this position, as do the first of the natural philosophers.[59]

Who were the 'first of the natural philosophers' here? The most natural assumption would be the Milesians, including Anaximander, especially as Aristotle uses a similar phrase at *Metaphysics* I/3 983b6 to refer to the Milesians.

## Cosmogony doxography

Let us now look at the other doxographical evidence. It is important to point out that the doxography can be wrong on cosmogony. Indeed it is now almost universally held that the doxography was incorrect in attributing a successive *cosmoi* view to Heraclitus. The passage in Aristotle which could be construed as attributing multiple *cosmoi* to Anaximander is *On the Heavens*, III/5 303b10–13:

Some hypothesize one alone, water, air, fire or something rarer than water but denser than air, and this they say is unlimited and surrounds all of the heavens (*pantas tous ouranous*).

The phrase 'all the heavens' here might attribute multiple co-existent worlds, but Aristotle separated three senses of *ouranos* (heaven) in *On the Heavens*, and he may have only intended to attribute 'heavens' in the sense of multiple rings, of stars, moon and sun.[60] Anaximander's celestial wheels are complex, well organized entities separate from each other which might well lead either Anaximander or Aristotle to term them *ouranoi*. Anaximander might use the plural to emphasize that his cosmos has depth (stars then moon then sun) in way in which previous cosmologies did not, there being a single vault of heaven.[61] With Aristotle keen to attack the idea of multiple *cosmoi*, it would be strange if Aristotle attributed multiple *cosmoi* to Anaximander here with no further comment here or elsewhere.

## Theophrastus

According to the standard reconstruction from the later doxography,[62] Theophrastus used the phrase 'all the heavens (*ouranoi*) and the *cosmoi* within them' (*hapantas ginesthai tous ournous kai tous en autois kosmous*), in reference to Anaximander.[63] Some of the later doxography explicitly attributes multiple *cosmoi* to Anaximander though Theophrastus did not. What might these *cosmoi* be? Anaximander had a strong sense of symmetry and his earth was shaped like a stone column drum, so had two sides. So if there were a human society on one side of the earth, making a political cosmos, there might very well be a society on the other side as well making political *cosmoi*.[64] There is also an interesting passage in the pseudo-Hippocratic *On Sevens*:[65]

> The *cosmoi* above the earth are equal in number and similar in form to those underneath the earth.[66]

Aristotle refers to different regions of the terrestrial realm as *cosmoi*.[67] Anaximander might have done the same, or might have a weather system associated with each side of the earth. We do not know if Aristotle and Theophrastus are quoting or paraphrasing Anaximander when they say 'all of the heavens (*ouranoi*)' and 'all the heavens (*ouranoi*) and the *cosmoi* within them'. If they are, Anaximander may have meant no more than political *cosmoi* or weather *cosmoi* on both sides of the earth within the rings of stars, moon and sun. If Aristotle and Theophrastus are describing Anaximander's view, it is not clear if they are attributing multiple worlds or not. It is significant that they say *en ouranois*, in the heavens, rather than *en tō kenō*, the atomist void, or even *en apeirō*, in the *apeiron*, when the meaning would be clear. It is also odd that *ouranoi* is a plural, as in a multiple co-existent world theory there are not 'heavens', there is a single space and if we try to push this on to Anaximander surely there should be a single *apeiron* which the supposed *cosmoi* are in.[68]

## Decay

I am sceptical about the cosmos terminally drying out for Anaximander. Aristotle is aware of drying out theories, but does not attribute this to Anaximander:

> At first the whole area surrounding the earth is moist, but due to the drying of the sun, that which is evaporated makes winds and the turnings of the sun and moon, they say, while that which remains is the sea. Thus they think it is becoming less through being dried up, and will at some point end up being entirely dry.[69]

At *Meteorology* 356b9 he does attribute this to Democritus but not to Anaximander. Alexander, *Meteorology* 67, 11 though tells us that:

> Of this view were Anaximander and Diogenes, according to the history of Theophrastus.

Theophrastus is simply wrong to attribute this to Diogenes. There is nothing in Diogenes to suggest any drying out theory. There is also nothing to suggest this in Anaximander. It is very important to distinguish between the earth drying out, which is all that is said here, and the cosmos drying out. If the earth were to dry out, but retain its position, and the celestial rings remain stable (which are fire and air, so no drying out applicable) why would that precipitate a new cosmos? A new earth, perhaps, so we have multiple civilisations (*cosmoi*?), but not a new cosmos. Would it be possible for the cosmos to dry out? Not if there is an equitable exchange of contraries as with the extant fragment. The essential question for any drying out theory, for earth or cosmos, is where is the moisture going? One further possibility to consider is that the earth was formed more moist than it is now, it dried out in the sense that moisture evaporates to form clouds in a weather system until an equilibrium of evaporation/ precipitation was achieved. Aristotle is aware that some places are drier than they were previously but puts this down to excess rain in some periods,[70] and argues that it is absurd to draw grandiose conclusions from small changes.[71]

There is also an interesting parallel between Diogenes and Anaximander. Both explain rain in terms of the sun and subsequent rainfall. So:

> Diogenes of Apollonia says that the water of the sea is drawn up by the sun, and then falls in the Nile. He believes that the Nile floods in the summer on account of the sun turning it into moist secretions form the earth.[72]

So did Theophrastus, on the basis that Anaximander and Diogenes believed that rain is generated by the action of the sun, then incorrectly attribute to them the full view that the earth is terminally drying out? There is also a deeper issue here about whether changes for Anaximander are synchronic or diachronic at the level of the cosmos. Granted that the earth might become drier or wetter, but can the cosmos as a whole become drier or wetter, or is it that a part of the cosmos becoming wetter entails that a part synchronically becomes drier?[73] If the latter, then the earth drying out has no consequence for the cosmos, it will not, as some have suggested dry out entirely and be re-absorbed in the *apeiron*.[74]

A second issue of decay arises if Anaximander's cosmos is thought to be organic. Mansfeld has commented that:

> Anaximander's explanation of the generation of the world as a natural process comparable to the generation of, say, a tree, or a marine animal, unavoidably suggests that, just as such a tree or animal, the world too will at one time come to its end.[75]

I agree with Mansfeld on the issue of the generation of the cosmos as a natural and biological process, but disagree on the implication. I agree with Kirk that:

> As for the argument that what was born must die, one has only to think of the widely scattered myths of the birth of Zeus, for example, to dispose of that.[76]

I would also note Aristotle, *On the Heavens*, III/1 298b29 as we have seen above saying that Hesiod and his followers and the first philosophers thought the cosmos generated but undying. Plato is an important contrary case. In the *Timaeus* we find a generated, organic living *cosmos* which will not decay or die, as the demiurge will not allow this. This is important in two senses, as a living cosmos that will not die, and as a cosmos under the care of a demiurge. If Anaximander's cosmos is under the care of the steering principle, particularly one which has responsibility for safety, it may not die either.

## The heavens

Anaximander held that there were separate rings for the stars, moon and sun. These rings encircle the earth, with the ring of the stars nearest and that of the sun furthest away. These rings consisted of a central core of fire, surrounded by air. With the rings of the sun and the moon, there is a single hole in the enveloping air, so what we see as sun and moon is in fact the central core of fire seen though this hole in the air. There is a great deal of symmetry to this arrangement, all of these rings being circles centred on the earth, so there is no reason for any of these rings to move. So too there is a great deal of *taxis*, good arrangement, both in the sense of the fire/air/hole structure of the rings and their distances from the earth, usually taken as 9, 18 and 27.[77] A small but important point here is that fire is not what is outermost in Anaximander's cosmos. The ring of the sun is outermost, but that is fire surrounded by air so there will be some air which is further away than the furthest fire. These considerations are important for cosmogony. We might attribute something like Aristotle's idea of natural place/motion to Anaximander, such that fire raises, but this will not produce his cosmos. It will not generate rings of fire surrounded by air nor will it generate air as the outermost element in the cosmos. So too attributing like to like to Anaximander would fail to produce the symmetry and *taxis* of his cosmos, and nor would attributing a vortex. Something more must guide the cosmos into its current order.

## Eclipses and phases

Anaximander has an explanation of eclipses and phases of the moon. This is important as a natural explanation of important phenomena. Hippolytus *Refutation of All Heresies*, I, 6 says that for Anaximander:

> When the mouths (*tōn ekpnoōn*) are closed eclipses occur. The moon appears to be waxing or waning in turns due to whether these pores (*tōn porōn*) are opening or closing.

The first thing to say is that the gap in the rings which we see as stars, moon and sun is described as an *ekpnoē*, a vent or breathing hole,[78] or a *stomion*, a mouth, or a *poros*, a pore through the skin.[79] It is important to recognize here that Anaximander's rings do not have mechanical parts. I used to translate *ekpnoē*, *poros*, and *stomion* as 'aperture', thinking that the closing for phases and eclipses could be likened to the shutter opening and closing across a camera aperture. I now think that is quite wrong, as there is no shutter and equally importantly, there is no mechanism to actuate the shutter. It is too mechanical a way of thinking about this for Anaximander. Furthermore, one would only get a small range of shapes for eclipses and phases out of a shutter. It is much better to translate *ekpnoē*, *poros* and *stomion* as 'breathing hole' or 'mouth' or 'pore' when one has no need of any mechanical parts and there is much greater flexibility in the shapes that can be generated for phases and eclipses. If we ask how the mouths open and close, steering is clearly one answer, albeit rather uninformative, although if we go in for the idea that the cosmos is steered as a seed steers a plant, we might say that the mouths open and shut in a way similar to the regular flowering of plants, or for some plants the regular opening and closing of their petals.

## The wheel analogy

The celestial rings in Anaximander are likened to wheels, *trochoi*. Does this constitute a mechanical analogy? It does not. The key issues here are how far this analogy can be pushed and what Anaximander gets out of this analogy. I agree with Berryman who says that:

> The question is whether artefacts and natural things were thought to *work like* one another. Not every artefact analogy would count as specifically 'mechanical'.[80]

The rings are like cart wheels, but how far does that likeness go? The key things which Anaximander gets out of this analogy are shape (circularity) and motion (circular around a central point). There are also clear dissimilarities with a wheel. No one could suggest that the celestial rings are made of wood, like the wheels of the time. A wheel would require something to connect the rim to the hub, either spokes or a solid wheel, which we do not get. A wheel would also require a hub, and an axle to turn on. We do not get either and it is inconceivable that we would.

I would also question the assumption that Anaximander's rings are rigid. They are in fact made of fire and air so they may be fluid. The difference would be that a rigid wheel would not deform if subjected to some force, where a fluid wheel would. However, if Anaximander's rings are set up such that there is no reason for them to move or to deform out of shape, fluid wheels would behave exactly as rigid ones do.[81] Whether the hole in a ring is fixed or can move relative to the ring is also worth consideration, the usual assumption being that the hole is fixed in a rigid ring. If the hole is able to move though, that would allow for some more flexibility in modelling some astronomical phenomena.[82] The conclusion from this is that the wheel analogy is certainly interesting, but is not a mechanical one.

## Astronomy or cosmology?

When we reconstruct Anaximander on the heavens, we have a choice. We can give him the best astronomy the evidence allows, or the best cosmology, this best being justified by historical generosity. These do not result in the same system! Couprie has championed the first approach and has highly ingenious suggestions which allow Anaximander to account for many astronomical phenomena, but the price is losing significant amounts of symmetry and *taxis*.[83] The heavens are no longer equally distributed around the earth all the time so the argument for the stability of the earth is lost too. I have championed the latter view, preserving symmetry and *taxis* while allowing that there are astronomical phenomena that Anaximander's system cannot account for.[84] There is a similar issue in Plato where re-constructing for best astronomy and best cosmology give very different results, where again I have argued that we should opt for the best cosmological reconstruction.[85] The tendency in the literature has been to go for the best astronomical reconstruction, possibly because we, or at least these scholars, have valued astronomy over cosmology. That may be a modern preference though and it is quite possible that the early Greeks valued cosmological principle over astronomical precision.

## Anaximander's numbers

There is also a more fundamental issue, which is Anaximander's numbers for the spacing of the rings of the stars, the moon and the sun. The standard reconstruction of the spacing of Anaximander's rings is from Tannery.[86] The first series of 9, 18 and 27 represents the inner diameter of the rings of the stars, sun and moon respectively. The second series of 10, 19 and 28 represents the outer diameter of the rings of the stars, sun and moon. The first series are all multiples of the diameter of the earth, which is said to be three times the depth of the earth. This forms a neat and attractive series, but we only have evidence for the figures 19, 27 and 28,[87] the other figures being conjectures to fit the supposed sequence. Indeed there are other ways of formulating a sequence and we need to be selective with the evidence to generate this sequence.[88] Do we overly modernize

Anaximander by generating this concrete sequence from a relatively small amount of evidence? It is certainly tempting to attribute such a neat, formulaic sequence expressing the distances of the heavenly bodies to Anaximander.

There has been debate as to whether these numbers are precise distances for the heavenly bodies or are something more figurative. West has suggested an oriental influence, Heath that these are sacred numbers, Diels that this is a poetic representation.[89] With Anaximander's numbers we see a 9 + 1 formula which is seen often in Homer and Hesiod to express a great amount of space or time. In Homer the siege of Troy takes 9 years before the fall in the 10th year, Odysseus roams for 9 years before returning home in the tenth. In Hesiod's a god who drinks from the river Styx is exiled for 9 years but can then return in the tenth.[90] In terms of cosmology, we have Hesiod, *Theogony* 720–725:

> As far below the earth as heaven is from the earth
> For this is as far as misty Tartarus is from the earth.
> Nine nights and days a bronze anvil
> Falling from heaven, will reach the earth on the tenth.
> Nine nights and days this bronze anvil,
> Falling from the earth, will reach Tartarus on the tenth.

The point of 9 + 1 in Anaximander may be to counter Hesiod rather than to give precise distances as in modern astronomy. The points here are that Anaximander gives depth to the heavens (the sun is further than the moon which is further than the stars), as opposed to all the heavenly bodies being the same distance, asserts the centrality of the earth and the no-existence of Tartarus, and asserts the symmetry of the cosmos such that not only the earth, but stars, sun and moon have no reason to move. So we may overly modernize Anaximander by treating his numbers as precise distances. One indication of this are the problems associated with angular size of the sun, which comes out too large if we take Anaximander's figures literally.[91]

## Conclusion

It is clear that Anaximander used *kubernan* in a significant cosmological context and that there was a tradition of doing so which included Heraclitus, a Hippocratic author, Parmenides and Diogenes, as well as Plato and Aristotle. It is also clear that there is significant work that this steering principle may be doing. The symmetry and *taxis* of Anaximander's cosmos cannot be generated by vortices, natural motion, chance or a like to like principle and we have no credible evidence that Anaximander was committed to any of these. The steering principle may then steer the parts of the cosmos into their proper order. So too the steering principle may play an important role in the ongoing stability of Anaximander's cosmos. There is a viable, organic interpretation of Anaximander which pays due attention to steering and situates Anaximander as engaging with Homer, Hesiod and other early poets. He does not, miraculously and without evident motivation, generate a mechanical account of the cosmos and its origins. Although I have argued against a mechanistic interpretation of Anaximander here, I would emphasize again that I see Anaximander as an important, original and seminal thinker, one trying to address important issues with the tools available to him.

# 5

# New Explanations, New Philosophies of Nature

We have seen how important the idea of steering was for Anaximander and how that may have grown out of an engagement with the ideas of Homer and Hesiod. In this chapter I want to look at some of the new explanations for natural phenomena that Anaximander gave. I will argue that they have further merits beyond naturalism. They are generalizable, have breadth, depth and economy and are invariant. Anaximander sets the parameters for those following him in the investigation of nature tradition, especially in meteorology and zoogony. If we drop superficial similarities between modern science and Anaximander, we find greater coherence and a strong methodology for investigating nature. This serves as a paradigm for approaching some other early Greek thinkers. Although Anaximander used a civil law model, this turns out to be surprisingly strong in its support for invariant behaviour. I argue that in an ancient context these give a much stronger model for regularities than any mechanical analogy would have done. The *kata* ... (according to ...) phrases that Anaximander and Heraclitus used show an interesting development on Homer and Hesiod without giving us *kata phusin*, according to nature. I will also argue that we can get important traction on understanding Anaximander if we are willing to consider some passages as allusions to and reactions to some of the poets.

## Meteorology

The key passage for Anaximander's meteorology is the following:

> Concerning thunder, lightning, thunderbolts, fire whirls and tornados.[1]
> Anaximander, all (*panta*) these come about because of wind. Whenever (*hotan*) it is enclosed in a thick cloud and then forcibly breaks out, due to its fineness and lightness, then the bursting makes the noise, and the rent against the blackness of the cloud is the lightning flash.[2]

It is sometimes said that these are the sorts of phenomena attributed to the gods of Homer and Hesiod. I believe we can say something stronger, which is that these are precisely the phenomena that Homer and Hesiod attribute to the gods and to Zeus in particular. In Homer, Zeus is commonly associated with thunder, thunderbolt, and lightning,[3] and we find this in Hesiod as well.[4] More particularly, in the battle of Zeus against the Titans in *Theogony* 845–6 we find that:

> The conflagration held the purple waters, from the thunder and lightning and the fire of the monster, from the tornado and the fiery thunderbolt.[5]

So we have thunder, lightning, tornado and thunderbolt, all as part of a battle of the gods. Zeus then uses his weapons of thunder, lightning and thunderbolt to defeat Typhoeus, who produces strong winds and wet winds. This passage is significant in that this looks like an allusion not just of the general views of Homer and Hesiod but of a specific passage. If Anaximander did allude to Hesiod in the thunder, lightning, fire whirls and tornados passage, this is neither unique nor unusual among presocratic thinkers. In *The Presocratics and the Supernatural* I argued that figures such as Anaximenes, Heraclitus, some of the Hippocratic authors, Xenophanes, Anaxagoras, Leucippus and Democritus all alluded to Homer and/or Hesiod in arguing for natural explanations for phenomena.[6]

I also argued there for what I called the 'targeting thesis'.[7] The targeting thesis is that among many of the early Greek thinkers, we find a comprehensive, consistent and targeted rejection of non-natural explanations. Comprehensive in that we find a great number of natural explanations of phenomena that had previously been explained in term of non-natural intervention. Consistent in that there are basic principles within each thinker used to explain the phenomena rather than ad hoc explanations. They were targeted in three senses. Targeted on what was commonly attributed to intervention by the gods. Targeted on most important cases and hardest cases to demonstrate natural explanation. Targeted in particular on Homer and Hesiod, both in terms of their general views and in terms of well-known passages. In particular the targeting thesis entails that there was a conscious and systematic rejection of non-natural explanation in favour of natural explanation.[8]

Specific important examples here are Anaximenes on rainbows and on earthquakes, Xenophanes on the rainbow,[9] on divination,[10] and on St. Elmo's fire,[11] the Hippocratic author of *On the Sacred Disease* and their rejection of any non-natural cause for the sacred disease,[12] Anaxagoras on rainbows, earthquakes and divination,[13] Leucippus and Democritus on the gods and on images.[14] Anaximander fits this pattern very well. It is also interesting that there are a number of early Greek thinkers following Anaximander who deal with thunder, lightning, thunderbolts, fire whirls and tornados. The same reservations about the evidence should apply as with Anaximander, but Stobaeus, who is the fuller source, mentions Metrodorus, Archelaus, Xenophanes, Diogenes, Empedocles,[15] Leucippus as having views on some of these phenomena. He has Anaximenes, and Anaxagoras as having views on all five, along with Aristotle, Chrysippus and Strato. Democritus is reported on four of these phenomena, but not on tornados and Heraclitus on three, again lacking tornados and slightly oddly thunderbolts as we know that Heraclitus did mention them.[16] Both Democritus and Heraclitus deal with winds though and as the passage in Hesiod has Typhoeus a god of winds that may be enough for all five.

Such allusions were not exceptional. Plato often alluded to early Greek thinkers without naming them.[17] There are passages in Aristotle that do not name early Greek thinkers but do give their views.[18] Did early Greek thinkers allude to each other? The simplest example here is Empedocles Fr. 17, 26, 'Listen to the undeceitful passage of my words' on Parmenides Fr. 8, 52, 'Listening to the deceitful *kosmos* of my words'.[19] Did early Greek thinkers allude to the poets? Xenophanes Fr. 11 is directly critical of Homer and Hesiod, as is well known. Xenophanes Fr. 1 does not name Homer or Hesiod, but its target is clear:

> Do not speak of Titans or Giants or Centaurs, fictions of old, or furious battles.
> In these there is nothing useful.[20]

There are also more subtle ways in which the early Greek thinkers alluded to the poets. Xenophanes says that:

> What is called Iris is also a cloud, red, purple and greenish yellow to see.[21]

Lesher also makes an interesting point about the closing words of this line.[22] Homer often finished lines with 'marvellous to see', with the gods being implicated in why this was marvellous. Here Xenophanes finishes his line with the same 'to see' but with simply the colours and no 'marvellous' and nothing about the gods. As Lesher comments those used to the rhythm and content of Homer would appreciate the difference here with Xenophanes.

## Lloyd's critique

Lloyd recognizes the possibility of Xenophanes' theory being an implicit rejection of the rainbow as a portent, but says:

> If that *may have* been the thrust of Xenophanes' point, that is just conjecture on our part.[23]

Lloyd generalizes this to 'other such ideas attributed to the early philosophers'.[24] This needs to be taken seriously, for as discussed in the introductory chapter, it would be very tempting to attribute a rejection of phenomena as portents and the full adoption of natural explanations to the early Greek thinkers. On the evidence that we have, it is impossible to prove conclusively that any single early Greek thinker consciously rejected portents and non-natural explanations. However, the considerations outlined above make it considerably more than conjecture. Allusion to the poets was on a wider scale than is generally recognized, it is more targeted on specific passages than is generally recognized and it consistently takes on difficult cases for replacing explanation in terms of the gods with natural explanations. Lloyd has also questioned whether for the early Greek thinkers it was:

> A mere act of faith – we might even say bluff – to claim to be able to explain, let alone control, the phenomena in question?[25]

This too merits serious consideration as again, it is very tempting to attribute decent, coherent explanations of phenomena to early Greek thinkers. There are important senses in which early Greek explanations were not acts of faith. Firstly, in the theological sense of an act of faith, it is not just that they do not cite any capricious gods in explanations, but they do not rely on asking gods as a means of investigation nor do they privilege their accounts by special access to gods or Muses. Secondly, in the sense of faith as belief without evidence or good reason, early Greek explanations were not acts of faith. It is again important here not to take explanations in isolation. The choice between, for example, gods and clouds splitting as an explanation of thunder may not *prima facie* give us great grounds for choice. In the next section I will argue that if we take Anaximander's meteorology as a whole though, we see greater depth, breadth and consistency in explanation.

A different reply here is that the new natural theories of the early Greek thinkers were at least the right type of theories, as they cited only natural entities. Better explanations, still citing only natural entities would follow. Lloyd's counter to this is that how natural explanation should be pursued was not at all clear and was contested, both in terms of content and methodology.[26] On this I agree and this is one reason why this book is *Early Greek Philosophies of Nature*, with the plural. I disagree on the initial choice of natural explanation being a matter of faith though, as while I think naturalism is a merit of Anaximander's meteorology, it is far from being the only merit. In relation to meteorology, it is also important in one sense that the early Greek thinkers made no claim to be able to control these phenomena. In Homer and Hesiod, as we have seen, the gods had at least partial control of meteorological phenomena. That control has now passed entirely to a realm of nature.

## Meteorology and explanation

Although Anaximander's meteorology is incorrect in modern terms, it does have considerable merits. It has both breadth and depth. In terms of breadth, Anaximander proposed to explain all of the phenomena of thunder, lightning, thunderbolts, fire whirls and tornados in terms of wind.[27] This is a broad spectrum of phenomena, which are being explained in terms of a single *explanans*, so we may say that Anaximander's theory is parsimonious as well. All instances of each of these phenomena are to be explained in terms of wind. The *hotan*, whenever, in each passage makes this entirely clear. Although such invariance might seem a small merit in modern theories, in context this is enormously important in relation to Homer and Hesiod. At *Theogony* 307 Typhoeus is referred to as *anomos*, lawless. At *Works and Days* 663 ff. sailing in the period of fifty days after the solstice is recommended, when the breezes are regular and the sea harmless. However, if Poseidon and Zeus, want to destroy you, their actions can override the normal behaviour of the winds. In *Odyssey* X Aeolus, the keeper of the winds gives a securely closed bag full of captured winds to Odysseus, so that Odysseus can sail home safely, only for Odysseus' crew to open the bag thinking it contained riches, unleashing the winds that blow in all directions. In Anaximander, winds behave in a perfectly regular manner. Anaximander's meteorology also has depth. What are winds for Anaximander?

> Anaximander believed wind to be flowing air, the finest and moistest parts of it being set in motion and melted by the sun.[28]

How do winds occur? According to Hippolytus, for Anaximander:

> Winds happen when the lightest vapours of the air are separated off and gathering together are set in. Rain is due to the vapour which comes up from things under the sun. Lightning happens when wind escapes by breaching clouds.[29]

If we want to know the cause of some meteorological phenomena, the answer is wind. If we want to know what wind is, or what causes wind, there are further answers. Effectively, Anaximander has given the *phusis* of these phenomena –

what they are, how they have developed, how they were generated in the first instance. This depth is in marked contrast to Homer and Hesiod's account of these phenomena being generated by the gods. It is also worth going a little further with the Hippolytus passage we just looked at for natural explanations for wind and rain, that Zeus as the cloud-gatherer is a standard epithet in Hesiod and in the *Iliad* and *Odyssey*,[30] Zeus also produces rain,[31] and generates storms.[32] That winds are caused by the gods is again standard in Homer and Hesiod.[33]

Anaximander's meteorology is a general theory of considerable scope. It is clear that where we cannot formulate general laws in Homer and Hesiod, Anaximander does formulate general laws of meteorology. These fit with the early Greek conception of *phusis*, explaining in terms of generation, development and current state rather than say a modern covering law model, but that is only to be expected.

Is Anaximander's meteorology fruitful? Anaximenes builds on it directly, if we accept the testimony of Stobaeus. He says the same as Anaximander but adds an interesting observation about oars and the sea.

> Anaximenes said the same as Anaximander, adding what happens with the sea, which flashes when broken by oars.[34]

Secondly, Anaximander's meteorology seems to set an agenda for many other early Greek thinkers who give natural explanations for thunder, lightning, thunderbolts, fire whirls and tornados, several of them taking on all five of these phenomena.

## Zoogony and observation

I have argued that Pseudo-Plutarch v, 19, 4 on zoogony in Anaximander is best translated as:

> Anaximander, the primary animals (*ta prōta zōa*) were generated in moisture enclosed in spine like barks, as they advanced in age they moved onto the drier and shedding their bark for a short time they survived in a different form (*metabiōnai*).[35]

I have also argued that this gives a very plausible fit for the life cycle of the caddisfly, whose larvae enclose themselves in 'spine like barks', attach themselves to the underside of stones ('the drier')[36] then shed their bark and emerge as caddisflies, which live for a few days. This passage is not then a 'genial fantasy' as Barnes has suggested, but may be based on observation or folk knowledge.[37] It is also important here to recognize that there may be further senses to *ta prōta zōa* (on my translation 'primary' rather than 'first') in that they may be the simplest animals or even primary in being bottom of the food chain. Some commentators have seen precursors of evolution or adaptation to environment here, the animals adapting in form as they move onto the drier.[38] I do not. I see the observation of what we would call metamorphosis. So Anaximander observed a natural process by which simple animals transformed into more complex animals.[39]

Some commentators have drawn tight parallels between Anaximander's cosmogony and his zoogony, in particular the idea that 'A sphere of flame was formed around the air around the earth like the bark around a tree (Pseudo-Plutarch *Stromateis* 2).'[40] Here we have the same word for bark as in the zoogony – *phloios*.[41] The cosmogony seems to offer a slightly more physical/mechanical approach to generation, the zoogony a slightly more biological one, with caddisfly larvae breaking the bark for themselves. Ought we to interpret the zoogony in terms of the cosmogony, seeing the zoogony as more mechanical, or vice versa seeing the cosmogony as more biological? Kirk, Raven and Schofield have taken the first option, emphasizing the physical aspects of both processes.[42] In relation to the caddisfly passage, KRS say that:

> The use of *phloiois* here reminds one of the bark-simile in the cosmogonical account; both ball of flame and prickly shell broke away from round the core (here *peri-* not *aporrēgnusthai*).[43]

This is why KRS have the barks being expanded and then split by heating.

> Moreover the general principles of the development of birth are similar: moisture is contained in a bark-like covering, and heat somehow causes and expansion or explosion of the husk and the release of the completed form within.[44]

This is a possible strategy for these passages, but we need to recognize that a choice has been made here. We could interpret the cosmogony in terms of the zoogony, giving us a more biological take on the cosmogony. If we do so, this may give a different perspective on how the earth forms for Anaximander. A key process in the generation of life is a model for change based on metamorphosis. So does the earth, inside its bark, undergo a change from a less complex arrangement to a more complex one as with the metamorphosis of caddisfly larvae? We need to beware of privileging the physical/mechanical approach to these passages. It is significant that 'bursting' as an explanation occurs frequently in Anaximander. We see it here in relation to meteorology, we have seen it in relation to zoogony, we will see it in relation to cosmogony and to the function of the heavens. There is then system and parsimony in the way that Anaximander explains natural phenomena. As with the meteorology, there is more merit to Anaximander's zoogony than simple naturalism.

One great advantage of the caddisfly view is that we do not have to suppose these first life forms to be exotic, rare creatures Anaximander had never seen nor do we need to say that his views are a 'genial fantasy'.[45] There were many species of caddisfly living in Greece/Turkey in Anaximander's time and 220 species are widespread throughout Europe today. They would have been well known to country people and fishermen. So a theory about the origins of life is generated by human investigation and contains no reference to the gods, unlike Homer and Hesiod.

## Anaximander's extant fragment

We have one passage from Simplicius that may preserve some of Anaximander's own words:

> Of those who say it is one, in motion and unlimited, Anaximander, son of Praxiades of Miletus, was a follower and student of Thales. He said that the *archē* and element of existing things was the unlimited, being the first to give this name to the *archē*. He says this is not water, nor any of the other so-called elements, but some other unlimited nature, from which are generated all the heavens and the *cosmoi* in them. The source of generation for extant things is that into which destruction occurs, **according to what is proper. For they pay penalty and retribution to each other for injustices according to the ordering of time (kata to chreōn. Didonai gar auta dikēn kai tisin allēlois tēs adikias kata tēn tou chronou taxin)**, as he says in a poetic fashion.[46]

The words in bold here are generally accepted as Anaximander's own.[47] On translation, *kata to chreōn* is interesting. It is usually translated 'according to necessity' but *chreōn* has another sense, of that which is 'right or proper'.[48] Mourelatos has argued that it is important to consider this sense in some passages in Parmenides and it is important to bear this possibility in mind here as well.[49] Translation here is an important decision. Necessity fits a more mechanical interpretation of Anaximander, dragging him towards a sense of necessity as supposedly found in the early atomists. What is proper fits better with the notion of steering as the *apeiron* may steer in a proper or appropriate manner.⁵⁰ Previously when I have discussed this passage I have presented these alternatives as a choice. I am now less inclined to do so and am more inclined to see 'according to what is proper' as the correct translation. It is significant here that Anaximander had a choice between *dei*, it is necessary, and *chrē* it is proper. Redard, Baratt and Benardete have all argued for slightly different forms of an important distinction between *dei* and *chrē* and their cognates. Redard distinguishes between 'it is appropriate' for *chrē*, with sense of adaptation, adjustment or accommodation and an overriding necessity for *dei*, where 'the obligation is external to the subject ... it is imposed on him'.⁵¹ Benardete distinguishes *chrē* as more subjective and more active, while *dei* has a more objective sense to which one submits passively. Baratt comments that '*dei* tends to stress the mere inevitability, *chrē* an accordance with the divine order'. So if Anaximander had wanted a clear expression of necessity here, there was an obvious option open to him, using *dei*, which he did not take. Alternatively, the three senses of *chrē* distinguished here all fit well with the idea of steering, with the *apeiron* steering appropriately, being more active and also being divine. If we see Anaximander as transferring some of the attributes of the poetic gods to the *apeiron*, especially the idea of the generation of order and *moira* being transferred from the gods to the *apeiron*, then these senses of *chrē* again fit very well. So too these senses of *chrē* help to tie the fragment together. If what happens is *kata to chreōn* then this fits well with paying penalty and retribution to each other for injustices. What is necessary does not have a normative force, what is proper does. This fits well with Anaximander modelling natural phenomena on civil law (see below), as does 'according to the ordering of time' if that has legal resonances (see below), and fits with the idea of the *apeiron* being divine and guiding intelligently.⁵² Finally 'according to what is proper' ties the fragment together in the sense that Simplicius' comment that it is said in a poetic fashion applies to the whole fragment, not just 'according to the ordering of time' or some other fraction of the fragment.

## *Chreōn* as proper

It is also significant that there is a Homeric formula *oude ti se chrē*.⁵³ It is clear that this does not mean 'it is not necessary for you' but means 'you ought not', or 'it is not proper for you to do so'. I take *kata to chreōn* to be Anaximander's own words rather than a later paraphrase. I also take these words to be mindful of Homer's use of *chrē* and of Homer's use of the phrase *kata moiran*. So perhaps

Anaximander is alluding to Homer and making a carefully worded statement: things happen according to what is proper, not according to *moira*. We do not yet have the later phrase *kata phusin*, according to nature, but we have an interesting development on Homer. Heraclitus also says that:

> It is proper (*chrē*)[54] to know the war is common and justice is strife and that all things happen according to strife and what is proper (*kat' erin kai chreōn*).[55]

Again it is important to translate *chrē* and its cognates as 'proper' rather than 'necessary'. I take this as an allusion to Anaximander, disagreeing on strife, justice and what is proper,[56] as do other scholars,[57] confirming that *kata to chreōn* are Anaximander's own words. A second interesting parallel is Euripides (*c*. 480–c. 406) *Iphegenia in Tauris* 1486:

> What is proper controls you and the gods (*to gar chreōn sou te kai theōn kratein*).

That is notable for giving 'the proper' control over both humans and gods and for using the language of *kratein* to express it.

At the other end of the extant fragment we have *kata tēn tou chronou taxin*, 'according to the ordering of time', which is also a phrase of considerable interest. Again, it has been suggested that *kata tēn tou chronou taxin* may be a peripatetic paraphrase, but I think we can make good sense of this phrase as Anaximander's original wording. Some commentators translate *chronos* as Time, along with translating *taxin* as ordinance or assessment, so we get 'according to the assessment of Time', with the idea of inevitable punishment over an unspecified period.[58] Kirk, Raven and Schofield take the view that *taxis* here suggests the punishment meted out by a judge. So we personify time and Time then acts like a judge in a court of law.[59] However, there is no reason to personify time in Anaximander, and both his ontology and cosmology would tell against this. There are no other such entities in Anaximander (and no need for them) and nowhere for any such entity to dwell. In Anaximander it is notable that not only are there no gods but no abode of the gods or place for human afterlife either. Nor is any such entity as Time mentioned in the doxography, even though Aristotle is happy to tell us that the *apeiron* is divine. There may still be important legal resonances here though in terms of Anaximander having a civil law model for phenomena and a normative sense of things happening 'according to what is proper'.

The majority of commentators take *taxis* in its primary sense of order or arrangement and leave *chronos* without a capital. This looks the most natural way to take the phrase. The problem then is, as Graham has phrased it, 'What power and authority does time have to maintain the balance of the opposites?'[60] One possibility here is if we take the passage of the seasons as a possible subject, with hot dry summer being succeeded by other seasons with other combinations of hot, dry, wet and cold being in the ascendency, then there is a poetic sense in which this might be said to be ordered by time. Alternatively, we can take up the suggestion that there was often an equation of time with the heavenly bodies, in particular the sun, and that there are two sides to Anaximander's earth. So while it is hot dry day on this side of the earth it will be cool wet night on the other side of the earth, and this will be ordered by time, and indeed we can say something similar of the seasons.

It is also worth placing Anaximander's extant fragment in the context of Hesiod. If it refers to the sequence of the seasons, then it forms a stark contrast with Hesiod, notably *Works and Days* where the cycle of the seasons is driven by the gods. A simple example here is that at *Works and Days* 415–16 it is Zeus who begins the autumn rain. The term *taxis* does not occur at all in Hesiod, but the term *dietaxis* does occur twice. *Theogony* 74–5 has Zeus destroying Kronos by force, and then says:

> He has appointed (*dietaxe*) their ordinances to the immortals, well in each detail, and assigned them their privileges.[61]

While *Works and Days* 276 runs:

> This was the rule for men that Kronos' son laid down (*dietaxe*).[62]

So again we can see the apeiron taking over a function of the gods, this time that of *taxis*. It is also worth comparing the extant fragment to a passage from Theognis,[63] a sixth century BCE poet, who wrote:

> They seize property by violence; kosmos has perished
> Equitable distribution no longer obtains.[64]

Against this decline in moral standards, where *cosmos* ought to be taken as organized society, we might see Anaximander asserting that there can be no such decline in the behaviour of the physical *cosmos*. Against the background of this passage from Theognis, translating *chreōn* as right/proper rather than necessary gives a stronger moral sense to the regularities of the *cosmos* for Anaximander. One can get similar considerations if there is allusion to Solon here as well, as Solon was noted for his dislike of a perceived decline in Athenian civil society. Anaximander imposes a stable, equitable, moral process on the *cosmos*, which society can then emulate. Finally, I agree with Vlastos that:

We may speak of this transition, the work of Anaximander and his successors, as the naturalization of justice. Justice is no longer inscrutable *moira*, imposed by arbitrary forces with incalculable effect. Nor is she the goddess Dike, moral and rational enough, but frail and unreliable. She is now one with 'the ineluctable laws of nature herself'; unlike Hesiod's Dike, she could no more leave the earth than the earth could leave its place in the firmament.[65]

It may be that the extant fragment is written 'in a poetic fashion' deliberately in order to evoke or allude to such ideas. The question then is, does Anaximander do that in order to agree with these ideas or in order to show how he transforms them? The evidence in relation to Hesiod would suggest that we need to keep the latter firmly in mind. On this view, Anaximander alludes to the earlier notions of *taxis*, *dikē* and *chronos*, but transforms them into something new.

## Steering again

If what steers has some form of intelligence and knowledge, with the gods of the poets and the Phaeacian ships being precursors here, it may steer justly. If it is an ideal, disembodied intelligence then it may steer both justly and invariantly, unlike the capricious gods of the poets. Both *kata to chreōn* and *kata tēn tou chronou taxin* can be taken to indicate law-like behaviour and can be seen as forerunners of the *kata phusin* expression. They are an interesting development from the Homeric *kata moira*. So 'what is proper' will be enacted on a regular basis. In addition, the *kubernētēs* was a person of authority who ought to be obeyed on matters of their craft. This gives considerable authority to the steering of the cosmos. It is something that could possibly be challenged, but really ought not to be. It is also something objective and something that humans can investigate. Xenophon 1. 6. 6. is interesting here:

> Those not knowing how to steer have no right to pray to save ships by taking over the steering.

This would be 'contrary to the ordinances of the gods' and those who pray to the gods for something that is not right will be disappointed. So the *kubernētēs* had significant authority and a moral right to exercise that authority. It is significant that at *Timaeus* 42e the demiurge steers (*diakubernan*) the cosmos and his children, the demi-gods, obey him. The authority of the *kubernētēs* is interestingly different model from how *moira* was thought of in Homer. The order of nature is now clearly invariable where that was at least not clear and probably not so in

Homer and the order of nature is now not open to challenge as *moira* in Homer could be. It is also open to being discovered and known by humans without recourse to the gods.

## Underpinning regularities?

How well could Anaximander's view support the regularities of nature? The idea of steering could be argued to require some act of conscious deliberation and choice on the part of the steerer. The extant fragment gives us a civil law rather than a geometrical or mathematical law conception, and a key distinction here is that civil laws are breakable whereas geometrical and mathematical laws are not. Here we come to an important point for this book, which is that the early Greek thinkers had different perceptions of how to model the regularities of nature. In the modern world, we contrast the regularity of machines against the frailty of humans. It is machines that are the paradigms of regularity. Arguably that has been so from around the seventeenth century onwards. A key phrase here is 'regular as clockwork' and it is no accident that the mechanical philosophy of the seventeenth century and beyond took clockwork as its key analogue for how the world worked.

The early Greek world though was without clockwork or any machine or contrivance that would give such a paradigm of regularity.[66] So instead we see an interesting reversal of modern intuitions. For some, it is human intelligence that is the model of regularity. A person who is intelligent will choose to do the same thing in the same circumstances. Alternatively, an early Greek *mēchanē*, whether we conceive of that as machine or contrivance, was something that was irregular. It was prone to rapid wear of key components due to issues of stress caused by poor design, poor lubrication and materials likely to wear rapidly, such as wood. It would occasionally be subject to unpredictable catastrophic failure due to indiscernible flaws in wooden components. So there is an interesting reversal of perceptions. Human intelligence is regular and reliable in contrast to the irregularity and unreliability of machines. Plato provides an interesting example of this. I have argued that in later Plato (at least from the *Timaeus* onwards) the motions of the heavenly bodies are entirely regular.[67] In the *Timaeus*, there is a hierarchy:

> A motion proper to its body, that of the seven motions which is best suited to reason and intelligence. Therefore he made it move in a circle, revolving of itself

uniformly and in the same place, and he took from it all trace of the other six motions and kept it free from their wanderings.[68]

To each of these he gave two motions, one being uniform and in the same place, always thinking the same thoughts concerning the same things, the other being a forward motion obeying the revolution of the same and similar. With regard to the other five motions, they were motionless and still, in order that each might attain the greatest possible perfection.[69]

At 34a Timaeus tells us that the universe revolves uniformly and has no trace of any wandering motion. At 40b Timaeus distinguishes between 'the stars which do not wander' and the planets 'which turn and as such wander'.[70] If the universe and the fixed stars have regular motion, there cannot be any metaphysical reason why the rest of the heavenly bodies cannot move in a regular manner as well.[71] At 39c Timaeus tells us that 'The wanderings of these stars constitute time.' If the wanderings of the planets constitute time, and these wanderings are irregular, then time will be irregular. There is no need for time to be irregular in the *Timaeus*. All that is needed for a distinction between time and eternity is that time flows while eternity stands still.[72] That time moves 'according to number' (*Timaeus* 37d, 38a, 38c) would also suggest it flows regularly. At 39d Timaeus tells us of the 'Great Year', the time taken for all the heavenly bodies to return to the same positions. This is a calculable amount of time, so the motions of the planets cannot be irregular. Finally, at *Timaeus* 47a ff. we are told that:

> God devised and gave to us vision in order that we might observe the rational revolutions of the heavens and use them against the revolutions of thought that are in us, which are like them, though those are clear and ours confused, and by learning thoroughly and partaking in calculations correct according to nature (*logismōn kata phusin orthotētos*), by imitation of the entirely unwandering (*pantōs aplaneis*) revolutions of God we might stabilize the wandering (*peplanēmenas*) revolutions in ourselves.

So the motions of the heavens ('revolutions of god') are entirely unwandering and we can make 'calculations correct according to nature' concerning the heavens. More important here is the question of why it is that the heavenly bodies move in an entirely regular manner. It is because each if these bodies have souls that guide them. So Plato says in the *Laws*:

> Those who engaged in these matters accurately would not have been able to use such wonderfully accurate calculations if these entities did not have souls.[73]

These underpinnings for celestial regularities are immensely strong. Not only will they generate absolute regularity in the motions of the heavens now, but because of the nature of the demiurge and his relation to the cosmos, these regularities will continue to be generated indefinitely. The principle here is that an intelligent entity or person will do the same thing in the same circumstances. It is significant here that these are ideal intelligences backing the celestial regularities. So while the cosmos is alive and has intelligence from *Timaeus* 33b onwards we are told that this 'animal' is perfectly spherical, has neither eyes nor ears as there is nothing external to see or hear, there is no air for it to breathe, no need of any organ to receive food or to excrete the remains, as it is entirely self-sufficient and nothing comes in or goes out. As it needs neither hands to defend itself nor feet to stand on, and has no need of legs or feet to propel itself, it has no limbs, and at 34b we are told it is a god. The planetary intelligences are similar. One interesting comparison here is that while Plato investigated the idea of an ideal intelligence generating absolute regularities, there is no parallel discussion of an ideal machine or *mēchanē* generating regularities in early Greek thought.[74] For Plato, entities not possessing an intelligent soul will tend to wander. So at least for some early Greeks, there is an interesting reversal of the modern contrast between the regularity of machines against the unreliability of humans. Their contrast is the reliability of intelligence against the unreliability of brute matter. Two closely related words illustrate this. One can apply the word *kosmiotēs*, to a person to show that they have propriety, decorum or good order, one can also apply the word *kosmios* to a person or a system indicating that it is well ordered, regular, orderly, or well behaved. So there is a close connection between propriety and orderly behaviour in persons and the good order and continuing regular behaviour of a system. Plato of course favoured the orderly soul over the disorderly one.[75] Previously we looked at this passage in relation to Plato recognizing prior traditions of investigation, but it is also important in this context. So *Gorgias* 508a1–5 runs:

> The wise (*hoi sophoi*) said this, Callicles, that heavens and earth and gods and humans hold together by partnership, friendship, propriety (*kosmiotēta*), self-control and justice. This is why they call this whole a cosmos, O friend, and not disorder or intemperance.

Again, we have the idea in a cosmological context that good behaviour, propriety, generates order and not disorder in the cosmos, and is indeed vital for a cosmos to be a cosmos.[76] So Anaximander's cosmos, guided by this steering principle, can display full regularities. I return here to the translation of *chreōn* in

Anaximander. What happens is 'according to what is proper', that is the right thing to happen, that is the choice of what is steering. This generality and invariance fits with the meteorology fragments.

## Invariance

If Anaximander did indeed envisage invariant natural law, how different is that from Homer and Hesiod? That depends on how strongly we take *moira* and how rigorous the justice of Zeus is. One can take the view that fate is absolute and so too in a sense is the justice of Zeus, in which case there is little difference. As argued in Chapter 2, I am inclined to take the view that *moira* is very strong and is very difficult to escape, depending on how specifically *moira* is phrased ('all mortals die' is different from 'you will die in battle' or 'you will die on a specific date') but in exceptional circumstances can be broken, perhaps requiring exceptional, heroic behaviour or the intervention of the gods. So too I would say the justice of Zeus is strong but not absolute and does not always occur immediately. We then have a contrast of a strong but not absolute order in Homer and Hesiod transformed into an invariant order in Anaximander. One might also contrast the rather unstable reciprocity of justice in Homer and Hesiod,[77] with the stable reciprocity projected by Anaximander.

A second aspect here is the epistemological one. In Homer and Hesiod, the gods set and know the *moira* of humans, but humans can only know their fate by being told by the gods. The mind of Zeus is inscrutable to humans, and indeed even to other gods. We can only know this by being told by the author, who has been told by the Muses. In Anaximander, the order and justice of the cosmos are common knowledge for humans.

## The divine *apeiron*

I will state something quite simply, which once said may indeed seem obvious, but nevertheless has some important consequences. For Anaximander, the *apeiron* is part of *phusis*. This must be so, for the *apeiron* is that out of which the cosmos is generated. So the steering principle is immanent in nature, even if it is not immanent in the *cosmos*.[78] Neither the *apeiron* nor the steering principle are metaphysical, in the sense of being beyond *phusis*. Nor is steering transcendent, in the sense that it is imposed on the physical realm from outside or beyond it.[79]

I do not see it as in any way problematic if Anaximander considered the *apeiron* to be divine. There is an old debate on theology and the divine in Anaximander. Burnet argued there was 'no trace of theological speculation' in Anaximander.[80] Jaeger argued that 'theology, theogony and theodicy' sat side by side in Anaximander's account of nature.[81] This debate was conducted in terms of the old conflict model of the relation of science and religion. The historiography of the relation of religion and science has undergone a significant transformation in recent years. The conflict thesis, that religion and science are always in conflict, is now seen as outmoded and has been superseded by a complexity thesis.[82] In the complexity thesis religion may promote science, may be neutral to it or may be in conflict with it, depending on specific circumstances.[83] This is important for Anaximander, as we need not be forced into a polarity where religious belief conflicts with a belief in natural explanation or vice versa, forcing us to question the genuineness of the religious belief or the commitment to natural explanation. A consequence of the move away from the conflict historiography is that we need not try to separate the 'religious' and 'scientific' aspects of Anaximander's thought, any more than we need to separate Empedocles' thought into different 'scientific' and 'religious' poems.[84]

That Anaximander, and other Milesians advocated some form of pantheism is now widely and in my view correctly accepted.[85] Although pantheism is a relatively modern term and modern pantheists generally see Spinoza as their philosophical founder, we may reasonably use the term for some early Greek thinkers and it is possible to be more precise about Anaximander's type of pantheism.[86] I take Anaximander to be a material pantheist,[87] and a collective pantheist, in the sense that he believed the universe as a whole to be divine. The alternative, distributive pantheism, where each individual entity is thought to be divine, would be a better description of Thales.[88] While panpsychism would be a good term for Anaximenes,[89] I would be cautious in applying this to Anaximander.[90] Anaximander could also be called a pankubernist, that is someone who believes that everything steers. Anaximander might also be described as a hylozoist, believing that matter is in some sense alive, though it is important here to recognize that matter is law like for Anaximander so the zoism is importantly circumscribed. I would also disagree with Cornford that matter for Anaximander is invested with the 'mythical properties' of life, divinity, soul and god.[91] It may have those properties, but in a very different way from how those properties were thought of in myth.

While some construction using pan-, whether it be pantheism, pandeism or pankubernism describes Anaximander reasonably well, there is one further point to address here. Does the pan- part of this description technically apply to Anaximander? The issue here is that it is the *apeiron* that surrounds all and steers all, and the *apeiron* that is the divine. What then of the *cosmos*? Clearly that does not surround, but is it not divine and does it do no steering? If so, technically the pan- attribution to Anaximander would be incorrect. Clearly one issue here is how different the *cosmos*, or its constituents, are from the *apeiron*. Whatever the answer to that, I would still suggest that using pan- remains a good first order description of Anaximander, which may need some revision when we take into account the relationship between the *apeiron* and the *cosmos*. The idea that Anaximander was really an atheist who hid his atheism under a veil of pantheism to avoid criticism or even prosecution should be rejected as entirely unsubstantiated. If Xenophanes could criticize Homer and Hesiod for attributing theft, adultery and deceiving each other to the gods,[92] then there must then have been a considerable degree of freedom to express views on matters of religion.

It is critical to recognize that this pantheism or pankubernism does important work for Anaximander's cosmogony.[93] Without steering, his cosmos would not be able to acquire the degree of *taxis* and symmetry that it exhibits. These will not come about by the simple actions of the elements and it is highly implausible that in a single cosmos they will come about by chance, nor is chance any part of Anaximander's vocabulary. It is because there is steering that the *cosmos* can have so much *taxis*. Without steering, or some similar principle, the order of the *cosmos* would be unexplained, or there would be a need for a multiple co-existent *cosmoi* view. Anaximander's pantheism is substantial. It is not merely the vacuous application of 'divine' to the universe, but involves steering and an explanation of the origins of order in the *cosmos*, an explanation that could not be had by an atheist in this context.

It is also important to recognize that Plato had an interesting and effective critique of purely physical cosmogonies. I have written about this extensively elsewhere, so I will be brief here.[94] If there is only matter and a like to like principle, that matter may well be sorted like to like but that sorting will only produce a separation of types of matter and not a cosmos. According to Plato a cosmos is a fitting and harmonious blend of opposites such as hot/cold, dry/moist and hard/soft.[95] A like to like principle on its own cannot produce such a result, as the opposites will not come together like to like. Plato had a good deal more to say about this (extending this cosmogonical critique to zoogony and stoichogony, the origin of the elements) again questioning the plausibility of purely physical accounts.[96] The key point here is that it was not immediately evident in the ancient world that purely physical accounts, like those of Leucippus and Democritus, were sophisticated enough to give a plausible explanation of the origin of the cosmos. Some form of steering seemed to be required to account for the current state of the cosmos.

## Conclusion

West has commented that:

> We can still see that Anaximander for his part was no vigorous rationalist. He allowed divinity an important place in his universe, major parts of his system had a visionary rather than a logical foundation, and he explained certain cosmic changes in terms of 'injustice', 'retribution', 'ordinance', language which Simplicius calls 'rather poetic' (DK12B1) but which it is much more meaningful to classify as theological.[97]

I believe this treats Anaximander in too binary a fashion, in that either he meets certain ideals of rationality or his thought is visionary and theological. So too I would reject the binary approach that Anaximander was either a mechanical thinker or a primitive thinker. There is a meaningful intellectual space between that which accords with modern science and the primitive. I also disagree that parts of Anaximander's system had a 'visionary rather than a logical foundation' or as Barnes has put it, 'was worked out with a dedicated mixture of mathematics, insight and fantasy'[98] as we have seen with the zoogony, when properly understood. I reject the 'conflict' historiography of the relation of science and religion that has been so influential up to the last twenty years or so. The notion that science and religion are always and have always been in conflict was a construction of late nineteenth-century historians such as Draper and White and is now widely rejected in favour of the complexity model.[99]

We see interesting new patterns of explanation with the Ionians. They explain phenomena without recourse to the gods of Homer and Hesiod and indeed take on the hardest cases. This is not something accidental. There is good evidence here that they target the difficult cases to explain and that they do so in a manner that alludes to Homer and Hesiod. This helps explain the content and nature of the examples they use and does away with any need to postulate a 'Greek Miracle' with Ionian thought being generated ex nihilo. The new explanations are not only free from reliance on the poetic gods, but are invariant, fully general, have breadth, depth and parsimony. There is a strong sense that humans can generate knowledge for themselves through an investigation of nature. We can see how those considerations have been generated through engagement with Homer and Hesiod and with the transfer of the attributes of the epic poetic gods to the new *archai*. What we do not see is any attempt at mechanical explanation, nor do we see any motivation for mechanical explanation. Indeed, mechanical explanations based on the machines available to the early Greeks would have generated far weaker models for the invariant behaviour of nature than those actually used. That is an interesting reversal of our modern suppositions, but one that is critical to understanding early Greek thought on nature.

6

# Anaximenes and the *Kratein* Tradition

We have seen that there was a substantial tradition using *kubernan* and its cognates, in this chapter we will look at *kratein* as a key term. First I want to link together the uses of *kubernan* and *kratein*, as some authors use them virtually interchangeably. As with *kubernan*, it is worth giving a list of those who used *kratein* in a cosmological context, to emphasize this is a significant portion of early Greek thinkers. In addition to Homer and Hesiod with *moira krataiē*, we have Anaximenes, some Hippocratic authors,[1] the Derveni papyrus author, Xenophanes, Heraclitus, Parmenides, Democritus, Empedocles, Diogenes of Apollonia and Anaxagoras.[2] It will be useful to look at the sort of analogies each of these early thinkers used for natural processes. In particular here I will be interested in the use of the macrocosm/microcosm analogy, which we first find with Anaximenes.

## *Kratein* and *Kubernan*

The Greek *kratein* was used in a similar manner to *kubernan* in some passages. Diogenes of Apollonia Fr. 5 says that:

> In my view that which has intelligence is called air by men, and all men are steered (*kubernasthia*) by this and it has a control (*kratein*) over all things. This seems to be a God to me and to have permeated everywhere, to arrange all things and to be in all things.

The Hippocratic author of *On Regimen*, I/ 10 tells us that:

> In a word, everything was arranged in the body by fire, in a manner suitable to itself ... The hottest and strongest fire, which controls (*epikrateitai*) all things, manages everything according to nature (*kata phusin*), it is imperceptible to sight or touch. In this are soul, mind, understanding, growth, change, diminution, separation, sleep, waking. This steers all things through all (*panta dia pantos kuberna*) both here and there and is never still.

So for Diogenes air both steers and has control over all men and all things. For the Hippocratic author, the hottest and strongest fire controls all things and steers all things, and it is worth noting that it does so *kata phusin*, according to nature. This is an important link between the two traditions.

## Anaximenes

The key passage in Anaximenes is:

> Anaximenes declared air to be the *archē* of existing things. From it all things come to be and into it all things are dissolved. He says **as our soul, being air, holds us in order (*sungkratei*), so wind and air envelop (*periechein*) the whole kosmos.**[3]

The section in bold here may be a direct quotation, or a paraphrase of something Anaximenes wrote, or it may continue reporting what the author believed were Anaximenes' views. Worries are that the passage is not in the Ionic dialect and that the 'He says' formula does not guarantee a direct quote in our sources. There are also worries concerning the use of the words *kosmos* and *pneuma* (for air) so early, though there are parallels for both at this stage among medical writers and the Pythagoreans.[4] As KRS argue,[5] *sungkratei* is not found in our sources until much later. They argue that *sungkratein* 'is really a compendium for *sunechein kai kratein*',[6] and could only have come about in the much later Koine Greek. Two possibilities here. Firstly, that this is virtually a direct quotation, but it is paraphrased into a later dialect and where Anaximenes wrote *sunechein kai kratein*, the doxography has *sungkratein*. Alternatively, this may be a later report on what the doxographer thought Anaximenes meant, and *sungkratein* expresses what he thought Anaximenes meant. Attested uses of *sungkratein* indicate that it means to keep troops together or to hold in, keep under control. The primary meaning of *sunechein* is to hold together, with a strong sense of continuity and the sense of *sunechein kai kratein* would be to hold together and control.[7]

Exactly what this means is not entirely clear, as KRS point out.[8] I agree with them that *periechein* may carry a sense of *kai kubernan* as in Anaximander (Aristotle, *Physics* III, 4, 203b, *kai periechein hapanta kai panta kubernan*). I am less concerned than KRS about a lack of early parallels to the idea that the soul holds the body together as all ideas have to start somewhere and we lack parallels for many well-attested and interesting early Greek ideas.[9]

## Macrocosm/microcosm?

Does this Anaximenes passage amount to a macrocosm/microcosm analogy? Although it is not phrased in that terminology, the structure certainly compares what happens in humans to what happens in the cosmos. Here again I make a plea for the recognition of some intellectual space between that which has affinities to modern science and the primitive. KRS comment here that:

> Although he introduced a thoroughly rational description of change, Anaximenes in some respects clung to the framework of the popular, non-philosophical world-construction, and so might retain more of the anthropomorphic attitude than at first sight seems probable.[10]

So are microcosm/macrocosm analogies always non-philosophical and anthropomorphic? It is important to recognize that there have been a wide range of macrocosm/microcosm theories and a similarly wide range of supposed relationships between the macrocosm and microcosm. On one level, one can explain the solar system, or the atom by saying that the electrons of an atom orbit the nucleus as planets orbit the sun and vice versa. That can be done without suggesting that there is any special relationship between planets and atoms or sun and nucleus, no causation from planets to electrons, any harmonic atunement, any sympathetic interaction or any anthropomorphism. The later natural magic tradition would suppose many types of relationship between the macrocosm and microcosm, such as sympathies, correspondences and harmonies and of course one can suppose non-natural relations between the two.[11]

Plato would disagree that a microcosm/macrocosm relationship is necessarily non-philosophical and anthropomorphic. As we saw in the last chapter *Timaeus* 47a ff. draws a macrocosm/microcosm relation between the motions of the heavens and the human mind, is specific in attributing orderly motions to the heavens and is critical for Plato's vision of the relation of humans to the world and how they might obtain knowledge of it. Related to this is the standard Platonic injunction that we ought to strive to be as much like god as possible. Humans should also imitate the cosmos to maintain good health, as the cosmos has a rocking motion in order to sustain its own good order. So humans ought to take a moderate amount of exercise in order to sustain their own good order.[12] There is also a macrocosm/microcosm analogy to do with the blood in Plato. Just as the cosmos confines and agitates the particles within it, so does the human body confine and agitate the blood.[13] The macrocosm/microcosm analogy then does some real work in Plato and has significant cosmological and ethical import.

Aristotle would also disagree that all microcosm/macrocosm analogies are non-philosophical and anthropomorphic. Aristotle, *Physics* VIII, 2, 252b24–7 says that:

> If this can happen to a living thing, what prevents the same thing happening to the universe? If this can happen in the small world (*en mikrō kosmō*) it can happen in the large (*en megalō*).[14]

While later macrocosm/microcosm analogies focused on the relationship between man and the cosmos, it is perhaps significant here that Aristotle phrases this in terms of living things and the cosmos. In Aristotle's *On Generation and Corruption* II, 10 and 11 we find a comparison of the cycle of the heavenly motions and the weather cycle, the weather cycle being said to 'imitate' the heavens.[15] Aristotle takes the weather cycle to be an interesting example of a cyclical phenomenon with the terrestrial realm.

To take a later example, William Harvey who discovered the circulation of the blood in the early seventeenth century suggested a similar relationship between the weather cycle and the circulation of the blood.

> Which motion (of the blood) we may call circular, after the same manner that *Aristotle* sayes that the rain and the air do imitate the motion of the superiour bodies. For the earth being wet, evaporates by the heat of the Sun, and the vapours being rais'd aloft are condens'd and descend in showrs, and wet the ground, and by this means here are generated, likewise, tempests, and the beginnings of meteors, from the circular motion of the Sun, and his approach and removal.[16]

In Harvey's system, the microcosm/macrocosm relation did real and important work. There are two types of blood in the human body and in Galen's cardiovascular theory there were two networks of blood vessels keeping these types of blood separate. With both types of blood in one system, Harvey had to account for how one type of blood could change into the other and vice versa, without the knowledge that this is done by oxygenation in the lungs and deoxygenation in other parts of the body. His model is Aristotle on the weather cycle, with water evaporating and the condensing being the model for change, with the heart acting as the heat source like the sun. This is a failed hypothesis, but also a philosophical and scientific one. Were macrocosm/microcosm relationships a dead end? Yes, of course. Their use had died out by the end of the scientific revolution of the seventeenth century. Plato, Aristotle and many others though were happy to use them as part of rational philosophies, doing important, non-primitive and non-anthropomorphic work within their systems prior to their being superseded by others forms of explanation.

It is possible to downplay the idea of a macrocosm/microcosm analogy in Anaximenes. Longrigg certainly does so, suggesting that the point of the passage is to emphasize that air is the *archē*, rather than to state any macrocosm/microcosm relation.[17] KRS canvass a variety of possibilities, although what I find most interesting about their discussion is that they reject *sungkratei* as impossible, in favour of *sunechei kai kratei*, which I find reasonable, and then focus entirely on *sunechei* to the complete exclusion of *kratei*. Their favoured solution is that *sunechei* means something like possesses, so as the soul possesses the body so air possesses the cosmos, possessing here having the sense of permeating the whole of.[18] As we have so little from Anaximenes on this, and what we have has probably been reworded at some stage, it is difficult to be sure, but my view is that Anaximenes probably originally wrote *sunechei kai kratein* that we should take due notice of the use of *kratein* within the tradition of its use. While Anaximenes does not use the terminology, he has some form of macrocosm/microcosm relationship in mind. That I take to be both rational, philosophical and unproblematic. It reflects well on him as an original thinker, not badly on him for failing to fit into a narrow and linear account of the early history of philosophy and science.

## Anaximenes and vortices

The evidence for Anaximenes using a vortex is the same passage that led to the suggestion that Anaximander used a vortex, that is, Aristotle, *On the Heavens* II, 13, 295a7 ff.:

> If the earth now remains in place by force, it was also assembled in the centre by being carried there because of a vortex. For this is the reason which everyone gives, through what occurs in water and around air. In these the larger and heavier things are always carried to the centre of the vortex. So all those who say that the heavens are generated have the earth being assembled in the middle.[19]

One might think the case is slightly stronger for Anaximenes, as he does have the earth held in place, and Aristotle classes him in this respect with the atomists. He tells us that:

> Anaximenes, Anaxagoras and Democritus say that it is the flatness of the earth which is responsible for it remaining in place.[20]

However, there is a simple reply here. This is that Anaximenes clearly does not have earth carried to the centre in order to generate the earth, he has air felting into earth to generate the earth. It is also the case for Anaximenes that a flat earth settles on air 'like a lid' that keeps it in place, without any contribution from a vortex. As with Anaximander, Anaximenes has no need of a vortex to hold the earth in place.

Anaximenes has no need of a vortex for cosmogony if he has a relation of *kratein* between air and the cosmos, just as Anaximander has no need of a vortex for cosmogony as he has the relation of *kubernan* between apeiron and cosmos. The *kratein* relation will allow the ordering of the cosmos. That the motions of the heavens are circular in Anaximenes ('like a cap being turned on a head')[21] does not necessitate a vortex. For Anaximenes:

> The earth is flat and is borne on air, and likewise the sun, moon and all the others heavenly bodies, which are all fiery, are carried on the air because of their flatness.[22]

This may only explain why the sun, moon and stars retain their relative position to the earth. If Anaximenes likens the heavenly bodies to leaves,[23] this does not mean that they are moved by currents of air. We are told that:

> According to Anaximenes the heavenly bodies make their turnings by being pushed by enclosed and rigid air.[24]

So the heavenly bodies may move of their own accord through stationary, evenly distributed air and then only change their course when meeting these pockets of air. There is no process in Anaximenes that we might suppose to be a vortex, there is no reason to suppose that Anaximenes, working before Parmenides, thought that matter was particulate and there is no mention in any of the doxographers of a vortex in Anaximenes. As with Anaximander, the simple conclusion is that Anaximenes did not employ a vortex. As with Anaximander, it is possible to try to force affinities with later developments which are seen as positive and generally more 'mechanical' (vortices, particulate nature of matter) but the basis is not really there if we look at the texts carefully and objectively.

## Anaximenes and analogies

We might also ask what sort of analogies Anaximenes used for natural processes. The most prominent one is a craft analogy, when he suggests that air 'felts' to become more dense substances. So Pseudo-Plutarch tells us that for Anaximenes:

All things are generated by a certain condensation of air, and again by its rarefaction. Motion has existed for all time. He says that when the air felts, firstly the earth is generated, entirely flat, and because of this, it rides on the air. So too sun, moon and the other stars have their origins in generation from earth. At any rate he declares the sun to be earth, as it acquires abundant heat by moving rapidly.[25]

That an early Greek thinker drew on the craft tradition for such an analogy can come as no great surprise. Hippolytus 1, 7, 6 also tells us that for Anaximenes:

> The heavenly bodies do not move under the earth, but go around it, just as a felt cap turns around our head.

Quite how one classifies that as an analogy is open to debate but it is clearly not a mechanical analogy. What Anaximenes gets out of it is circular motion for the heavenly bodies. An interesting comparison is then with Anaximander's wheel analogy. Both give circular motion, both are clearly not mechanical as soon as one looks at them more closely. Stobaeus also tells us something very interesting about Anaximenes in relation to Anaximander and his views on meteorological phenomena. We saw that in Stobaeus' section on 'Concerning thunder, lightning, thunderbolts, fire whirls and tornados' Anaximander's view was that all these come about because of wind. Stobaeus then goes on to say that:

> Anaximenes said the same as Anaximander, adding what happens with the sea, which flashes when broken by oars.[26]

So we can add a maritime analogy for Anaximenes, and again for an early Greek that is no great surprise. There is also a culinary analogy, which when pressed further becomes a little contentious. Anaximenes has the earth as being flat and supported by air. Plato in the *Phaedo* 99b6–8 says that:

> This is why one man surrounds the earth with a vortex, making the earth remain still because of the heavens, while another supports it on a base of air, as though it were a broad kneading trough (*kardopō*).

I do not think we have quite the right text here with *kardopō*, which usually means 'kneading trough', and is certainly open to question. I would certainly consider *kardopiō*, the lid of a kneading trough, as a more plausible alternative in the context of something broad being supported by air. In relation to this, Aristotle makes the same point at *De Caelo* 294b13–30:

> Anaximenes, Anaxagoras and Democritus say that it is the breadth of the earth that is the reason for its immobility. It does not cut, but covers the air below it like a lid, as it seems that broad bodies have this ability. Even winds find them

hard to move due to this resistance. This same effect, they say, is produced by the breadth of the earth in relation to the underlying air, which not having sufficient room to change place rests on the mass below, like with the case of the clepsydra and water. They cite many proofs that air, when cut off and at rest, has the ability to carry much weight.

However we take *kardop(i)ō*, either as kneading trough or lid, here we have a culinary analogy, which again is entirely natural for an early Greek thinker.

## Xenophanes

Xenophanes is interesting in that he may give us another verb to go along with *kubernan* and *kratein*. In Fragment 25 Xenophanes' says of his god that:

> Entirely without effort he agitates (*kradainei*) all things by the thought of his mind.[27]

The primary meanings of *kradainein* are to swing, to wave, to vibrate and to agitate. There are some interesting comparisons with Zeus in Homer, as at *Iliad* I, 530, Zeus bows his head and makes Olympus tremble, while at *Iliad* VIII, 443 it is Zeus' feet that make Olympus tremble. Xenophanes' god by comparison agitates all things and does so with his mind rather than moving any part of his body. So in fragment 26:

> Always he remains on one place, not moving, nor is it proper to go to other places at other times.[28]

If we take Fragment 25 reflexively, then there is a question of whether Xenophanes' god agitates himself, so contradicting Fragment 26. We might read 'all things' as 'all other things', though Aristotle *Metaphysics* 986b says Xenophanes made nothing clear but did say 'the one is god' implying some form of pantheism. Alternatively, we might allow Xenophanes' god to vibrate with changing place. Whether Xenophanes was aware of these reflexivity issues is another matter. Xenophanes also used *kratein* in several passages. Simplicius *Physics* 22, 22ff says:

> Xenophanes says that god is one and everything, which he demonstrates from god being the most controlling (*kratiston*) of all things. If he were many, he says, the control (*kratein*) would in like manner belong to them all, but god is the most controlling and best of all.

Pseudo-Aristotle, *On Melissus, Xenophanes and Gorgias*, 977a25–9:

If god is the most controlling (*kratiston*) of all, he must be one. If there were two or more gods, he would no longer be the most controlling (*kratiston*) and best of them. Each god of this many would have a like share. This is what god and gods capability is – to control (*kratein*), but not to be controlled (*krateisthai*) and to be the most controlling (*kratiston*) of all.

Pseudo-Aristotle, *On Melissus, Xenophanes and Gorgias*, 978a13, says that it is part of Xenophanes' god:

> To see, hear and control (*kratein*), every part.

There is not much to be gleaned from Xenophanes' Fragments on analogies for how the natural world functions, but it is clear that Xenophanes' god controls but is not controlled and also agitates the cosmos as necessary.

## Heraclitus

There is an interesting use of *kratein* in Heraclitus Fr. 114:

> For those who speak with intelligence it is proper to rely on what is common to all, as a city must rely on its laws, but to an even greater degree. All human laws are nourished by the one divine law (*trephontai gar pantes hoi anthrōpeioi nomoi hupo henos tou theiou*).[29] This controls (*kratein*) as much as it wishes, and is easily sufficient for all things.

I would agree with KRS that this passage should be seen in the context of two other fragments, firstly Heraclitus Fr. 2:[30]

> It is necessary to follow the common. Although the logos is common the many live as if they have an idiosyncratic understanding.

Secondly, Heraclitus Fr. 50:

> Listening not to me but to the logos it is wise to agree that all things are one.

The key point for Heraclitus being that there is objective law. I would add two other passages here. Heraclitus Fr. 102:

> To the gods all things are beautiful and just, but humans have assumed some things to be unjust and others just.

Heraclitus Fr. 89:

> For those who are awake the cosmos is one and common, but those who sleep turn away each into a private world. We should not speak and act like sleeping men.

I take the second part of this to be important in rejecting dreams as critical to knowledge or some form of privileged mind state, and also important in rejecting the idea of the gods either appearing in dreams to humans or sending dreams to humans. Heraclitus Fragment 35 also tells us that:

> According to Heraclitus it is proper for humans who love wisdom to investigate (*historas*) many things.[31]

I do not have space here to enter the complex debates about the nature of logos for Heraclitus, I just want to emphasize that there is objective law in Heraclitus and that Heraclitus uses *kratein* and *kubernan* in interesting ways. In this context it is no surprise that Heraclitus frequently uses the phrase *kata logon*, according to the logos. Heraclitus also has some interesting analogies for how natural processes work, as in Heraclitus Fr. 30:

> This cosmos, the same for all,[32] was not made by Gods or men, but has always existed and will always exist. It is an everliving fire, kindling in measures and going out in measures.[33]

So the cosmos is a fire, but one which acts in an invariant manner, 'kindling in measures and going out in measures'. Heraclitus possibly wants to emphasize the ever-changing nature of the cosmos with his use of fire here, but also wishes to emphasize the invariance lying behind that. It is also interesting in this context that Heraclitus Fr. 90 says that:

> All things are an equal exchange for fire and fire for all things, as property is for gold and gold is for property.

This further emphasizes the importance of the fire analogy and invariance and interestingly does it with a commercial analogy. Heraclitus Fragment 31 is also interesting in equating fire with lightning:

> Fire's reversals: first sea, though half of sea is earth, and half lightning. Earth is dispersed as sea, and measures up to the same ratio as before it became earth.[34]

This brings us back to Heraclitus in steering, Fragments 64 and 41:

> The thunderbolt steers (*oiakizei*) all things.

> Wisdom is one thing – to be acquainted with judgement, how all things are steered (*ekubernantai*) through all.

Heraclitus Fragment 94 also says that:

> The sun will not overstep his measures. If he does, the Erinyes, the defenders of justice, will find him out.

This is very interesting, as here Heraclitus is operating with a civil law conception of physical behaviour, rather than a mathematical law conception. That is a reasonable possibility for understanding how the world works at this stage of the development of philosophy and science. With civil law, breaches are conceptually possible and are met with punishment. If we model physical behaviour on the mathematical/geometrical law breaches are conceptually impossible.[35] It is possible to have civil law conceptions of physical behaviour where breaches are conceptually possible but do not actually happen as we have seen with Plato on astronomy. With the emphasis that Heraclitus lays on measure and logos, particularly in Fr. 30, and the notion that all is steered through all in Fr. 41, I do not think the sun will overstep his measures. The reference to the Erinyes then is metaphorical rather than stating the actual existence and vengeance of the Erinyes.

The last analogy to consider in Heraclitus is that of parenting. So Heraclitus Fr. 53 tells us that:

War is father of all things and king of all.[36]

This should not be taken lightly as an analogy, as Plato uses parenting analogies in describing the receptacle and its relation to what is in it in the *Timaeus*. So the receptacle is mother (*mētēr*, *Timaeus* 50d2, 51a4) and nurse (*tithēnē*, *Timaeus* 49a6, 52d6) and there is also consideration of the role of a father (*patēr*, *Timaeus* 50d2).[37] Heraclitus also says in Fr. 80:

It is necessary to know that war is common, and strife is justice, and that all things occur according to strife and what is proper (*kat' erin kai chreōn*).

As with Anaximander we find neither *kata moira* nor *kata phusin*, but we do find the interesting *kat' erin kai chreōn*. We also find *kata logon* and *kata phusin* in Fragment 1:

For although all things occur according to this logos (*kata ton logon*) they are like un-experienced people, even when they experience words and deeds and I distinguish in detail how each thing is according to nature (*kata phusin*) and tell what characteristics it has.

So in Heraclitus we find no machine analogies. We find him using both *kubernan* and *kratein* in significant circumstances and a key cosmological analogy for him is that the cosmos is like a fire, kindling and going out in measure. A final comment on Heraclitus on Fr. 123, *phusis kruptesthai philei*, often translated 'Nature loves to hide'. I agree with Graham that this is better translated 'nature is hidden'.³⁸ As Graham points out, *philein* + *infinitive* does not mean loves to ..., and *phusis* at this stage means a nature (as in the nature of something) and not Nature as a whole. Whether a nature hides itself or is hidden (*kruptesthai* as middle or passive), there is a need to investigate it.

## Parmenides

As we have seen, Parmenides used *kubernan* (Fr. 12, 'In the middle of this there is a goddess, who steers all things (*panta kubernai*))'. He also uses *kratein*. At Parmenides Fr. 8, 29–31 we have:

> Remaining the same and in the same, it lies by itself
> And remains firmly in place. For controlling Necessity (*kraterē Anankē*)
> Holds it in the bonds of a limit (*peiratos en desmoisin echei*), which fences it in.

Here we might discuss whether *kraterē anankē* should be translated as 'mighty' or 'strong' necessity, or as 'controlling', as we did with *moira krataiē* in relation to Homer and Hesiod. It must be said that most scholars have gone for the first option here, but in relation to this, Parmenides Fr. 10 is interesting:

> You will learn the works and nature of the wandering round-eyed moon
> you will know the surrounding heaven
> whence it grew and how Necessity led and bound it (*agous(a) epedēsen Anangkē*)
> to hold the limits of the stars (*peirat echein astrōn*).

Here we have Necessity leading, and the verb is *agein*, which is familiar from *Odyssey* XVII/ 218 and Homer's like to like principle. So as Necessity leads in Fr. 10, and we can also note the similarity of the following lines where a limit is held, I am strongly inclined to translate Fr. 8, 30 as 'controlling Necessity' for *kraterē Anankē*.³⁹

I take it that Mourelatos has shown that there are significant allusions and interesting similarities of Greek usage from Parmenides to Homer.⁴⁰ Certainly we can point to *kraterē anankē* at Fr. 8, 30 as resonances in Homer and Hesiod. At *Odyssey* X, 273 Odysseus says that he must act in a certain way as 'a controlling necessity has come upon me (*krateres de moi eplet' anangkē*), while at *Iliad* VI, 458 a 'controlling necessity will be laid upon' (*kraterē d' epikeiset' anangkē*) the captured Trojan women. At Hesiod *Theogony* 517 'Atlas holds the broad sky with controlling necessity' (*krateres hup anangkēs*). It is also interesting that *moira* in Homer seems to be referenced by Parmenides as well. So Fr. 8, 37 speaks of 'What is' having been 'shackled by Moira' (*moira epedēsen*). In Homer, at *Iliad* IV, 517 Diores is 'snared by *moira*' (*moir' epedēse*), hit by a stone and killed in battle, at *Iliad* XXII, 5 Hector is snared by *moira* (*moir' epedēse*) and stays in front of Ilios at the Scaean gates, at *Odyssey* III, 269 Aegisthus[41] is ensnared by 'a *moira* of the gods' (*moira theōn epedēse*) and at *Odyssey* XI, 292 Melampus is ensnared by a 'hard *moira* of the god' (*chalepē de theou kata moira pedēse*). At Parmenides Fr. 10, 6 we also have *agous(a) epedēsen Anangkē*, 'Necessity led and bound it'. There is no exact match in Homer but as Mourelatos has pointed out, there are interesting similarities with Fr. 8, 37 'shackled by Moira' (*moira epedēsen*) and Homer and Hesiod's use of *kraterē Ananke* and *moir' epedēse*. The important point for this book is that Parmenides associates *moira* with necessity, uses the important verb *agein* (as well as *kubernan* and *kratein*) and all this is part of his account of the order of the world. There are also clear references back to Homer in relation to these words.

As Parmenides' attitude to the world around us is unclear, and so little of the third part of his poem still exists, it is difficult to talk of the analogies that Parmenides used. However, the beginning of Fr. 8 is significant. When Parmenides talks of change, he does so in an organic rather than a mechanical manner. So in Fr. 8 line 6 Parmenides asks what birth (*gennan*) we might seek, line 7 asks in what way would it grow (*auxēthen*) and lines 10/11 ask why it would grow (*phun*) from nothing sooner rather than later.

## Derveni papyrus

There is an interesting passage in the Derveni papyrus that gives us a link between spinning Moira, Zeus and Zeus exercising his power by means of *kratein* and a transfer of the attributes of the gods to a substance. Column 19 of the Derveni papyrus tells us that:

> Existing things have each been called a single name on account of what controls (*epikratountos*) them, all things being called Zeus for this reason. Air controls (*epikratei*) all as far as it wants to. When they say that Moira span (*epiklōsai*) they say that the understanding of Zeus sanctions how the things that are, that have been generated and the things that will be must come to be and cease. He likens him to a king (for this appeared to him the most appropriate of all the names that are said), saying this: 'Zeus the king, Zeus the ruler of all with the shining thunderbolt.' He said he is king because of many ... One rule controls (*kratei*) and accomplishes all.[42]

So as with Anaximenes, air controls (*kratein*) though it is less clear here exactly what the nature of that control is. Zeus is here equated with air, so in a sense it is Zeus who is controlling, and in a second sense it is air that is controlling, a good example of the transfer of the attributes of the gods on the issue of order. Zeus is also equated with Moira. A further significant point here is that air/Zeus has a considerable amount of knowledge, 'the understanding of Zeus sanctions how the things that are, that have been generated and the things that will be must come to be and cease'. We might compare here Anaxagoras' *nous*, which has knowledge of what was, what is and what will be.[43] Column 18, 2–12 is also important in making the connection between Moira, Zeus and order:

> Orpheus named this breath (*to pneuma*) Moira. But other humans, according to common usage, say Moira span (*epiklōsai*) and that those things which Moira span (*epeklōsen*) will be, speaking correctly but not knowing what Moira and spinning (*epiklōsai*) are. Orpheus called Moira understanding. This appeared to him as the most suitable of all the names humans had given. Before Zeus was called by name, Moira was the understanding of the god always and through everything. Since Zeus was called by name, he believed he was born, though he existed before but had not been named.

The second sentence here, that 'other humans, according to common usage, say Moira span and that those things which Moira span will be, speaking correctly but not knowing what Moira and spinning are', is interesting in relation to some of the things that I argued in Chapter 3. It seems that the nature of Moira and spinning were not clear to many of the Greeks. There are some other significant passages in the Derveni papyrus as well. So in the context of cosmogony, Column 21:15 tells us, albeit rather fragmentarily that:

> Controlled (*ekratei*) such that they were separated out.

The final part of Col. 21 concerns cosmogony but is rather fragmentary by line 15, so it is difficult to tell what was controlled and why. In Column 9:9 fire is controlled:

> Whatever is kindled is controlled (*epikrateitai*) and when controlled (*epikratēthen*) it mixes with the other things.

In Column 25:5 the sun controls the 'thing suspended in the air':

> Those things which make up the moon are the whitest of all, and are distributed according to the same *logos*. There are other things which are now in the air, suspended far away from each other, though in the day they are invisible due to being controlled (*epikratoumena*) by the sun, while at night it can be seen they

exist. They are controlled (*epikrateitai*) due to their smallness. Each of them is suspended in necessity, such that they do not come together with each other.

Col. 4 of the Derveni papyrus both quotes and alludes to Heraclitus approvingly.[44] Lines 5–6 say:

> Similarly Heraclitus... the common... overturns the private.[45]

This would seem to be an allusion to Heraclitus Fr. 89 above, on the cosmos being one and common to those who are awake, unlike the private world of sleep. Derveni papyrus Col. 4 lines 7–10 then goes on to give us some quotations from Heraclitus:

> The sun according to nature (*kata phusin*) is the width of a human foot[46]
> and does not exceed its boundaries. If he oversteps,
> the Erinyes, the defenders of justice, will find him out.[47]

So like Heraclitus, the Derveni author is operating with a civil law conception of physical behaviour, rather than a mathematical law conception. This passage is fundamental to the stability of the cosmos in the Derveni papyrus cosmology because of the critical role that the sun plays. Derveni papyrus. Col. 9 tells us that:

> Realizing then that fire, when mixed with the others, disorders these things and prevents them from being set together by heat, he removed it sufficiently so that once removed it did not prevent the things that are solidifying.[48]

Derveni papyrus, Col. 25 tells us that:

> If the god had not wished the things now existing to be, he would not have made the sun. However, he made it of such a type and of such a size as was explained at the outset of this account.[49]

The sun has a specific size and a specific role to play. There is a critical balance whereby the sun dissolves the things that are now and the moon re-constitutes them.[50] If the sun grows too large, this endangers the stability of the cosmos. The continual growth of the sun could lead to a widespread degeneration. The sun then has a constant size and will not overstep its measures. As argued with Heraclitus, here we have an assertion of regularity in the cosmos. Betegh has commented that in the Derveni papyrus:

> First, we have the obviously dialectical, polemical use of the cosmological and physical doctrines in critical discussions about the theoretical foundations of the craft. Second, and more important, these texts show a conscious use of concepts

and explanatory methods developed from the 'inquiry into nature' tradition, among which, first and foremost, there is the unifying concept of nature, and the conviction that the world is an ordered whole within which one can account for the diversity of phenomena and processes with a reductionist, mechanistic causal explanation, built on a few basic principles.[51]

Betegh has also argued that the Derveni authors' criticism of religious and magical practitioners has parallels in the Hippocratic corpus.[52] On much of this I would agree with Betegh, except that I do not find the explanations of the Derveni papyrus to be mechanical. As with Heraclitus, there are no machine analogies, we have *kratein* being used in critical cosmological passages and the author is operating with a civil rather than a mathematical conception of natural laws.

## Empedocles

With Empedocles, we have both Love and Strife controlling and we also have the four elements being said to control in turn. So Simplicius *Physics* 158, 28, talking of earth, water, air and fire says that:

> These are all of like and equal age, but each has a different prerogative, and each a different disposition, and each in turn controls (*krateousi*) as time moves around.[53]

Simplicius *Physics* 33.18, is identical from 'each in turn', except for *kukloio* for *chronoio*, so 'each in turn controls as the cycle moves around'.[54] Simplicius' next line is:

> They shrink into each other and grow in turn according to *aisa*.

That could mean simply 'each in their allotted turn',[55] or it could mean 'each in its destined' turn,[56] in which case we would have an interesting association of *kratein* with *aisa/ moira* as we did in Homer. Simplicius, *On the Heavens* 530, 5, says that:

> At this time Kupris, busy generating forms, moistened earth with a storm, and gave it to fire to control (*kratunai*).

Our key word here *kratunai* could mean to harden or to strengthen, or could mean to rule, govern or control.[57] So in Empedocles the elements can control, as can Love and Strife. Aristotle *Physics* 252a7 says that:

> Love and Strife in turn control (*kratein*) and produce motion (*kinein*).

So too Philoponus, *On Generation and Corruption* 19, 3 says that:

> When Love controls (*kratousēs*), all things become one and generate the sphere.

Simplicius *Physics* 160, 26 also says that:

> Intelligible things have been made like by Love, while perceptible things have been controlled (*kratēthenta*) by Strife.

So there can be no doubt that both Love and Strife control at certain stages of Empedocles' cosmos cycle. There is one more use of *kratein* in Empedocles, where Aristotle reports his views on breathing, in *On Respiration* 273a29, and has Empedocles using *kratunōn*, controlling.

Empedocles did invoke the Muses, though as ever with Empedocles, it is difficult to be sure of his exact intent in doing so. Fragment 4 says that:

> The bad are much inclined to disbelieve the strong
> But know, according to the assurances advised by my Muse,
> By sifting[58] the account in your heart.

Fragment 9 asks the Muses 'What is it right for the ephemeral to hear?' while Fragment 131 invokes the Muses, for the sake of the ephemeral, so there can be a 'revelation of a good account concerning the blessed gods'. This is too complex a matter to discuss fully here, but I am inclined to agree with Tor that it is Empedocles' claim to great experience that privileges his writing rather than an appeal to the Muses.[59] With Empedocles on nature, a critical passage is Empedocles Fr. 111, which says that:

> All the remedies (*pharmaka*) which exist as a defence against evils and old age
> You will learn, as for you alone will I accomplish all these things
> You will stop the might of tireless winds which over the earth
> Sweep and destroy fields with their gusts
> Then again, if you wish, you will bring on the requiting winds
> You will make, from a black rainstorm seasonal drought
> for men, and out of a summer drought you will generate
> Tree nourishing streams that dwell in the aether
> and you will bring back from Hades the strength of a man who has died.[60]

One can read this magically or naturally.[61] Read magically, the *pharmaka* are magic potions, the learning in line 2 is akin to mage an adept, the control of meteorological phenomena is in the magical weather-working tradition and we take literally the final line about bringing someone back from Hades.[62] Read naturally, *pharmaka* are natural medicines,[63] line 2 is simply learning and the claim is to exert some control over the weather through a knowledge of nature.[64] With Hades, possibly this is a reference to resuscitation and near death experiences, possibly Empedocles thinks we currently are in Hades and his teachings will show the way out.[65]

## Love and Strife

Sometimes Love and Strife are referred to as forces.[66] I have very strong reservations about this and would much prefer to call them principles of association and dissociation. Love and Strife are entities on their own rather than properties of matter. They do not generate attractive or repulsive forces between matter, they just effect association or dissociation. Contrary to what we understand as forces, their effect varies over time. Their effect also discriminates between different types of matter.[67] It is better to refer to love and strife as principles of association and dissociation respectively. This is not to single out Empedocles, as I have reservations about using the word force in this sense in relation to any of the early Greek thinkers. As we will see with Leucippus and Democritus, I also object to calling the like to like effect a force. It is a sorting principle, which operates only when the correct type of motion (vortex motion) occurs, and not a force that operates between atoms.

## Like to like

Nor is like to like in Empedocles a force; indeed like to like is not a force in any of its incarnations in early Greek thought, though one can find comments like:

> The attraction of like for like was an important force in the cosmology of Empedocles.[68]

Here it is of the utmost importance to differentiate between different instances of like to like principle, as like to like associated different types of things in different ways. The first use of a like to like principle, as we have seen, is *Odyssey* XVII, 218 where 'As always, the god leads (*agei*) like to like'. How general this leading of like to like together is has to be a matter of speculation. In this instance, it is the leading together of like people. Odysseus has a swineherd as his companion and is insulted by Melanthius, and the preceding line is:

> Now very much we have the vile leading the vile (*kakos kakon ēgēlazei*).

Whether we can generalize this as all like things are led together by the gods or by a god in Homer is another matter. Whatever the answer to that, a more precise description for this principle would be that like is led to like and not like is attracted to like. There is clearly no force in operation in Homer.

It is possible to read a like to like principle into Parmenides, although he does not explicitly mention one. Fr. 8, 22 tells us that:

> Nor is it divisible, since it is all alike (*epei pan estin homoion*).

Fr. 8, 25 further says:

> Thus it is all continuous. For what is draws near to (*pelazei*) what is.

Fr. 4 also says that:

> You will not cut off (*apotmēxei*) what is from holding fast (*echesthai*) to what is. It does not disperse itself in every way and everywhere according to order nor does it set itself together.[69]

This is tricky to interpret if for Parmenides (at this point in the poem at least) there is only one thing and there is nothing to separate any putative multiplicity of things. This cannot be a like to like principle in the sense of many like things being drawn spatially together, so this is perhaps best phrased as a 'like coheres with like' principle.

Plato at *Lysis* 214a quotes Homer's like to like principle exactly. He also mentions 'those who have written and debated concerning nature (*peri phuseōs*) and the whole (*holou*)' who hold the view that 'of necessity like is always friendly with like' (*to homoion tō homoiō anangkē aei philon einai*). In this context Plato is again talking about people, how good people can be friendly with one another, but disagreeing that bad people will be friendly as one will injure the other. At *Symposium* 195b Plato says that:

> The old saying has it well, that like always draws near to like (*ho gar palaios logos eu echei, hōs homoion homoiō aei palazei*).

The context here is that Plato is arguing for the view that love is for the young as Love is youngest of the gods and so consorts with the young. Similarly, at *Phaedrus* 240c2 Plato says that:

> As the old saying has it, those of the same age enjoy those of the same age (*hēlika gar kai ho palaios logos terpein ton hēlika*).[70]

Again, the context is love between humans. Protagoras 337d has a different theme. Plato has Hippias say:

> For like is of similar kind to like by nature (*to gar homoion tō homoiō phusei*) not by law, whereas law, the tyrant of humans, often constrains us contrary to nature (*para tēn phusin*).[71]

Here he is emphasizing that all here, including Protagoras and Socrates are fellow citizens by nature and not law and so should not quarrel, but discuss matters properly.

I have quoted all of these passages to show that there is no single like to like principle and certainly no like to like force, so we must look carefully at each instance of the like to like principle. This is especially so in Plato's *Phaedo*. At *Phaedo* 67a, there is a similarity of purity of the body and purity of knowledge. At *Phaedo* 79c, when there is enquiry with the senses, then the soul is dragged (*elketai*) by the body to things that do not stay the same and wander, while when the soul enquires by itself, it goes to (*oichetai*) the pure, everlasting, immortal and changeless, and itself becomes unchanging and free from wandering. In both cases, some form of like to like principle seems to be in operation, though exactly how we phrase that in each case is open to debate, some possibilities being like is known by like or like perceives like or like cognizes like. This brings us to Empedocles Fr. 109, which tells us that:

> It is with earth that we see Earth, and Water with water; by air we see bright Air, by fire destroying Fire. By love do we see Love, and Hate by grievous hate.

There is some debate here on whether this is a physical or mental perception,[72] but what should be clear is that this is not a like is led to like or a like coheres with like principle, indeed it has nothing to do with the distribution of the elements at all. It is best termed a like is perceived by like principle. Certainly, it does not state a force of attraction between like things. This is important to recognize for Empedocles, but this section has also laid the groundwork for arguing that like to like is not a force operating between atoms in the early atomists, Leucippus and Democritus either. It is a principle of how atoms are sorted within a vortex and does not operate outside vortices. I will argue this in greater detail in the next chapter and conclude that there is no like to like force in any early Greek thinker.

## Anaxagoras

Anaxagoras did not use *kubernan* at all, but *kratein* does play a very important role for him as this is the term used for the relation of nous to the rest of the universe. Anaxagoras Fragment 12 says that:

Other things have a portion of everything, but *nous* is unlimited, rules itself and is unmixed, being alone by itself. If it were not by itself, and mixed with other things, it would have a share of all things, if it mixed with any. In everything there is a part of everything, as I said previously. Mixed things would hinder it, with the result that it would be able to rule nothing in the same way as it does now, alone and by itself. *Nous* is the finest and purest of all things, it has all knowledge concerning everything and it has the greatest power. *Nous* controls all things (*pantōn nous kratein*) that have life, both the greater and the smaller. *Nous* controlled the revolution of the whole (*kai tēs perichōrēsios tēs sumpasēs nous ekratēsen*), such that it revolved in the beginning. At first it revolved in a small region, but now it revolves in a greater, and will revolve in a greater still. The things which are mixed and separated and divided are all known by *nous*. *Nous* ordered them all, this revolution in which the stars and the sun and the moon and the air and the aether which are being separated off. This revolution produced the separation. The dense is separated from the rare, and the hot from the cold, the bright from the dark and the dry from the moist. There are many parts of many things. Nothing is entirely separated or divided from anything else except *nous*. *Nous* is entirely alike, both the greater and smaller parts of it. Nothing else is like anything else, but what is most in each single entity is most clearly what it is and was.[73]

So *nous* controls all things (*pantōn nous kratein*) that have life and nous controlled the revolution of the whole (*kai tēs perichōrēsios tēs sumpasēs nous ekratēsen*), such that it revolved in the beginning. As Broadie among others have pointed out, given that *nous* knows all things and controls all things, attributes that might lead one to expect that *nous* would be described as divine, it is not.[74]

If we are looking for other analogies for natural processes in Anaxagoras, then Fragment 4a talks of 'the seeds of all things' (*spermata pantōn chrēmatōn*) and Fragment 4b speaks of 'seeds of unlimited number' (*spermatōn apeiron plēthos*) in significant cosmogonical context where the seeds are clearly going to form all of the things we find in the current natural world.[75] That *nous* is the key factor in cosmogony for Anaxagoras should be enough to rule out any mechanical interpretation of him, even given Plato's critique in the *Phaedo* that instead of using *nous* and explaining why things were for the best, Anaxagoras explained many phenomena simply in terms of 'air, aether, water and other absurdities'.[76]

It is possible to try for a more mechanical interpretation of Anaxagoras, which results in a debate like that over Anaximander. With Anaximander one can downplay *kubernan* and push for a multiple worlds interpretation. With Anaxagoras the aim is to downplay the role of *nous*, and so the importance of *kratein* and again push for a multiple worlds view. So one can try to minimize the role of *nous* and maximize the independent role of the vortex, which can then be seen as mechanical once it has been started. However, if we look at the use of *kratein*, we have *pantōn nous kratein* (*nous* controls all) where *kratein* is a present infinitive and *kai tēs perichōrēsios tēs sumpasēs nous ekratēsen,* (*nous* controlled the revolution of the whole), where *ekratēsen* is an aorist indicating an incomplete action. There is no reason then to suppose that *nous* relinquishes its full control of everything. Plato may criticize Anaxagoras for not using *nous* enough in explanation, but that is another matter. On multiple worlds, the key passage is Anaxagoras Fr. 4:

> If this is so, it is right to believe that there are many things of all types in all that has been separated, seeds of all things and all sorts of shapes, colours and tastes and men have been formed and animals have souls, and that men have lived in cities and established farms, as with us, and have sun and moon and the others as with us, and the earth grows for them a great amount of many sorts of things, of which they harvest the useful and take into their houses to consume. This then I have said concerning separation, that separation would occur not only with us, but elsewhere too.

It is possible to offer a solution parallel to that which I suggested for Anaximander. Anaximander believed in a flat earth, as did Anaxagoras. With Anaximander, I suggested that the *cosmoi* in the phrase *cosmoi en ouranoi* were related to the two sides of the earth, perhaps *cosmoi* in the sense of civilisations, perhaps in the sense of separate weather systems. So for Anaxagoras too, there may be a civilisation on the other side of the earth. There would be 'sun and moon and the others, as with us', the same bodies but seen from the other side of the earth. Cornford and Guthrie have previously suggested other places on the earth, which Vlastos objected to as the last sentence in the fragment is clearly cosmogonical and clearly occurs in a different place.[77] Here there can (and indeed ought to be) be a parallel cosmogony on the other side of the earth. I doubt that we can read much into 'the earth' having a definite article and 'sun, moon and others' not as unique entities did not always have definite articles. Simplicius rejects the elsewhere on earth theory, but does not discuss the under the earth theory.

There are many theoretical grounds for rejecting multiple worlds in Anaxagoras.[78] It is unclear why Anaxagoras would need to postulate multiple worlds or what they would help explain for him, while those issues are very clear for Leucippus and Democritus and for Empedocles. More *cosmoi* would presumably mean more vortices, otherwise it is not at all clear how those extra *cosmoi* would function. In Anaxagoras Fr. 12 it is clear that *nous* begins the motion of one vortex, but there is no mention of *nous* beginning the motion of any other vortex and there is no mention of other vortices at all in Anaxagoras. As we saw in Chapter 4, in Leucippus and Democritus, and in Empedocles, there are very clear individuation and boundary conditions for *cosmoi*. We find nothing of this sort in Anaxagoras. This is a problem in particular for the idea that there are *cosmoi* of varying sizes for Anaxagoras. Aristotle and most of the doxography is against the idea of multiple worlds in Anaxagoras. It is also significant that while Plato criticizes Leucippus and Democritus and Empedocles for their multiple world ideas, Plato does not criticize Anaxagoras on these grounds despite the fact that he has a long and famous critique of him in the *Phaedo*.

## Democritus

We do find *kratein* in Democritus, though not in any strong cosmological contexts. Democritus Fragment 29 tells us that:

> Humans ... their own lack of intelligence. For by nature (*phusei*) judgement clashes with luck (*tuchē*). This same thing, which is most hostile to understanding, they say controls (*kratein*).

So too Democritus Fragment 100 says:

> It is hard to fight against spirit (*thumō*), but to control (*krateein*) it is to be a prudent human.

I will have a great deal more to say about analogies in Leucippus and Democritus in the next chapter. The final issue to consider for Democritus here is Fragment 34 and another possible macrocosm/microcosm relationship:

> In man, who is a small cosmos (*en tō anthrōpōi mikrōi cosmōi onti*).[79]

It is interesting to note that this fragment is in Diels, is not in Bailey's *The Greek Atomists and Epicurus*, is not in Kirk, Raven and Schofield *The Presocratic Philosophers* and is not in Taylor's *The Atomists: Leucippus and Democritus*, though it is in Freeman's *Ancila to the Pre-Socratic Philosophers*, it is in Graham's *The Texts of Early Greek Philosophy* and it is in Laks and Most's *Early Greek Philosophy*. Unfortunately, we have no idea how, or how extensively, Democritus employed this principle. Other early Greek usage would suggest man as microcosm and cosmos as macrocosm, but if that is so for Democritus, we do not know what the aspects were for comparison or how that comparison was mediated. It may simply be that like Democritean *cosmoi*, humans have an origin, grow taking in atoms, reach an acme then decline and die. Alternatively, something more elaborate may have been envisaged but we simply do not have any evidence.

## Conclusion

As well as there being a significant tradition based around *kubernan* as a key verb for the steered order of the cosmos, there was also a significant tradition based around *kratein* for the controlled order of the cosmos. Those two traditions were clearly related and there were thinkers who used both *kubernan* and *kratein* or used *kubernan* and *kratein* synonymously. Both traditions have their ultimate roots in Homer and Hesiod, though the first in the philosophical tradition to use *kratein* in this way was Anaximenes. It is also important to look at the other analogies for natural processes that the early Greek thinkers used. We have found no machine analogies, but many analogies drawn from everyday ancient Greek experience. We have the craft analogy of felting, culinary and maritime analogies in Anaximenes, pyrotechnical, commercial and parenting analogies in Heraclitus and agricultural analogies in Anaxagoras. We also have the question of the macrocosm/microcosm analogy. One can see why those trying to see mechanism in early Greek thought want to downplay this, but it does play an important role, and if we recognize an intellectual space between the primitive and modern science, an interesting and unproblematic role. As with Anaximander, if we drop superficial similarities with modern science, the thinkers in the chapter come out as stronger and more coherent, and we get a more plausible history of the development of early Greek thinking on nature.

7

# Leucippus and Democritus

The best candidates as mechanists among the early Greek thinkers are the first atomists, Leucippus and Democritus. It might be thought that their ontology of necessity gives them a mechanical view, but this is not so. This chapter aims to show that in three key senses – the supposed use of machine analogies, a supposed deterministic system and the supposed application of mathematical mechanics – they were not mechanists. I prefer to call the entities of the early atomists' ontology 'what is' and 'what is not'. The reason for this is that 'atoms and the void' tend to obscure the full force of the '*ou mallon*', the 'not rather' arguments that are critical to early atomism.[1] Atoms and void also suggest a continuity with seventeenth-century atomism such that while the early atomists may not actually have applied a mathematical mechanics to their system, in principle it would be simple to 'retrofit' a mechanics to it. However, the *ou mallon* stance of the early atomists creates problems for the application of mechanics and for determinism. Critical here is whether the early atomists system conforms to 'Laplace's Demon', that if we know all the positions and motions of the particles in one state, we can then in principle predict all future states.

## Like to like

I begin with the like to like principle, because it is important to be rid of a popular misconception. Like to like in the early atomists was not a force of attraction that acted between atoms. It is a principle of sorting that only occurs in conjunction with certain types of motion. The key passage here is Sextus Empiricus *Against the Mathematicians* VII 116–18:

> Democritus founds his argument on both animate and inanimate things. For animals, he says, flock together (*sunagelezetai*) with animals of the same kind – doves with doves, cranes with cranes, and so with the other irrational animals.

> Similarly in the case of inanimate things, as can be seen from seeds that are being winnowed and from pebbles on the sea-shore. For in the one case the whirl of the sieve separately arranges lentils with lentils, barley with barley, wheat with wheat; and in the other case, by the motion of the waves, oval pebbles are pushed into the same place as oval pebbles, and round pebbles as round as pebbles, as though the similarity in things has some sort of ability for leading things together (*hōs an sunagōgon ti echousēs tōn pragmatōn tēs en toutois homoiotētos*).

The translation of the last phrase here is critical. Taylor has: 'as if the similarity in things had a kind of attractive force'.[2] However, *sunagōgon* does not have this sense of force, rather it is a leading together, as at *Odyssey* XVII, 218 the god leads like to like (*ton homoion agei theos hōs ton homoion*). There is no suggestion here that if we leave a mixture of lentils, barley and wheat in a sieve, that they will separate out without the sieve being whirled, or that similar stones on the beach will separate out if they are not agitated by the waves.[3] It is better to think of like to like as a sorting principle, or an effect of motion, rather than a force in itself.[4]

Plato too advocated a like to like sorting principle and required specific types of motion for this to work.[5] In the pre-cosmic chaos, it is the fact that the receptacle shakes like a winnowing basket that produces a separation of like to like. At *Timaeus* 57c and 88de we are told that this shaking continues in the cosmos. At *Timaeus* 58a ff. we are told of the compressive effect that the rotation of the cosmos has on the elements, making them intermingle. Like to like here is dependent on specific types of motion. There is no universal attraction of like to like, nor is there any force that operates at a distance. Similarly, at *Timaeus* 80bc electricity and magnetism are explained as due to contact action and mutual replacement, and there is an outright denial that any attraction is involved.[6]

Two modern parallels here. Why do larger breakfast cereal flakes come at the top of the packet and smaller ones at the bottom? If the packet has been transported upright, agitation in transportation means the smaller but not the larger flakes can drop through the gaps between flakes. No one would suggest that there is a like to like attractive force between same sized breakfast cereal flakes! Note that the sorting will only occur when there is agitation of the packet. Secondly, a modern centrifuge, which in some ways moves in a similar manner to a vortex, will very efficiently separate the components of a solution/suspension by density. Again, there is no permanent like to like attraction between the components, the sorting happens only when the centrifuge is rotating.

## Like to like and vortices?

Pseudo-Plutarch tells us that, for the early atomists:

> The cosmos as it is now was formed in a curved manner in this way.[7] The atomic bodies were in an un-providential, chance, continuous and extremely rapid motion at the same time, and many of these bodies gathered together, having a variety of shapes and sizes.[8]

While Pseudo-Plutarch gives us four descriptions of motion prior to cosmos formation (un-providential, chance, continuous and extremely rapid), there is no mention of the like to like principle. On the contrary, it is a variety of shapes and sizes that come together to generate a cosmos. Simplicius also tells us that:

> When Democritus says that 'A vortex of all shapes is separated off from the all' (how or by what cause he does not say), it appears that this occurs spontaneously or by chance.[9]

So according to Simplicius it is by chance and not by like to like this occurs.[10] Aristotle has a discussion of the motion of atoms outside the vortex at *De Caelo* 300b8 ff. Here there is no natural motion outside the vortex and according to Aristotle this view is incoherent. If there was like to like motion outside the vortex, Aristotle would have recognized that as natural motion, but he does not even mention like to like outside the vortices. So the sorting of like to like only occurs within vortices. A consideration of the early atomists' ontology should also rule out any permanently acting like to like attraction. The ontology is simply what is, and what is not. Nothing else is mentioned and nothing else is needed. Democritus Fr. 9 says:

> By convention sweet, by convention bitter, by convention hot, by convention cold, by convention cold, but in reality atoms and the void.[11]

If that sets out a general programme of reduction, rather than merely the reduction of perceptual qualities, then non-reductive forces are ruled out.[12] The doxography is unanimous on the ontology of the early atomists and the reductive nature of their explanations.

## Mechanical philosophies

There is a sense in which this discussion of like to like in the early atomists cuts both ways. Early versions of the seventeenth-century mechanical philosophy had no forces that acted at a distance at all. So gravity was an effect of vortices, electricity and magnetism due to the motion of screw shaped particles through a plenum of finer particles. Later versions of the mechanical philosophy, in particular that of Newton, had gravity as an intrinsic force of matter acting at a distance. At the time, Newton was criticized for reintroducing occult and scholastic qualities, which the early mechanists opposed. His ideas were allegedly scholastic in the sense that gravity was an irreducible quality of matter, where the mechanical philosophy programme was to reduce everything down to matter and motion. They were allegedly occult in the sense that Newton's conception of gravity was action at a distance and was inexplicable in mechanical terms. Pyle believes that in defining the mechanical philosophy it is best to follow Thomas Hobbes and that means rejecting action at a distance.[13] It can be argued that in a truly mechanistic system, the constituent particles must be entirely passive, with no forces of attraction or repulsion between them.[14] If Leucippus and Democritus supposed there to be a force of like to like attraction acting between atoms, this disbars them from being mechanists in this sense. There is no like to like attraction, so in this sense it is possible that Leucippus and Democritus were mechanists. This is also important in relation to some other definitions of what it is to be mechanistic. Hesse stresses the ideas of inanimate and passive matter and forces of expansion, contraction, suction, pressure, centrifugal force, taking these to be the mechanical properties of matter.[15] We find very little of this in Leucippus and Democritus. Salmon alternatively stresses the importance for the mechanical philosophy of explanation in terms of 'levers, springs, pulleys, wheels, gears, deformable jelly etc.', and we find none of this either in the early atomists.[16]

## Like to like and congregation

There is a further reason to reject the idea of like to like as a force in Leucippus and Democritus. There is no beginning to the universe for the early atomists, even if individual *cosmoi* come and go. So time stretches back indefinitely and forward indefinitely. If like to like operated outside of vortices, then all the atoms would have clumped together by now. One might object that this is too modern a consideration for the early atomists, but something similar was considered by Empedocles, Plato and Aristotle. Empedocles believed that Love and Strife would eventually produce perfect association and perfect dissociation of the elements, Plato that like to like on its own would produce only a sorting of the elements and not a cosmos, and Aristotle that the natural motion of the terrestrial elements would sort the elements into four concentric shells if left to its own devices.[17]

## Taylor's forces

On the issue of forces in Democritus, Taylor says there is:

> Some evidence that Democritus' dynamics postulated three fundamental forces, a repulsive force which plays the role of impact in conventional corpuscular theory and two kinds of attractive force, one which draws together atoms of the same shape and another which holds together atoms of a different shape in an atomic aggregate.[18]

Taylor's motivation here is Philoponus' concern that if atoms did actually come into contact with one another,[19] nothing would separate them, and they would coalesce into a single body. That Philoponus was concerned about what he thought the unfortunate consequences would be if the atoms should collide does not mean that Leucippus and Democritus shared his concerns. There is no evidence they did and Aristotle, who wrote a lost work *On Democritus*, does not seem to have been bothered by these concerns either. Given Aristotle's critical attitude that is very surprising if there is a problem here. As Bodnar has argued, in the absence of any other source for such a critical idea, it is best to see Philoponus inferring what the atomists might have said to resolve this supposed difficulty rather than reporting what they actually said.[20] There is also significant evidence that the early atomists considered their atoms to be solid.[21] The word used is *nastos*, for which LSJ give 'close pressed, firm' and 'solid'. If so, they may have simply taken the view that when atoms collide, they rebound. It is best then to retain the orthodox view that atoms can collide and entangle, when we do not have to postulate short range forces, either attractive or repulsive. Aristotle says that:

> Leucippus and Democritus say that the one does not come from many nor the many from one but that all things are generated by entangling (*sumplokē*) and scattering.[22]

Here *sumplokē* has a primary meaning of to twine or plait together or to entangle and is also used of wrestlers when they become locked together, so there is no question of Aristotle's meaning here. Simplicius quotes Aristotle's lost *On*

*Democritus* to make the same point,[23] and in his commentary on Aristotle's *On the Heavens* has the intertwining of atoms due to their shape, some being hooked, some convex, some concave and so on.[24]

There is an issue with the magnitude of the forces. There has to be a balance between them for the interactions between atoms to work. So, for example, if the repulsive force is too strong relative to the attractive forces, atoms will not come into structures. Alternatively, if the attractive forces are too strong all the atoms will already be in structures (there being infinite past time) and will never come out of them either. Why then is there a balance between these forces, that balance allowing structures and human life? The reply cannot be design, nor can it be that the order of this universe is accidental and is explained as one in an infinite array of universes. That is a modern reply to issues of why the gravitational constant and the speed of light have specific, undetermined values that allow our universe to develop in a certain way, but the early atomists theorize many *cosmoi* in one universe, not many universes. There is a more subtle concern here as well, which is that the early atomists often say '*ou mallon*', not rather, in relation to key questions in cosmology as I discuss below.

## Mechanical analogies?

What sort of analogues do the early atomists use for natural processes? At no point did they employ a machine analogy. In the passages we have looked at so far, animals flocking together is a biological analogy, seeds being winnowed is an agricultural analogy and like shaped pebbles gathered together on the shore is a maritime analogy. The vortex itself is meteorological or maritime analogy, depending on whether one is thinking of a whirlwind or a whirlpool. Metrodorus of Chios, in relation to the many *cosmoi* theory, says that:

> It is strange for one ear of corn to be produced in a great plain, and for one world in the boundless.

That gives us another agricultural analogy. Seneca *Natural Questions* V, 2, reporting Democritus' view, has the origin of winds likened to the behaviour of humans in a crowded market place, so we have a human analogy.[25] Diogenes Laertius IX, 31 gives this account of early atomist cosmogony:

> Leucippus holds that the whole is infinite ... part of it is full, and part void ... from these innumerable *cosmoi* come to be and are dissolved into these again. The *cosmoi* are generated in this manner. By cutting off (*apotomēn*) from

the infinite many bodies of all shapes move into a great void, where they are crowded together and produce a single vortex, where colliding with each other and circulating in all manner of ways, they separate out like to like. When, because of their great number they are no longer capable of moving around in equilibrium, those that are fine spread out into the outside void, as if sifted, while the rest hold together and becoming entangled, they unite their motions and create the first spherical structure. This stands apart like a membrane (*humena*), containing in itself all kinds of bodies. As they whirl around, due to the resistance of the middle, the surrounding membrane (*humena*) becomes thin, and the close packed atoms flow together due to touching the vortex. In this way the earth came into being, the atoms which had been borne in to the middle remaining there together. Again the surrounding membrane (*humena*) itself is increased, due to the influx of external bodies.[26]

So all of the *cosmoi* have surrounding membranes, *humena*. LSJ give *thin skin, membrane, caul*, of those that enclose the brain and heart, so again we have a biological analogy at the heart of cosmos formation. So there are no machine analogies in Leucippus and Democritus. We get what we might expect from Greeks of their time – biological, agricultural, meteorological, human and maritime analogues, and as we saw in the last chapter, they used a macrocosm/microcosm analogy.

Some commentators have taken the winnowing of seeds and the sorting of pebbles on the beach to be mechanical analogies. The reason for this, other than a desperate desire to see the early atomists as mechanists, is that both can be analysed solely in terms of particles interacting with each other mechanically. That is true, but this mistakes analysis for analogy. Whether we in the twenty-first century can analyse these phenomena in this manner is not the issue. The question is whether the early atomists did and as far as we know they did not. Rather, they present these agricultural and maritime analogies as the way in which the particles interact with each other. Even if there are only particle to particle interactions, this does not of necessity give us a mechanical view. The popularity of the mechanical view since the seventeenth century may have rendered other views of how particles might interact implausible or redundant to us, but that is not the case for the early Greeks. There is no machine analogy here. The sea can hardly be thought of as a machine, but is the winnowing basket a *mēchanē*? In the sense that it is a contrivance, yes. Is it a machine? No. It has no moving parts and it has no interacting parts. I also go back to a point made in the methodology chapter about Unguru on Greek mathematics. Greek mathematics had a geometrical form, which is not reducible to algebra, nor is it algebra dressed in a different language. So too these analogies are not mechanical, nor are they mechanical analogies dressed in a different language. We need to recognize they had a nature of their own appropriate to the thought of the time. They do important work in providing contextually plausible analogies for how atoms are sorted in a vortex, something a machine analogy would not have been able to do at the time.

## Machine analogies?

I agree with Berryman that:

> There is little credible evidence before Aristotle's time that might count as the use of working artefacts in understanding the functioning of nature.[27]

In line with one of the historiographical themes of this book, I would ask why the early Greeks would have used machine analogies rather than why they did not use such analogies. I also agree with Furley that the available Greek *mēchanē* of the time did not display the characteristics of regularity or reliability that later machines, in particular clocks, came to exhibit.[28] The materials, design and lubrication technologies of the time meant that key components were subject to considerable forces and were prone to rapid wear and failure. So if your axle end is wood (too soft) in an axle hub that is a hole in wood (with no bearings), your lubrication (if any) is animal fat and your cart is un-sprung when travelling on unpaved or rudimentary roads, it will wear and unless regularly serviced it will fail. I would be very interested to see the maintenance and safety records of the early Greek cranes used to place column drums in place and to know how often key components had to be replaced or failed.

One reason I have mentioned carts here is that it might be suggested that the chariot in the first part of Parmenides' poem is an example of good machine technology as it goes swiftly and gets to its destination. However, on closer examination this chariot is subject to rapid wear in key parts and failure is imminent. Parmenides Fr. 1, 6–8 tells us that:

> *Axōn d' en chnoiēisin hiei suringos autēn aithomenos (doios gar epeigeto dinōtoisin kuklois amphoterōthen)*
>
> The axle glowing in the sockets, gave out a shrill whistle (for it was hard pressed by two well turned wheels).

If the axle is glowing in its sockets then it is overheating, wearing rapidly and will fail soon. A second indication of this is the shrill sound made by the axle. Remarkably little has changed here in vehicle diagnostics. The first signs of wheel bearing failure in a modern car is a shrill whistling noise from the bearing and overheating. To check the diagnosis, jack up the vehicle, place your hands on opposite sides of the road wheel pushing with one and pulling with the other to see if there is excess movement on the bearing. I would expect Parmenides' chariot to fail an MOT (British annual vehicle roadworthiness test) on this criterion. On translation for this passage, *aithomenos* actually means burn or blaze but the weaker 'glowing' seems appropriate. Even if we take this poetically rather than literally, the axle will still be overheating. The noise made, *suringos*, can mean a shepherd's pipe, so a pleasing musical sound, or a cat-call or shrill whistle. Given the overheated nature of the axle shrill whistle seems appropriate, but even a musical whistle would be indicative of rapid wear. The axle is *epeigeto* 'hard pressed' by the wheels. Another possibility is 'urged on' but 'hard pressed' gives a stronger sense of the axle being pushed to its limits, which I think is proper given that Fr. 1 line 5 has the horses straining to pull the chariot, *harma titainousai*. So even in poetry, in an imaginary journey to meet a goddess who will discuss metaphysics and ontology, there is still a recognition that a Greek *mēchanē* would wear out rapidly.

One reply here is that of course the early atomists did not get the machine analogy idea from these examples, which clearly do not give the regularity or reliability required. The onus would then be to specify which ancient Greek *mēchanē* did give rise to any machine analogy. There was none suitable for this purpose. Alternatively, one might argue that the machine analogy arose before technology was advanced enough to generate suitable machines. Here again we come to the issue of why such an idea would arise rather than why not. It is very easy to treat the machine analogy and the mechanical view more generally as natural, obvious or in a sense transparent and so ask why it would not have been adopted. If we look across the many cultures of ancient science (Babylonian, Egyptian, Chinese, Indian etc.) we do not see the easy emergence of this supposedly natural idea. There is any 'Platonic form' of the machine analogy or the mechanical philosophy, such that it might be easily thought up even in the absence of suitable machines. One thing I have tried to point out in this book is that both come in many forms and it is by no means clear that there is a single correct mechanical philosophy or machine analogy.[29] I would also emphasize that the mechanical philosophy is long dead. Seventeenth-century mechanical philosophers may have thought in terms of 'levers, springs, pulleys, wheels, gears' as explanations for everything, including living entities, but modern science does not and has not for a long time. One does not have to be a technological determinist to believe that sufficient sophistication in the construction of machines is required before there can be the idea that the world can be likened to a machine.

## Divine mechanism?

Dijksterhuis has commented that:

> This use of the term mechanistic does not imply any connexion with the concept of a machine. Indeed, when speaking of a machine, we think of a consciously designed implement with which a clearly defined object is achieved, and its mechanical, soulless character is due merely to the fact that it can be left to itself, provided the requisite motive power is supplied. This however, is in every respect the opposite of the Democritean world-picture. The term mechanistic is rather intended to convey that the motions of the atoms are governed by the laws of a science of mechanics which recognizes no forces beyond those exerted during the mutual contact of the bodies.[30]

On one point I entirely agree with Dijksterhuis here, that the machine analogy is 'in every respect the opposite of the Democritean world-picture'. It is important to take 'world' in the sense of universe rather than cosmos. The universe for the early atomists is a chaos of atoms in motion, from which *cosmoi* are generated by chance. If the universe functioned in the manner of a machine, this would invite the question of why it does so. Who has designed and made this contrivance and for what purpose? The early atomists though lack a creator god or any reason why the universe should function like a machine.

There is an important contrast here with the mechanical philosophies of the seventeenth century, which were underpinned by the idea of the Christian god. These philosophies were often one-world philosophies in that there was no need to explain the order of our cosmos by making it one of an infinite array of *cosmoi* that have been generated by chance. The omnipotent, omniscient Christian god could make the appropriate choices for the one cosmos (particle shapes, sizes, distribution etc.), and the order of our cosmos can be explained with reference to that god. The cosmos can be machinelike because the Christian god has decreed that it should be so.

## Application of mathematical mechanics?

The following passage from Seneca *Natural Questions* V, 2 has been discussed in relation to mechanics in the early atomists:

> Democritus says that when in an empty space there are many small corpuscles, which he calls atoms, then there is wind. On the contrary, the air is placid and static when in a large space there are few small corpuscles. For example, when there are not many people in the market or a street, they can walk without tumult, but when a crowd comes together in a small place, they bump into each other and there is a commotion. The same thing happens in the space which surrounds us. When many bodies fill a small space, they of necessity bump and push each other and are knocked back, entwined and compressed. Winds are produced from this, particles jostling with each other and pressing hard for a long time begin to move in one direction. When only a few bodies move in much space, they cannot bump into one another or be impelled.

It is important to recognize here that the behaviour of the particles is being modelled on the behaviour of humans, not on any *mēchanē*. The main issue, as discussed by several commentators, is whether the behaviour of the particle accords with Newton's first law of motion, that 'Every object in a state of uniform motion tends to remain in that state of motion unless an external force is applied to it', though I would also question whether there is a breach of the second and third laws, 'The relationship between an object's mass m, its acceleration a, and the applied force F is F = ma' and 'For every action there is an equal and opposite reaction'. According to Balme here:

> The extra jostling does not merely determine them to move in the same direction: it also generates momentum, just as it excites people in a crowd. The more jostling, the more speed: *collision generates motion.*

Does this breach Newton's first law? If collisions generate motion, which seems the clear import of this passage, then yes it does.

Balme also notes that Newton's first law was not commonly held by those after Leucippus and Democritus, indeed many thought that motion could peter out.[31] However, Simplicius tells us that the atoms are always in motion.[32] Parallel to the consideration that like to like would have already caused everything to come together over an infinite amount of past time, so a petering out of motion would have caused a total standstill by now if there has been an infinite amount of past time. One possibility here is that there is both the generation of motion through collision and that motion peters out, but that they balance each other out. I am very doubtful about this solution, along the same lines as some of my doubts about Taylor's forces. There are many possibilities for an imbalance here and a perfect balance cannot be explained either by there being a designer or there being a multiplicity of universes.

There is also an important historiographical issue about how we approach the atomists, and indeed how we approach ideas on motion in any of the ancients. It is very tempting to think of them looking forwards and trying to see them as anticipators or progenitors of ideas that are thought to be progressive. It is also very tempting to read back later ideas into their thought, or try to see them as addressing later problems. Alternatively, we can view them looking backwards to the sort of problems they were actually trying to solve, rather than the problems we would perhaps like them to be trying to solve.

A related issue here is the early atomists conception of the vacuum. Sedley has distinguished between the ideas of void as empty Newtonian space containing the atoms and the idea of atoms (what is, or the full) and voids (what is not, or the empty) on an equal footing in space.[33] The modernizing view, which would make mathematization easier for Leucippus and Democritus and make them more continuous with seventeenth-century atomism is clearly the first view of atoms and void. However, I am very much inclined to support atoms and voids in space view. There is clearly a parity between what is and what is not, which is why I prefer to use that terminology rather than atoms and void. It also makes their reply to Parmenides more coherent. Parmenides did not deny that what exists is somewhere, but did deny that there could be somewhere without what exists.[34] So the early atomists do not need to assert that place exists, but do need to assert that what is not exists in the sense that it can occupy a place.

## Aristotle and change

Were the early Greeks concerned with the quantification of motion? This is important with Aristotle on motion and change. Debate here used to centre around how close Aristotle's supposed dynamics were to those of Newton, and what prevented Aristotle getting any further.[35] More recent work by Wardy,[36] Lloyd[37] and Gregory[38] has taken a different historiographical line that has emphasized the context of Aristotle's comments on motion. Attempts to see these as general laws are for Lloyd 'in some respects clearly, and in others very probably, an overinterpretation',[39] while Wardy urges a 'minimalist' interpretation and attacks the 'Whiggism' associated with the older view.[40] I have argued that one of Aristotle's projects is to try to solve the problems of change bequeathed by Parmenides and Zeno. This is a broad project encompassing many types of change and we should not construe his goal as an attempt to found a mathematical science of bodies in motion. Did Aristotle have an integrated theory of force, mass and motion that could be considered to be dynamics? His comments are scattered through the *Physics* and *De Caelo*, and at no point did he present his relevant views as a whole.[41] Aristotle was quite aware that bodies in free fall move more quickly as they approach the ground, and so accelerate.[42] However, he made no attempt to synthesize this insight with his other views or to develop a theory of acceleration. He is also slack in his usage of key terms, such as *ischus*, *dunamis* and *rhope*,[43] and one might contrast the approach of the *Metaphysics* to defining key philosophical terms.[44] Aristotle's remarks on motion do not appear as conclusions but as premises where he is oriented to generating anti-infinity and anti-void conclusions.[45] There are several examples where Aristotle is quite happy to talk of *alloiosis* using just greater than, equal to and less than. From elsewhere in the *Physics*:

> Let the greater *dunamis* always be the one which accomplishes the same act in a shorter time, whether that be heating, sweetening, throwing or any sort of change.[46]

Aristotle's comments often seem to be pitched at the wrong level, appearing to be concerned with change in a more general sense. Was Aristotle incompetent at constructing a dynamics? Or did he have a more fundamental purpose in mind, that of giving an account of change that avoided the problems raised by Parmenides and Zeno? Certainly the latter seems to fit better with what Aristotle actually says when we read his works as wholes rather than select out certain passages. So too Leucippus and Democritus. They are best seen as reacting to Parmenides with important new ideas in an ancient Greek context rather than viewed with the end point of seventeenth-century mechanical philosophy in mind.

## Early atomists and motion

It is questionable whether the preservation or generation of motion were issues for Leucippus and Democritus. It is not clear whether, in modern terms, they considered the collisions of atoms to be 'perfectly elastic', that is, there is a coefficient of restitution of one such that motion is neither gained nor lost in a collision. There is another possibility that leads to an interesting historiographical issue. The early atomists might say yes, we believe that motion peters out, here is an invariant function that precisely describes that petering. Yes, there is energy gained in collisions, here is an invariant function that precisely describes that energy gain. Would that be an application of the mathematical science of mechanics to the particles or not? Or does the application of the mathematical science of mechanics have to be the application of the correct mathematical science of mechanics in order to count? If the latter, there are two difficulties. Descartes is notorious for stating that he had derived six laws of particle interaction *a priori* and with certainty, but five of them are wrong. Does Descartes then not count as a mechanist? Here is important news for those who do not know. Newton's physics is generally a good approximation for the behaviour of slow-moving macro objects, but it is not correct. For micro objects quantum mechanics is an important improvement; for objects moving rapidly (approaching the speed of light) relativity is an important improvement. Newton's formula for gravity is reasonable as an approximation for weak gravitational fields; general relativity much better in strong fields.[47] Even $F = ma$ is not correct (there is a corresponding but different relativistic formula). So is Newton's system mechanistic or not? I would drop the idea that the application of the mathematical science of mechanics has to be the application of the correct mathematical science of mechanics in order to count. It seems implicit in some writing on the topic though that we are talking of the application of a correct mathematical science of mechanics.

## Historical application of mathematics?

As a simple matter of historical fact, as far as we are aware, Leucippus and Democritus did not apply any mathematical mechanics to their particles. In this sense, their view was not mechanical. If we ask whether mathematical mechanics could be applied to their view, then that question has some different senses. Could a contemporary mathematical mechanics have been incorporated in their view? No, as there is no evidence of the existence of such a discipline at this stage. As we have seen Aristotle, some time after Leucippus and Democritus, did not have many of the key concepts for a mathematical science of motion. There is also a more fundamental issue, which is the mathematization of nature. Did the early Greeks conceive of nature in such a way that mathematics was applicable to it in the sense required for a mathematical science of motion? That is at least questionable. Some Pythagoreans may have held the view that everything consisted of number, but I do not see that helps a great deal. One important contrast here is that where the early atomists say *ou mallon* in relation to atomic shapes and do not apply number to the atoms, Plato is very precise in applying mathematics. Again, with the early atomists we should be asking why they should be applying a mathematical mechanics, or indeed numbers at all, to their atoms rather than why not. With Plato, I have argued elsewhere that the reason he applies numbers to his basic triangles is so that his demiurge can make a choice of the best triangles for the cosmos, not because he wants to found a mathematical mechanics.[48]

Can we 'retrofit' a mathematical science of mechanics to the early atomists? I have phrased this in a slightly pejorative manner as there are considerable perils of anachronism involved in such an approach. If we only look at the similarities of early atomism with its seventeenth-century counterpart, it is easy to assume we can retrofit, and of course tempting to do so, as in one sense this would be a very positive thing to say. However, we need to be suspicious of such an approach and recognize the differences as well, especially the import of the *ou mallon* approach of the early atomists. More controversially I will question whether the system of Leucippus and Democritus is deterministic in the sense that early modern mechanical philosophies claimed it to be. It has generally been assumed that the early atomists' system was deterministic, but in what follows I raise some difficulties for that view.[49]

## Laplace's demon?

Is the system of the early atomists mechanistic in the sense of being amenable to Laplace's demon? That is, if everything about particles (position, velocity, mass, shape) is known at any one moment, can all past and all future states then be calculated? The original Laplace is:

> We may regard the present state of the universe as the effect of its past and the cause of its future. An intellect which at a certain moment would know all forces that set nature in motion, and all positions of all items of which nature is composed, if this intellect were also vast enough to submit these data to analysis, it would embrace in a single formula the movements of the greatest bodies of the universe and those of the tiniest atom; for such an intellect nothing would be uncertain and the future just like the past would be present before its eyes.[50]

The common assumption is that the system of the early atomists is indeed amenable to Laplace's Demon. I disagree, as I think there is a fundamental aspect of early atomist thought that means that the application of any mathematical science of mechanics is problematic, and that their system does not conform to Laplace's Demon and does not do so for interesting reasons.

## Reply to Parmenides

Parmenides had a brutally simple ontology. What is, is. What is not, is not. Out of this he concludes that what is, is unitary, motionless and unchanging. The early atomist reply is also well known. There is a multiplicity of atoms, which are *atomos*, 'uncuttable', and they in some way assert the existence of not being, allowing the atoms to move. The atoms do not change in themselves, but their configurations do, and this is what we perceive as change at the macro level. On the question of the shapes of the atoms, Simplicius tells us that:

> Leucippus supposed there to be an infinite (*apeira*) number of atoms that are always in motion and have an infinite (*apeiron*) number of shapes on the grounds that nothing is this rather than such (*dia to mēden mallon toiouton ē toiouton einai*).[51]

I take this reply to be of fundamental importance for the early atomists. Aristotle's evidence suggests that this *ou mallon* approach was taken to atomic sizes as well.[52] Parmenides' view in Fragment 8 is that:

> It is complete, from all directions like the bulk of a well-rounded sphere, equivalent in all ways from the centre. For it must not be any larger or any smaller here or there.[53]

As soon as we move away from that, then there is need for some justification of the new distribution. The early atomists assert that there is a new distribution, in that there are all sorts of shapes of atoms, but in terms of justification simply say *ou mallon*, effectively that there is no preferred distribution so there are many different shapes of atoms. It is no surprise that we do not find *ou mallon* arguments in cosmogonical contexts prior to Leucippus and Democritus (no trace in Homer, Hesiod, Anaximander, Xenophanes, Heraclitus etc.) as they are a specific reaction to a Parmenidean issue. I have argued elsewhere that cosmos formation is *ou mallon* for the early atomists as well with respect to space and time.[54] So there are no preferred times for cosmos formation and no preferred places to cosmos formation. Again, this can be seen in relation to Parmenides. Parmenides says that:

> It never was nor will be, as it is now, all alike,
> one and continuous. What birth will you seek for it?
> In what way, from what source did it grow? I will not allow you
> to think or say from not being, for it is not to be thought or said
> that it is not; and what necessity would have driven it
> later rather than sooner, beginning from nothing, to grow?[55]

One can read this as asserting that there is no reason to prefer any one instant to another for cosmos formation, though of course the formulation is more general and applies to all change. One can also read Parmenides Fragment 8 above as posing a similar problem about where in a homogenous whole cosmos formation might begin.[56] There is considerable support for the idea that vortex formation is random in the doxography. Simplicius tells us that:

> Democritus says that a vortex of all shapes is separated off from the all (how or by what cause he does not say), it appears that this occurs spontaneously or by chance.[57]

We have to be careful with 'chance' here, as the contrast was often between teleology and what we would consider to be a straightforwardly causal account rather than chance, but the 'spontaneous' here is suggestive that this is a genuine chance occurrence. As we saw above with the passage from Pseudo-Plutarch, vortex formation is not a matter of like to like attraction but rather 'unprovidential, chance, continuous and extremely rapid motion' and the gathering together of a variety of atomic shapes and sizes.[58]

This leads us to the key question in relation to Laplace's Demon. What of the distribution of atoms in the void? There is good reason to believe this is *ou mallon*. Plutarch says that:

> He said that thing exists no more than nothing, 'thing' being the name of body and 'nothing' of void, the latter having a nature and substance of its own.[59]

Here I follow Barnes' paraphrase that:

> There is no more reason for there to be occupied than for there to be unoccupied areas of space.[60]

So the distributions of atoms in void is *ou mallon*. That, on my reading of the replies of the early atomists to some of the issues raised by Parmenides is no surprise and is fully in tune with the rest of their thinking. Although there is no specific evidence on this, I would suggest that the motions of the atoms are also *ou mallon* in magnitude and direction. This has significant implications for the possibility of applying a mathematical science of mechanics to the motions of the atoms. Can such a science be applied if the positions, and quite possibly the motions as well are *ou mallon*? Certainly there is an epistemological issue here. If we take it that the atoms cannot be perceived by humans, there is no empirical means of applying the mathematics and there can be no *a priori* means if positions and motions are genuinely *ou mallon*. We need to take this issue in conjunction with the question of whether vortex formation is *ou mallon* with respect to space and time. If it is genuinely *ou mallon*, then here are future states of the system, which cannot be predicted. In this sense the system is not deterministic and does not conform to Laplace's Demon. It is of course tempting to read determinism into the early atomists as a precursor of the strongly deterministic mechanical philosophies of the seventeenth century and beyond. I doubt that, in formulating a reply to Parmenides it was an important issue for them though. As ever, I would ask why it would be rather than why it would not be.

For the relation of Leucippus and Democritus to Parmenides, Parmenides Fr. 4 is very interesting:

> You will not cut off (*apotmēxei*) what is from holding fast (*echesthai*) to what is. It does not disperse itself in every way and everywhere according to order nor does it set itself together.[61]

This is precisely what Leucippus and Democritus do, however. If we go back to the Diogenes Laertius passage on cosmogony, atoms are cut off (*apotomēn*) from each other, they are dispersed and do come together. Granted the cosmogonic sense of *apotomēn* here, where atoms are cut off from each other to form a vortex, is different from Parmenides metaphysical sense of what is being cut into pieces, but the use of *apotomēn* may well be an allusion to Parmenides insisting that atoms can be cut off from each other in the void and that presupposes a metaphysical cutting as well. The use of *apotomēn* here has puzzled scholars, but if it is an allusion to Parmenides, in a place where there is a denial of key Parmenidean ideas, that would make sense.

## Laplacian disconnections

There are further significant disconnections with the ideal that Laplace sets out. One important sentence is:

An intellect which at a certain moment would know all forces that set nature in motion.[62]

The early atomists though did not envisage a beginning to the universe where nature is set in motion. There is no first state for them. I have significant doubts that Leucippus and Democritus understand force in the way that would be required for Laplace's demon. There is also the question of the nature of this intellect. As there are an infinite number of atoms, this may well have to be an infinite intellect. To Laplace, firmly rooted in a Christian tradition of an omnipotent and omniscient god the idea of an intellect that would be capable of comprehending and calculating on this sort of scale would come relatively naturally. However, we find nothing of this sort among the early Greeks and certainly nothing of this sort in the early atomists. One can of course define determinism in other ways to Laplace, but this case is interesting in bringing out some of the difficulties of applying modern concerns to ancient thinkers.

## Chance and necessity

How does this discussion of *ou mallon* fit with Leucippus Fr. 2, which allegedly says that everything happens by necessity and nothing happens by chance? To give this fragment its full context:

> Democritus says everything happens by necessity. This is the same as fate, justice, providence and cosmos making (*kosmopoion*). Leucippus says that everything happens by necessity, which is the same as fate. He says in his *On Mind*, 'Nothing happens at random (*matēn*),[63] but everything for a reason and by necessity.'[64]

It is the *ou mallon* distribution and motions of atoms in the void that give rise to *ou mallon* times and places of vortex formation. I do not attribute a theory involving chance to Leucippus and Democritus. However, I do think there is an interesting contrast between what happens in the void and what happens in vortices. In a centrifuge, the distribution and motion of what is in the fluid does not matter, it will separate the contents to the same result. So too, I suggest, with the vortices of Leucippus and Democritus. The position and motion of the atoms does not matter, a similar like to like sorting will occur. We get different cosmoi dependent on the number and shape of the constituent atoms. In this sense, what happens after a vortex forms is necessary. Position and motion does matter for what happens outside the vortex, but these are *ou mallon* and vortex formation is *ou mallon* with respect to time and place. This would agree with the evidence of Diogenes Laertius, who says that for Democritus:

> Everything occurs by necessity, the vortex being the cause for the coming into being of all things, and this he calls necessity.[65]

We have to read the first 'everything' here in a slightly restricted way as meaning everything in the cosmos (or perhaps everything in any cosmos) rather than everything in the universe. That though seems justified by the second clause, where the vortex is the cause for everything coming to be. In *Physics* II, 4 Aristotle contrasts the chance formation of vortices with the subsequent formation of animals and plants for them, which he says happens 'by nature' and not by chance.[66] Simplicius backs Aristotle on this point, and says that the 'ancient theory which denies chance' refers to Democritus, who made use of chance when explaining the formation of *cosmoi*, but then says that Democritus did not use chance to explain anything subsequent to cosmos formation, always citing normal causes.[67]

It is easy to see how the doxographers could have interpreted Leucippus and Democritus as having a theory involving chance.[68] What we get in the doxography then depends on what the doxographers think about the nature of chance and necessity. Certainly there are those who emphasize the role of chance and they are usually hostile to Leucippus and Democritus.[69] The move away from universal determinism in Leucippus and Democritus may seem quite radical, but it is clear that if the positions of what is in what is not are *ou mallon*, and so cosmos formation is *ou mallon* with respect to space and time, then determinism in the sense specific by Laplace cannot hold for them.

## The rejection of determinism

One objection to this rejection of determinism for Leucippus and Democritus might be who are Epicurus and Lucretius objecting to when they postulate an atomic swerve? As Sedley has commented:

> Epicurus inherited Democritus' atomic system, but modified it in a number of respects. In particular, he so vehemently objected to its rigidly deterministic laws as to postulate a minimal 'swerve'.

So Epicurus and Lucretius allow for some freedom in human cognition by postulating the atomic swerve. Here we must once again distinguish what happens in vortices and *cosmoi* and what happens outside of them. Outside of the vortices, where the like to like principle does not operate, the *ou mallon* considerations mean that future states, in particular vortex formation, are not predictable. However, inside the vortices, where like to like does operate, then as we have seen things happen by necessity. A parallel. If we dip a test tube blindly into a murky, non-homogenous puddle of water in a field, the contents of that tube will in one sense be random. When the test tube is run through a centrifuge, of necessity the centrifuge separates out the components from the puddle of water. As humans exist only in the *cosmoi* generated by vortices, what happens to them, and ultimately their thoughts as well would be necessitated, hence the objection from Epicurus and Lucretius.

One might also be concerned about the following tension. The *ou mallon* consideration, when applied to atomic shapes, appears to generate infinite shapes of atoms, usually taken to mean that all shapes of atoms are instantiated. However, when the *ou mallon* consideration is applied to the distribution of the atoms, it does not generate atoms in every place, but a distribution of atoms. Aristotle's comment in the *Physics* seems particularly pertinent:

> Why should there be void here rather (*mallon*) than there? If an entity is in one place, should it not be in all places?[70]

Previously I have argued that:

> The two uses of *ou mallon* are not identical but are related. For shapes and sizes we get all shapes and sizes of atoms, but we do not get vortices forming at all places and at all times. Perhaps this difference is not so great though in that if the universe does exist for an infinite amount of time, then ultimately all places will be sites for vortex/cosmos formation, though not all at a single moment of time. So too in an infinitely large void with an infinite amount of matter, there will be vortex/cosmos formation at all times, though not in all places at a single time. So Leucippus and Democritus do treat space and time slightly differently from size and shape in respect of *ou mallon* considerations, but perhaps justifiably so.[71]

There is another solution, though, which is radical and intriguing. In the Simplicius passage on shapes and *ou mallon*, the phrase usually translated as 'infinite in number' is *apeiron to plēthos*. What, though, if we translate that as unlimited in number? There would then be no limit to the number of shapes of atoms, but it might well be the case that not all shapes are instantiated. One can do the same thing for size as well. Then the *ou mallon* consideration would work in the same way for the shape and size of atoms as for the distribution of atoms and for the times and places of vortex formation. A further implication of this if we are going to read *apeiros* as unlimited rather than infinite for Leucippus and Democritus would be that instead of an infinite number of atoms in an infinite space there would be an unlimited number of atoms in an unlimited space.

This in some ways would make a very interesting reply to Parmenides. Parmenides in several places emphasizes the importance of *peras*, limit, and one might argue that the idea of limitation runs through Fr. 8.[72] The early atomist reply then might be seen as denying limit where they see that as appropriate rather than asserting infinity. Parmenides can be seen as promoting sufficient reason considerations, and one can argue he does that with the shape, number and homogeneity of his entity as well as the issues concerning time and place of cosmos formation discussed above. If so, then this would make Leucippus and Democritus' use of *ou mallon* and unlimited more radically anti-sufficient reason. Do we overly modernize Leucippus and Democritus by taking *apeiros* in relation to them to mean infinite?

One objection to consider here, though, is Aristotle *On Democritus* from Simplicius *De Caelo* 295, 5, which says that for Democritus there are atoms of:

> All sorts of forms and all sorts of shapes and differences in size (*pantoias morphas kai schēmata pantoia kai kata megethos diasphoras*).

The question here is the precise meaning of *pantoias*. Does it imply that all shapes are instantiated or that a wide variety of, but not all possible shapes are instantiated? Aristotle's other uses of *pantoias* would incline one to the latter. He uses this only in *Nicomachean Ethics*. 1100a5–6 has 'many changes and all kinds (*pantoiai*) of chance occur in life', 1101a24–5 has 'Events occur which are numerous and admit of all kinds (*pantoias*) of difference', 1178a12 has 'all sorts of manners of action', and 1164b28–30 has examples that are 'many and admit of all sorts (*pantoias*) of differences of smallness, largeness, goodness and necessity', each of which suggest we actually get some of an array of possibilities and not all possibilities. So I would take this passage as supporting the idea of unlimited rather than infinite shapes and sizes of atoms. Aristotle may be quoting or paraphrasing Leucippus and Democritus here.

The rejection of determinism for Leucippus and Democritus may seem a radical step but once the historiographical decision is made to take the *ou mallon* considerations seriously and as critical to Leucippus and Democritus, then it is an inevitable conclusion. The distinction between what happens inside and outside of vortices must be born in mind. Outside of the vortices, the distribution of atoms is *ou mallon* as are the time and places of vortex formation. Inside the vortices the like to like principle operates and we have a necessity that will apply to humans.

## The seventeenth century and Plato?

Plato has an interesting critique of his predecessors, which can be taken as a confirmation of early atomist ideas on atomic shape. *Timaeus* 53d4–54a6 says that:

> This we hypothesize as the principle of fire and of the other bodies ... but the principles of these which are higher are known only to God and whoever is friendly to him. It is necessary to give an account of the nature of the four best (*kallista*) bodies, different to each other, with some able to be produced out of the others by dissolution ... We must be eager then to bring together the best (*kallei*) four types of body, and to state that we have adequately grasped the nature of these bodies. Of the two triangles the isosceles has one nature, the scalene an unlimited number. Of this unlimited number we must select the best (*kalliston*), if we intend to begin in the proper manner. If someone has singled out anything better (*kallion*) for the construction of these bodies, his victory will be that of a friend rather than an enemy. We shall pass over the many (*tōn pollōn*) and postulate the best (*kalliston*) triangles.

The last line here, passing over the many in favour of the best, can be taken as a critique of Leucippus and Democritus' *ou mallon* view of atomic shape. Seventeenth-century atomism does not have this issue, as the Christian god could select appropriate shapes for the atoms. So we find Robert Boyle telling us that:

> The provident demiourgos wisely suited the fabric of the parts to the uses that were to be made of them.[73]

We can also find Newton saying:

> It seems probable to me that God in the beginning formed matter into solid, massy, hard, impenetrable movable particles, of such sizes and figures and with such other properties and in such proportion in space, as most conduced to the end for which he formed them.[74]

When there is a Platonic demiurge or a Christian god to order the atoms, then there is no longer a need for *ou mallon* considerations. We should be cognisant of the dissimilarities as well as the similarities between early atomism and the mechanical philosophies of the seventeenth century, and we should be careful not to privilege the similarities. With Plato, we often have the reverse situation, especially if commentators are hostile to or dismissive of Plato's views on the natural world, such that we need to be conscious of the similarities as well as the differences with later views and not privilege the differences.

## Conclusion

Like to like in the early atomists is a sorting principle that operates in vortices but not elsewhere, and is not a force that acts at a distance. The early atomists had a physical ontology of what is – the atoms – and what is not – the void. They were anti-teleological and, contrary to some commentators, there was a target for this anti-teleology in the *kubernan* and *kratein* traditions.[75] The early atomists were also strongly reductionist. However, they were not mechanists. They did not apply machine analogies, but did use meteorological, biological, human, agricultural and maritime analogies. Indeed, it is doubtful that there were any meaningful machine analogies they could apply at this stage of technological development. Certainly there is nothing like the clockwork analogy or the pneumatic analogies that were so important for seventeenth-century mechanical philosophies. They were not mechanists in the sense of an application of a mathematical science of motion. As a matter of historical fact, they made no such application and indeed it is again doubtful that there was any meaningful mathematical science of motion at this stage. Contrary to the view taken by many commentators, such a mathematical science of motion cannot be 'retrofitted' to the system of the early atomists. The positions, and most probably the motions too of the atoms, as well as their shapes and sizes, are *ou mallon*, so they cannot be treated mathematically. The time and place of vortex formation is also *ou mallon*, with the result that the system is not deterministic in the sense specified by Laplace's Demon. One can see why on some historiographies mechanism and determinism have been attributed to Leucippus and Democritus, but it is critical that we recognize the role of *ou mallon* as part of an interesting, consistent and coherent response to Parmenides on multiplicity, change and cosmos formation. It is also important to ask why the early atomists would have been mechanists, rather than exclusively to ask why not. There are of course important similarities between the early atomists and some of the mechanical philosophies of the seventeenth century and beyond. There are also important dissimilarities, notably in the role that a Christian god can fulfill in setting shapes, sizes, positions and motions of particles. In the previous chapter I argued that it is important to recognize the reversal of a modern prejudice in the ancient world, that intelligence rather than mechanism was the key paradigm for regularity. Here it is important to recognize, contrary to some scholars, that analogies used by many early Greeks were strong rather than weak,[76] and that machines, such as Parmenides' chariot, would have provided a poor analogy for natural regularities.

8

# The Hippocratic Authors

The Hippocratic authors are another interesting case, and again there are debates about how great an affinity they have to modern ideas, what they have to say about nature and disease and to what extent their ideas ought to be construed as mechanical. They had a great deal to say about *phusis*, both in the sense of things, and in particular diseases, having a *phusis* and behaving *kata phusin*, according to nature or senses in which they may be *para phusin*, contrary to nature. They also made use of *kubernan* in a key cosmological passage and made abundant use of *kratein*. They made use of a like to like principle and also used the macrocosm/microcosm analogy. I reject any sharp division between a philosophical tradition and a medical tradition, or even a *peri phusis* tradition and a medical tradition. Some medical writers addressed philosophical issues and some discussed how to enquire into nature, while some philosophers discussed medical issues.

## Epilepsy and disease

There has been considerable debate about epilepsy in *On the Sacred Disease*. Contrary to how epilepsy was previously considered, did it offer an entirely natural conception of the disease and its treatment? Scholars have been divided on this issue.[1] Babylonian sources treated epilepsy as inflicted by the gods, indeed they treated all diseases in the same manner.[2] Early Christian sources too treated epilepsy in terms of possession by a devil.[3] That diseases were caused by the gods was also prominent in Homer and Hesiod, for example, the plague of *Iliad* I,[4] Pandora's jar in *Works and Days* and Zeus punishing a whole city with famine and plague in *Theogony* as we have seen.[5] So epilepsy, and disease more generally, was attributed to the actions of the gods prior to the Hippocratics. Epilepsy might be thought to be a difficult and important case for natural explanation. As Temkin comments:

> Showing both physical and psychical symptoms, epilepsy more than any other disease was open to interpretation both as a physiological process and as the effect of spiritual influences.[6]

The symptoms of epilepsy can be quite alarming, and one can see how someone in an epileptic fit could easily be thought to have been affected by the gods.

## The sacred disease and nature

The opening passage of the Hippocratic *On the Sacred Disease* is:

> Concerning the disease which is called 'sacred'. In my view it is no more divine or sacred than any other disease, but has a nature and a definite cause (*alla phusin men echei kai prophasin*). Men have called it divine due to their inexperience and great wonder, it being unlike other diseases.

The start of *On the Sacred Disease* V says something similar:

> This disease in my opinion is no more divine than the rest, but it has a nature (*phusin*) as do other diseases and each occurs due to a definite cause (*prophasin*).

So it is clear that the supposed sacred disease has a *phusis*, has a definite cause (*prophasis*) and is no more sacred than any other disease. The next section of *On the Sacred Disease* begins:

> In my opinion the first men to consider this disease to be sacred were like those we now call mages, purifiers, vagabonds and quacks. These people claim for themselves great piety and much knowledge. They used the divine as a cloak, having no treatment or anything useful to offer, and in order that their lack of knowledge should not be evident, they called this condition sacred.[7]

*On the Sacred Disease* XVI further tells us that:

> This disease is born and grows from that which enters and leaves (the body), it is no more intractable than the others, nor is it incurable or unintelligible, and is no more divine than the others.[8]

So it looks, from these passages, that *On the Sacred Disease* gives an entirely natural account of the cause, nature and proper treatment of epilepsy. One might also argue that epilepsy is targeted because it is a difficult case.

## The issue

However, matters are not quite so simple. The final section of *On the Sacred Disease* opens with:

The so-called sacred disease is produced by the same causes as other diseases, from what enters and leaves the body, from cold, sun and the changing winds which are never resting. These things are divine, such that there is no need to distinguish this disease from the other diseases, they are all divine and they are all human (*alla panta theia kai panta anthrōpina*).

So all diseases are divine and in an important sense *On the Sacred Disease* does not deny the divinity of disease. Does this compromise the idea that each disease has a nature and a natural cause? No, and this passage should very much be seen in context with other passages in *On the Sacred Disease* and some from other Hippocratic works as well. Directly after this passage we are told that:

> Each disease has its own nature (*phusin*) and power (*dunamin*) and none are intractable or untreatable (*ouden aporon... oude amēchanon*).[9]

The closing lines of *On the Sacred Disease* are also significant:

> Anyone who knows how to produce in men dryness or wetness, cold or heat by means of regimen, can cure this disease as well, if he can distinguish the due times for treatment, without needing purifications or magic.[10]

So too *On the Sacred Disease* II, 45 is very specific and programmatic:

> It is the foods that cure or harm, and the power of the god disappears.

On the Sacred Disease XIV also says that:

> This is best seen with cattle who are attacked by the disease, especially goats. They are most commonly seized. If you cut open the head you will find that the brain is wet, full of fluid and foul smelling, so clearly one recognizes that it is not a god which is harming the body, but the disease. So too with humans.[11]

What is important here, and indeed throughout *On the Sacred Disease*, is that while the disease is thought to be equally sacred and divine with other diseases, there is never any sense of there being anything other than entirely natural cause or treatment for the disease.

## Context and targets

It is important here to keep the comments in *On the Sacred Disease* in context and to recognize the targets of these comments. A key target here is those who thought that epilepsy is special in being sacred. This view is attacked throughout

*On the Sacred Disease* as being incoherent. So section V asserts that epilepsy attacks the phlegmatic more than the bilious, yet if the disease were divine it should attack each type equally. The attacks on some types of practitioner are quite clear. *On the Sacred Disease* IV says that:

> They have instituted a mode of treatment which is safe for themselves, namely, by applying purifications and incantations,[12] and enforcing abstinence from baths and many articles of food which are unwholesome to men in diseases ... And they forbid to have a black robe, because black is expressive of death; and to sleep on a goat's skin, or to wear it, and to put one foot upon another, or one hand upon another; for all these things are held to be hindrances to the cure. All these they enjoin with reference to its divinity, as if possessed of more knowledge, and announcing beforehand other causes so that if the person should recover, theirs would be the honour and credit; and if he should die, they would have a certain defence, as if the gods, and not they, were to blame, seeing they had administered nothing either to eat or drink as medicines, nor had overheated him with baths, so as to prove the cause of what had happened.[13]

A further important aspect of *On the Sacred Disease* is its critique of magical practitioners. Critiques of individual, allegedly incompetent magical practitioners had been seen before, but not an assault on magical practitioners as a whole.[14]

> If a human by magic and sacrifice can bring down the moon, eclipse the sun, make storm and good weather, I will not call these things divine, but human, since the ability of the god is overpowered and enslaved by the knowledge of humans.[15]

The Hippocratic author continues:

> But perhaps this is not true and these men, being in need of a living, fashioned and embellished many tales of all types, about many things and about this disease in particular, placing the blame for each form of this condition on some god.[16]

## Other passages

We might also consider two passages from other Hippocratic works. Firstly, from *Airs, Waters, Places*:

> I believe that these conditions are divine and so are all others, none being more divine or human than any other, all are alike and all divine. Each of them has its own nature (*phusin*) and nothing occurs without a natural cause (*phusios*). How, in my view, this disease occurs I will now explain.[17]

As with *On the Sacred Disease*, *Airs, Waters, Places* goes on to give entirely natural explanations of the causes and proper treatment of diseases. The position of *Airs, Waters, Places* is perhaps best encapsulated by the comment at XXII, 53 that:

> As I said earlier, these diseases are divine like the others. Each occurs according to nature (*kata phusin*).

Our second passage is from *On the Art*:

> Under closer examination the spontaneous does not appear, as everything which occurs does so on account of something, and this 'on account of' shows that the spontaneous has no existence and is just a name. Medicine, though, as it acts on account of something and its actions can be predicted has substance as is evident now and always will be evident.[18]

I would not go so far as to associate this with a fully deterministic world view, though one can see the temptation to do that. Jouanna has commented that:

> One of the greatest virtues of the physicians of the Hippocratic Collection is to have stated, in its most universal form, what was later to be called the principle of determinism. All that occurs has a cause. It is in the treatise of The Art that the most theoretical statement of this principle is to be found: 'Indeed, under a close examination spontaneity disappears; for everything that occurs will be found to do so through something [*dia ti*].[19]

Here we must be careful of exactly what we mean by determinism. The Hippocratics would clearly fail the 'Laplace's Demon' test, which we discussed in the previous chapter, but the claim that every disease has an explanation is important.

## Pantheism

If we are prepared to allow such an intellectual space for early Greek thinkers, then the resolution to the issue of diseases being both divine and natural for the Hippocratics is straightforward. The Hippocratics were pantheists. So everything was divine, and the divine was everything. No disease will be any more divine than any other disease, all will be divine, human and natural. This may take the Hippocratics out of a linear narrative of the ascent of medical science and lessen their affinities with modern thought, but it does give them a coherent and interesting position. One thing I would emphasize here is the orderliness of the

Hippocratic world. Each disease has a nature and there is no question of any god interfering or intervening with the nature of that disease. There is a proliferation of the term *kata phusin*, 'according to nature', throughout the Hippocratic corpus and at key points so we can expect phenomena to occur in a predictable manner. So too the *On the Art* passage we just looked at would suggest an entirely orderly cosmos for the Hippocratics. What is of greater importance than this discussion about divinity for the Hippocratics are the clear differences with their predecessors both on issues of magic and the role of gods in disease. There is absolutely no sense that individual gods are the cause of diseases or that any appeal to them will help in the treatment of diseases.

## Prayer

Within a pantheistic context, I do not see it as at all problematic that the Hippocratics, or at least the author of *On Regimen*, called for prayer.[20] Here it is important to recognize that there are many types of prayer and that we should not immediately assume that the call is for intercessory prayer, for the gods to intervene and change a situation. Kierkegaard famously took the view that the purpose of prayer is to change oneself, not the mind of any god being prayed to.[21] One can find similar approaches among the early Greeks. So Xenophanes Fragment 1:

> Having poured a libation and prayed to be able to achieve what is right.[22]

Democritus prays, in a deterministic context, to meet good things and to be able to choose the good and the intellectual.[23] In relation to this one might consider the final part of *On Regimen* IV, 87:

> To pray to the gods is good. However, while calling on the gods it is necessary to contribute yourself.[24]

In Homer, of course, it is common to pray to a god in order to try to make them change their mind or to ask them to intercede in human affairs.

A different reason for recommending prayer is the morale of the patient. The doctor's opinion on whether there are gods or whether they can intervene in disease is irrelevant.[25] Asking the patient to pray can be a placebo as far as the doctor is concerned. What matters is that the patient believes in the efficacy of prayer, prays and so has their morale raised, which may help the doctor in effecting a cure. Can a pantheist be pious? Yes, certainly they can. They may hold that there is a properly divine conception of nature and that there is a proper, duly reverential attitude that one should have to divine nature.

## Pantheism and explanation

One objection to this pantheist view is what Hankinson has termed 'The Explanatory Vacuity of Pantheism'.[26] He writes that:

> One might argue, either on positivist or pragmatist grounds, that unless the hypothesis that there is a divine component to things can make some difference, either to what (in principle) verifiable predictions we can make or to our actual practice, then such suppositions are devoid of content.[27]

Certainly one might be concerned about what difference it makes whether the world about us is considered to be divine in the pantheist sense or not. Hankinson's reply to this is that:

> Nature is divine because of its intricacy, regularity and teleological structure; natural processes, in their goal-directedness and their striving for a type of immortality, seek to emulate the divine condition. Yet even if nature is divine in more than merely a metaphorical sense, there is still no point in appealing to it as one might a powerful patron. This sort of divinity, in sharp contrast with the angry, engaged, interventionist gods of epic and tragedy, is not open to plaint or suasion, much less magical coercion.[28]

I would add to this the issue of cosmogony, where if there is steering, an account can be given of how an orderly cosmos can come about. An atheist would not have this option. It is significant that no one in early Greek thought believed that matter on its own could generate a single, well-organized cosmos. Either there was steering that generated a single cosmos, or there was the generation of multiple different *cosmoi* (co-extensively or successively), of which our own cosmos was one instance.

It is also important to recognize that the historiography of the relation of science and religion has shifted significantly in recent years, from the conflict model of Draper and White to the new complexity model.[29] So instead of seeing religion and science always in conflict, the relation is now seen as complex where religion and science may have many different and more complex relationships to each other in different situations.[30] This has helped, for instance, with Empedocles and the question of whether he wrote two works or one, defusing the need to separate the 'religious' and the 'scientific' fragments into two different works. It helps in this case, as we can much more easily accept that someone who thought of nature or the *apeiron* as divine can have a rational and naturalistic view of the world. As ever, this book is seeking to avoid binary categories such as the old approach to the relation of science and religion. There is some interesting intellectual space, which allows their fruitful interaction. The Hippocratic idea that nature is divine does not reduce to primitive or animistic ideas.

## Nature and healing

One further aspect of what a divine nature might be able to do is brought out at *On Regimen* I, 15, which says that:

> Cobblers separate wholes into parts and make wholes from parts, they make sound what is unsound. Humans have the same experience. Wholes are separated into parts and from the bringing together of parts wholes come to be. By cutting and stitching, that which is unsound in men is made sound by the physician's skill. This is physicianship: to relieve pain and to make sound by taking away the problem. Nature herself knows how to accomplish these things (*ē phusis automatē tauta epistatai*). When sitting it is problematic to stand up, when moving it is problematic to come to rest, and in other ways nature (*phusis*) is the same as the physician's skill.

Is the steering ability of nature active here in nature being able to heal? That 'Nature herself knows how to accomplish these things' could be taken as metaphorical, or could well be literal. The verb of knowing may be very significant here, if steering is modelled on the Phaeacian ships, which did indeed know many things. One might also argue parallel to the above comments on cosmology. Can the healing we see in nature be explained without supposing this sort of steering on nature's part? We might also look at the general cosmological context set by *On Regimen* I, 10. Here we may have another explanatory use for the steering function.

## Macrocosm/microcosm and steering fire

*On Regimen*, I, 10 tells us that:

> In a word, everything was arranged (*diekosmēsato*)[31] in the body by fire, in a manner suitable to itself, in imitation of the whole, small to large and large to

small (*mikra pros megala kai megala pros mikra*). The belly is the largest, a reservoir for water dry and moist, giving to all and taking from all, with the power of the sea, nourishing creatures suited to it, killing those not suited. Water cold and moist is arranged around this, a passage for cold breath and warm breath, an imitation of the earth, which alters everything which falls to it. Consuming and increasing it scatters fine water and aethereal creative fire, the visible and the invisible, separating from that which has been set together, in which things are brought into a state of clarity, each according to its destined role. In this fire made for itself three circuits bounded by each other internally and externally. Those towards the hold of the moist have the power of the moon, while those towards the outer circuits, towards the surrounding mass, have the power of the stars and those in the middle are bound internally and externally. The hottest and strongest fire, which controls (*epikrateitai*) all things, manages everything according to nature (*kata phusin*), it is imperceptible to sight or touch. In this are soul, mind, understanding, growth, change, diminution, separation, sleep, waking. This steers all things through all (*panta dia pantos kuberna*) both here and there and is never still.[32]

The Hippocratic author of *On Regimen* goes in for a full macrocosm/microcosm analogy, with large related to small and small related to large (*mikra pros megala kai megala pros mikra*).[33] Here too we see an important application of the steering principle at the cosmological level, as all is steered through all (*panta dia pantos kuberna*). We also have fire controlling (*epikrateitai*) all things and doing so 'according to nature' (*kata phusin*). The term *diacosmein* is also interestingly strong, suggesting a thorough ordering. There are of course interesting relations to Heraclitus here. That macrocosm/microcosm is an important explanatory analogy for at least this Hippocratic author is undeniable. This approach to heat or fire, and to the macrocosm/microcosm analogy is not restricted to *On Regimen*. *On Breaths* XV, discussed in more detail below, has macrocosm and microcosm, though this time with breath as the key constituent. *On Fleshes* II begins with:

> In my opinion that which is called heat (*thermon*) is immortal (*athanatos*) and it apprehends (*noeein*), sees, hears and knows (*eidenai*) all the things that are and all those that will be.

This is also interesting in relation to the attributes of the gods being transferred to *archē* theme of this book. Here heat is described as immortal (*athanatos*) just as the gods are in Homer and Hesiod and heat also has many of the intellectual attributes of the gods as well. That can be seen in the latter part of the *On Regimen* I, 10 passage as well. That is important if there is to be intelligent steering or control.

## Dreams

The macrocosm/microcosm analogy is also put to use for the explanation of dreams. *On Regimen* IV, 89 says that, when dreaming:

> Seeing the sun, moon, heavens and stars clear and undefiled, each in their proper order, is good. This indicates bodily health, but it is necessary to guard this state by following the current regimen. If something contrary to this occurs, this indicates some illness in the body, a strong contrast a strong illness, a weak contrast a mild illness. The stars are in the outer orbit, the sun in the middle, the moon nearest the hold. If one of the stars should appear to be disabled, or to disappear or to be obstructed in its orbit, if this is due to mist or cloud the influence is weak, but if through water or hail, stronger. It indicates that a moist and phlegmatic secretion has been generated in the body and has fallen to the outer orbit.[34]

The foundation here is the macrocosm/microcosm cosmology from *On Regimen* I, 10. So dreams are indicative of state of health, depending on if we see the heavens as clear and undefiled or not.[35] What the mediation is between macrocosm and microcosm is not specified. Dean-Jones has suggested sympathy.[36] That is possible, though I disagree with the view that:

> Here the rationalist account of cause and effect has not entirely superseded the traditional belief in the sympathy of the macrocosm and microcosm.[37]

Such sympathy can be rational but incorrect. If such a sympathy is invariant then what else is there to distinguish it from what is natural?[38] That fire arranges everything *kata phusin* in *On Regimen* I, 10 would suggest invariance. It is slightly odd here to refer to the 'traditional' belief in the sympathy of macrocosm and microcosm, as that analogy was one that was generated by early Greek thought. To set up a succession account of traditional belief to rationality one then has to push back the macrocosm/microcosm analogy so that it becomes 'traditional'.

Hankinson has also suggested that there is a 'physical, causal relationship' here between macrocosm and microcosm.[39] Another possibility is correspondence. If 'everything was arranged in the body by fire' (*On Regimen* I, 10), our dreams may correspond with or be signs of our state of health without there being any causal link, as with the Stoic account of astrology, where the heavens are signs of rather than causes of events. That may be too deterministic for the Hippocratics, but a steering fire might be able to set up dreams as signs without such determinism.

From a modern perspective, this attempt to explain dreams seems odd. In context though it is highly significant. This gives a natural explanation of dreams, where if we look to Homer, we find dreams as visitations from the gods. It may also be significant that these Hippocratic dreams are veridical (there is no question of a 'false' dream here) in sharp contrast to the deceptive dreams that are sent by the gods in Homer.

## Hippocratic use of *kubernan* and *kratein*

The Hippocratic author of *On Regimen* makes a significant cosmological use of *kubernan* and *kratein* as we have seen at I, 10. The other Hippocratic use of *kubernan* is *Ancient Medicine* IX, where we are told that:

> Most doctors, it seems to me, are like bad steersmen (*kubernētēsi*). When they steer (*kubernōntes*) on a calm sea, their errors are not evident. However, when they held in a great storm with a violent wind, it is clear to all humans that their errors have driven the ship to ruin.

So again we have an association of *kubernan* and its cognates with safety and with medicine and health. Clearly here a good doctor should act like a good steersman. There is also considerable Hippocratic use of *kratein*. One significant example is *On Regimen* I, 2:

> I say that it is necessary if someone wishes to write correctly about human regimen first to have knowledge and discernment concerning the nature of the human as a whole. Knowledge of how it is put together from its basic constituents (*ex archēs*) and discernment concerning the parts by which it is controlled (*kekratētai*). If they do not know the synthesis of the basic constituents, they will be unable to know how things come about. If they are ignorant of what controls (*epikrateon*) in the body, this will be insufficient to treat humans.

Basic constituents are fire and water as *On Regimen* I, 3 makes clear, and fire is hot and dry while water is cold and moist as I, 4 makes clear.

> Each in turn controls (*kratei*) or is controlled (*krateitai*) to the greatest or least extent. Neither is capable of controlling completely.

There is an interesting parallel here with Plato, *Republic* 444d:

> To make healthy is to set things up according to nature (*kata phusin*) such that they control (*kratein*) or are controlled by (*kratesithai*) each other, while for

disease things are contrary to nature (*para phusin*) ruled (*archein*) or ruled (*archesthai*) by each other.⁴⁰

These are the most significant uses in cosmological contexts or in the context of control related to the body. One might argue that other uses are less loaded, in the sense of more technically talking about one part of the body controlling another. However, that is still significant as that sort of use of *kratein* cannot be construed as denoting a mechanical relationship.

The Hippocratics also made considerable use of the phrases *kata phusin*, according to nature, and *para phusin*, contrary to nature, again in more instances than I can detail here. These phrases are used in two senses. First, there is the cosmological sense where everything occurs *kata phusin* and nothing is *para phusin*. This gives us an entirely orderly cosmos. Second, *kata phusin* can refer to the healthy state of the human body, such that it is according to the nature of humans to be healthy, and unhealthy states of humans are *para phusin*.

## Justification?

It is remarkable that there are no references to the Muses at all in the Hippocratic corpus. On what sort of authority do the Hippocratic authors then write? *On Ancient Medicine* II has this to say:

> Medicine has everything ready of old, and has discovered a basic principle and method (*kai archē kai hodos heurēmena*), according to which many and excellent discoveries (*heurēmena*) have been discovered (*heurētai*) in a long period of time, and the rest will be discovered (*heurethēsetai*), if someone is adequate, and they hold these discoveries (*heurēmena*) in mind and begin their enquiry from these.

One reason for quoting this passage is the proliferation of *heuriskein*, 'to discover' and its cognates. The author here holds the optimistic view that medicine has discovered a basic principle and method, that many excellent discoveries have been made and the rest will be made.⁴¹ If we dig a little deeper into *On Ancient Medicine*, then that method is clearly an empirical, practical method of observing how different foods affect different people and people suffering from different diseases. There is no mention here of the gods or any medical knowledge being acquired from the gods as there is in Homer and Hesiod, and that is so for the rest of the Hippocratic corpus as well. Earlier I noted that *historia* and *skopein* are absent from Homer and Hesiod, along with any sense of enquiry. *Airs, Waters, Places* starts with:

Whoever wishes to investigate (*zētein*) medicine correctly must do this.

*Airs, Waters, Places* III begins with:

> I will now set out clearly how it is proper to investigate and test (*skopein kai basinazein*) these matters.

That is interesting relative to Homer where testing was *ad hoc*, often based on military or athletic prowess and certainly was not part of a broader, systematic investigation.[42] *Places in Humans* states that:

> The nature (*phusis*) of the body is the beginning for medical knowledge.

*On Fleshes* I begins with the author saying that he will employ assumptions that are generally held, his own and those of other people, as it is necessary to establish a common starting point if one wishes to discourse of the skill of medicine. Directly following this we have the passage from *On Fleshes* II on the immortality and capabilities of heat, which we looked at earlier. *On Crises I* begins with:

> A large part of the skill [of medicine] is to be able correctly to examine thoroughly for yourself (*kataskopeesthai*) what has been written.

*On Crises* goes on to say that one needs to understand thoroughly (*katamanthanein*) the constitution (*katastasin*) of the seasons and of diseases, which are the good factors and which the deadly. The order of critical days also needs to be examined thoroughly (*taxin tōn krismōn ek toutōn skopeesthai*). *On Young Women's Issues*[43] I begins with:

> The start of my thesis is what is eternal (*aieigeneōn*) in medicine. It is not possible to know the nature (*tēn phusin*) of diseases, which it is the task of the skill [of medicine] to discover (*exeurein*), if one does not know that which is partless at the beginning, out of which it is separated.

There is also *Ancient Medicine* XX, which insists that a doctor must know about humans, must know about the investigation of nature, and that it is not enough to think that something is a bad food or drink, one must know how it interacts with the constitution of different humans, all taken as things that can be learnt. So unlike Homer and Hesiod, the Hippocratics rely on making an investigation to generate medical knowledge, knowledge that will be tested in practice and that they are optimistic about acquiring. Medicine is now a discovery of humans, not a gift from the gods, as at *Iliad* XI, 831.[44] They have a conception of what is and what is not *phusis*, and they can distinguish magical practitioners and reject them, not because they are individually incompetent, but because they reject magic entirely. A final difference with Homer and Hesiod here is with prognosis. So *Prognostic* I begins:

> It appears to me a most excellent thing for the physician to cultivate Prognosis; for by foreseeing and foretelling, in the presence of the sick, the present, the past, and the future, and explaining the omissions which patients have been guilty of, he will be the more readily believed to be acquainted with the circumstances of the sick; so that men will have confidence to intrust themselves to such a physician. And he will manage the cure best who has foreseen what is to happen from the present state of matters.[45]

What the Hippocratics are at pains to emphasize is that their prognoses are based on evidence and experience and are not based on divination, magic or any form of visitation from the gods. Both *Iliad* and *Odyssey* make use of seers and foresight,[46] and in both *Iliad* and *Odyssey* they are implicated in attempts to relieve disease.[47] In Hesiod, early on we have a famous passage setting up Hesiod's account in the *Theogony*,[48] when the Muses appear to him and they:

> Breathed into me a divine voice to celebrate things that shall be and things there were aforetime.[49]

The Hippocratics are careful to justify their writings and prognoses by other means than some form of divine revelation either from Gods or Muses. It is also significant that they mention the 'the present, the past, and the future'. A theme in Homer is that gods can, but humans cannot see or think of what has gone before or what will come after.[50] Doubtless telling 'the present, the past, and the future' impressed the patient and gave them faith in the Hippocratic practitioner, but it is also an important move away from Homer for a human to be able to claim to do such things on a systematic basis.

## Hippocratic like to like

We do find a like to like principle in the Hippocratics. Section XVII of *On the Nature of the Child* begins by saying that:

> As the flesh is augmented it is articulated by breath (*pneumatos*) and each of its parts moves like to like (*to homoion es to homoion*), dense with dense, rare with rare and moist with moist. Each moves to its idiosyncratic place according to type and from which it was generated.

*On the Nature of the Child* then goes on to describe an experiment. It reiterates its like to like principle:

> All of these things are articulated by breath. For blowing separates everything according to type (*kata sungenian*).[51]

It then says place earth, sand and lead filings in water in a bladder. Attach a pipe to the bladder and then blow through the pipe. First the ingredients will be mixed with the water, but eventually they will separate out like to like. This can be confirmed by allowing the bladder to dry out and dissecting it. This section of *On the Nature of the Child* ends:

> In the same manner, the seed and the flesh are articulated (*diarthrountai*) and each part moves like to like (*homoion es to homoion*).

In relation to the Sextus passage on like to like in Democritus Lonie comments that:[52]

> This passage suggests a deliberate attempt to give a mechanistic motive cause for a principle which was essentially animistic. Such a motive cause is also provided in the Hippocratic passage, where the movement imparted by the breath is an essential element in the sorting process.[53]

While I agree that the breath is an essential element in the sorting process here, as again there is no evidence that there will be any like to like effect in the absence of breath,[54] Lonie is too quick to assert that the breath gives 'a mechanistic motive cause'. In some early Greek thought (for example, Anaximenes) breath may have a significant role to play in control of the body/cosmos, but even outside of that breath can be seen as something human and animistic rather than something mechanical. With the Sextus passage on Democritus, sieve whirling is an agricultural analogy and waves sorting pebbles is a maritime analogy.[55] There is no reason to suppose an early Greek would think either mechanical, whatever we in the modern world think of these examples, and it is important to note that these analogies are treated on a par with animals flocking together. Like to like may be a little more widespread in the Hippocratics. *On Diseases* IV, 51 has an interesting process, which while not called like to like, has interesting similarities. Just as milk shaken in a container will separate out into heavier and lighter fractions, so when moisture is agitated in the body there is a similar separation. This is a slightly different process from the seeds and winnowing basket in Leucippus and Democritus, but still relies on an agricultural analogy. *On the Nature of Man* 6 is similarly interesting, suggesting that just as a plant will draw to itself what is most akin to it, so will drugs in the human body. Again, this is not specifically called like to like, and is this time a botanical analogy for how this works.

## Mechanisms in the Hippocratics?

There have been suggestions that the Hippocratics at times gave mechanical explanations or thought of some physiological processes in terms of mechanisms. One can see why this might be thought of as an attempt to bring the Hippocratics further in line with a narrative of the founders of rational medicine. Alternatively, this might be motivated by an attempt to justify a mechanistic approach to the body and medicine by location in a tradition of mechanical medicine traced back to supposedly mechanical aspects of Hippocrates. Whether there is a sound basis for this is another matter. Lonie has written a very interesting study on Friedrich Hoffman (1660–1742), who was an influential iatromechanist at a time when a mechanical approach to medicine and the body was trying to establish itself.[56] Hoffman saw mechanical aspects in Hippocrates and used those to justify his own approach. Lonie analyses what Hoffman saw in Hippocrates and then looks at Hippocrates to see what, if anything, could be considered mechanical in his work. I agree with Lonie that we can rule out anything mechanical for the Hippocratics in the sense of the application of a mathematical science of mechanics to particles. As Lonie puts it:

> This has to be excluded, since there was nothing at the time which we could regard as a science of mechanics with coherently formulated laws.[57]

There is nothing at all in the Hippocratic corpus to indicate any move to begin any such application of a mathematical science of mechanics to particles, nor is there any reason to suppose that any of the Hippocratics had an ontology involving particles. I also agree with Lonie that mechanism in the sense of the human body being treated as a machine or as an automaton is entirely absent from the Hippocratic corpus.[58] Nor is there any real reductionism in the Hippocratic corpus, and certainly we do not find bodily processes being explained in terms of atoms.[59] The body is always treated as a biological entity, not one that is at root physical and mechanical. However, Lonie does find mechanical explanations in the Hippocratics, as he puts it 'In terms of the mutual contact and pressure of bodies, both solid and fluid'.[60] He cites the Hippocratic *On Breaths* VIII, which says:

> The blood fears (*to haima phobeumenon*) the shivers which are present and so gathers together and shoots (*suntrechei kai diassei*) through the whole body to the warmest parts of it. As the blood leaps (*kathallomenou*) from the extremities of the body to the inner parts, there is trembling.

If this is mechanical, then the blood should not be fearing. One might take that fear as metaphorical, but there is never any sense of a further, reductive account of that fear. So too if this is mechanical, the blood should not be instigating its own motion, just as we saw that particles should not be instigating their own motion in the previous chapter. Yet here it gathers together, shoots through the body and leaps from the extremities because it fears. It is not forced to do so by something else. *On Breaths* VIII continues:

> Much air gathers together and going upwards in a mass, levers open (*exemochleuse*) and separates (*diestēse*) the mouth.

This happens in the same way that boiling water releases a great deal of steam, which rushes upwards. A *mochlos* was a lever used for moving ships, so I would agree with Lonie that 'levers open' is the best translation for *exemochleuse*.[61] Whether that should be seen as mechanical we will come back to in a moment. It is important to note though that at the end of this work we have *On Breaths* XV:

> I have given an account of the causes of diseases, and I have shown how wind (*pneuma*) controls (*dunasteuon*) in things as wholes and in the bodies of animals.

One can go two ways with *dunasteuon* here. One can take it in the same sense as I have been taking *kratein*, as I have translated here, such that wind exercises control and so should certainly not be seen as acting mechanically. Alternatively, one can translate *dunasteuon* as 'influential' when wind is then important for the account of diseases, but nothing is said about the active nature of wind. One might argue though that the first part of 'things as wholes and in the bodies of animals' is then otiose. One might also note that 'things as wholes and in the bodies of animals' is reminiscent of Anaximenes' 'as our soul, being air, holds us in order (*sungkratei*), so wind and air envelop (*periechein*) the whole *kosmos*.'[62] This raises a second point, as to whether there is a macrocosm/microcosm relationship being alluded to here between things as wholes and the bodies of animals. I doubt that we can be entirely determinate on these issues, but we should certainly be aware that there may be rather more in play in relation to the nature of air in *On Breaths* than any simple mechanical or physical account. Lonie is also interested in the Hippocratic *On Regimen* II, 66:

> If the secretion becomes abundant, then it controls (*ekratēse*) even the healthy, with the result that the whole body is heated and a strong fever ensues. When the blood is drawn in (*epispasthentos*) and heated, the things in the body make a rapid circulation, and the body is cleansed by the breath, that which is combined is thinned and forced out (*exōtheitai*) of the flesh and onto the skin and is called hot sweat. When the secretion ends, the blood establishes (*kathistatai*) its natural motion (*tēn kata phusin kinēsin*).[63]

In favour of a mechanistic reading, we have the heating of the blood, an ensuing rapid circulation of things in the body and sweat being forced out and onto the skin.[64] Here I am happy that *exōtheitai* means 'forced out'. Alternatively, we have this phrased in terms of Hippocratic excretions with no sense that they might be reduced to something physical rather than biological, and we have the secretion controlling, *kratein*. We also need to put this in the broader perspective of the cosmology of *On Regimen*, where we have fire controlling (*kratein*) all things and everything being steered (*kubernan*) through everything. Whether we take *kratein* in this passage to be control in this sense or a more innocent, medical sense of control, the broader context of *On Regimen* is certainly not a mechanical one.

## Humours

Lonie takes the view that the Hippocratic humoral system can in some respects be seen as mechanical. The balance of the humours is responsible for the health of the body, and according to Lonie, those humours are transported around the body in an interconnected system of vessels. The humours are subject to heating, cooling, coagulation and compacting, and may pressurize or be pressurized. So Lonie says that:

> Since this is a system in which fluids move through tubes and may exert pressure upon or suffer pressure from their containing vessels, it is recognizably mechanistic in at least one sense.[65]

Lloyd supports this view with an example from the Hippocratic *On Diseases* IV, 39. The author describes an experiment where three copper containers are placed on level ground, and pipes are connected between them. If we then fill the first one, the others will be filled as well. If we then take water out of one of them, the water level will drop in the others. He then says, 'In the body it is the same (*houtō de kai en tō sōmati echei*)'. Lloyd states that:

The writer illustrates a highly conjectural theory concerning physiological processes with a comparatively simple mechanical one.[66]

As ever, I would question whether the eclectic use of technological analogies amounts to the use of a mechanical analogy. It is interesting that the Hippocratics use a physical analogy here, but physical analogies cannot immediately be taken to be mechanical analogies.

## Hippocratic analogies

In one sense I agree with Lonie that of course there are analogies that we might consider to be mechanical in the Hippocratics. I also agree with Lonie that:

> The combination of animistic (the blood 'runs away' from the cold) with mechanistic (particularly the 'levering' open of the jaws by the air) features is characteristic.[67]

The Hippocratics took an eclectic approach to using analogies for the body. That is so not only across the corpus but in any groups of texts within the corpus and indeed within any one given text. So in *On the Nature of the Child*, we find a culinary analogy (a membrane is formed around the room in a similar fashion to how the crust forms around a loaf of bread), the like to like analogy that we saw above, and also considerable use of botanical analogy, in that humans are compared to plants.[68] *On the Nature of the Child* 27 is quite specific on this, stating that everything that grows in the earth derived moisture from the earth, in the same way that the human foetus lives in the mother. The section ends with the author stating that the growth of things from the earth and the growth of humans are exactly parallel (*pasan paraplēsiēn*). Like other early Greek thinkers, they used whatever analogies were to hand. What I do not see in the Hippocratics is any sense that the supposedly mechanical analogies are in any way dominant or privileged relative to other analogies. In *On the Nature of the Child* 27 the dominant analogy is the comparison of the growth of plants to the growth of humans in the womb. Nor do I see any attempt at reduction, either in the sense that other analogies or explanations reduce to mechanical analogies or explanations.

Technological or physical analogies are not necessarily mechanical analogies, nor, to parallel Unguru on the geometric rather than algebraic nature of Geek mathematics, are these technological or physical analogies at root mechanical but dressed up in another language. We may look at Greek technological analogies, such as the use of a *mochlos* for levering a ship and see a mechanical analogy, especially if for certain historiographical reasons we are looking to talk up supposed mechanical analogies for the early Greeks. So too we might look at early pneumatic technology such as the clepsydra or the containers and levelling experiment in the Hippocratics. Did the early Greeks, and in particular here the Hippocratics consider these to be mechanical analogies though? The way they use these analogies along with other analogies that are clearly not mechanical would suggest not. Certainly, this is not part of a grander scheme to generate a mechanical account of the body or a mechanical account of the cosmos. There is no sense in the Hippocratic corpus as a whole, or in any individual work, that these sorts of analogy are in any way the key analogies, the dominant analogies or in any sense are privileged analogies. Nor is there any sense that other analogies can be reduced to or replaced by these sorts of analogies.

We might also consider whether we in the twenty-first century consider pneumatic analogies to entail a mechanical account of the body. The reason why this is an issue is that the mechanical philosophies of the seventeenth century used clockwork as their primary analogy, but also used pneumatic analogies. Hence this association with a supposed mechanical approach in antiquity. If one used a clockwork analogy for the human body now, that would be dismissed as too crude. If one used a pneumatic analogy now, would that entail a mechanical view of the human body? Given advances in the understanding of the human body and the sophistication of pneumatics, it would not. Certainly, the early Greeks used some pneumatic analogies, particularly in relation to the clepsydra, but that did not entail a mechanical understanding of the body.

## An Empedoclean parallel?

Lonie has also argued in favour of a relation with Empedocles Fragment 84, which compares the human eye to a lantern someone would use on a stormy night:

> His comparison of the whole structure to a lantern with its horn shutters, may fairly be called mechanistic.[69]

First, I see nothing particularly mechanical about a Greek storm lantern, rather it is simply a piece of early technology. The early Greeks would not have seen it as mechanical. Second, 'horn shutters' is an overly mechanical translation. Inwood and Wright both have 'linen screens' here, but whether the material is horn or linen, the point is that it acts as a screen to let light out and not let wind in, not as a shutter as in a window shutter.[70] Third, there is the immediate context of this passage. If we read on in Fragment 84, it is Love who has fashioned the human eye, and if we look to Fragment 86 and 87, it is the divine Aphrodite who generates the eyes with love. Many scholars believe that this is a teleological fashioning. So Sedley has argued that:

> Even if one strips from this the figurative personification of Love as a divine artisan, one is left with the impression of an intelligent and purposive creative force. The architectonic role of Love in Empedocles' cosmic cycle makes it a very hard task indeed to portray him as a pure mechanist.[71]

There is not teleology or design here, but there is a perennial difficulty in talking about something as complex as the eye without invoking purpose, an issue still in modern biology.[72] However, it is Love, a non-material, non-mechanistic principle that does the work here. Here it is important to escape the binary of teleology or mechanism for the early Greeks. In my view, Empedocles was not a teleologist (certainly not in Plato's sense) nor a mechanist. Fourth, we must look to the broader context of Empedocles. Are Love and Strife mechanistic principles? What were the dominant metaphors for him?[73] Like other early Greeks, he drew on technological analogies for the human body.

## William Harvey

In my first chapter on methodology, I drew some parallels between how historians of science have recently revised views about William Harvey, who discovered the circulation of the blood in the seventeenth century and what I am trying to do in this book. Harvey was seen as someone who drew strongly on mechanical analogies and the application of quantification and mathematics to the body, and so was seen as positive, progressive and an important factor in the supposed scientific revolution of the seventeenth century. Harvey's supposed mechanical analogies, under closer, inspection, turned out to be no such thing. My reason for returning to Harvey here is that it is clearly possible to attempt to read mechanical analogies into Harvey, in the same way as it is for the Hippocratics, and with Harvey we have an overt rejection of mechanical ideas. So Harvey says that:

> They that argue thus, assigning only a material cause, deducing the cause of natural things from an involuntary and causal occurrence of the elements, or from the several dispositions or contriving of atoms, do not reach that which is

chiefly concerned in the operations of nature, and in the generation and nutrition of animals, namely the divine agent, and God of nature, whose operations are guided with the highest artifice, providence, and wisdom, and do all tend to some certain end, and are all produced, for some certain good.

He also said that:

It is a common mistake with those who pursue philosophical studies in these times, to seek for the cause of diversity of parts in diversity of matter whence they arise ... Nor do they err less who, with Democritus, compose all things out of atoms; or with Empedocles, out of elements.[74]

On the blood Harvey says that:

Seeing therefore that blood acts above the powers of the elements and is endowed with such notable virtues and is also the instrument of the omnipotent Creator, no man can sufficiently extol its admirable and divine faculties. In it the soul first and principally resides, and that not the vegetative soul only, but the sensitive and the motive also.

Aubrey wrote a biography of Harvey and he reports that Harvey:

Did bid me go to the fountain head and read Aristotle, Cicero and Avicenna and did call the neoteriques [newcomers, i.e. believers in the new mechanical philosophies] shitt breeches.

A little crude in expression perhaps, but it shows clearly the hostility that Harvey had towards the new mechanical philosophies of his time. Harvey was also appalled by the mechanistic interpretation of the circulation put forward by Descartes.[75] In relation to the supposed mechanical analogies in his work, Harvey clearly did not see them as such.

In relation to Lonie's comments on the Hippocratics, Harvey's account of the cardio-vascular system is considerably more mechanical than the Hippocratic account of the humours and their transportation around the body. It is also more mechanical than the Galenic account. Rather than the blood being attracted to the heart in its active phase, as for Galen, blood is forcibly expelled from the heart for Harvey. The blood is transported around the body rapidly and under pressure. Harvey, though, would utterly reject any suggestion that his account of the cardio-vascular system was mechanical. Should we then understand the Hippocratic use of technological analogies as mechanical? Harvey too took an eclectic approach to the analogies he used, drawing on the technology of his time.

In view of the disproportionate attention that has been paid to Harvey's supposed likening of the heart to a pump, it is worth emphasizing that the macrocosm/microcosm analogy is central to the original conception of the circulation and appears at critical points in *De Motu Cordis*. Harvey did not in fact liken the heart to a pump, but to a pair of water bellows, and did so only in his lecture notes.[76] He said that:

> From the structure of the heart it is clear that the blood is constantly carried through the lungs in to the aorta as by two clacks of a water bellows to raise water.[77]

A water bellows has significant differences from an orthodox pump in that its body is collapsible, while the cylinder and piston of an orthodox pump are rigid. So too the clacks were pieces of leather placed over the entrance and exit of the main chamber so placed to allow one-way flow only. Like the triscupid and biscupid (right atrioventricular and left atrioventricular (or mitral)) valves of the heart, these are flexible, rather than the rigid valves found in orthodox pumps.[78]

It is important to recognize though that there are some critical dissimilarities to the heart too. In particular, a water bellows is operated by an external agent, and the heart valves are more complex and active than the clacks (they operate themselves, where the clacks are opened by the water). Nevertheless, this is significantly less of a mechanical analogy than might be suggested by a direct analogy with a pump. Aristotle likened not only the lungs but also the heart to a pair of forge bellows:

> It is necessary to regard the structure of this organ [the lung] as very similar to the sort of bellows used in a forge, for both lung and heart take this form.[79]

While Aristotle of course does not have a mechanical account of the heart, and in particular would object to the idea that it is moved by an external agency,[80] he is quite happy to use this analogy with a forge bellows to get across the basic structure and functioning of the heart. Although Harvey's analogy is slightly more sophisticated, involving leather clacks (simple one-way valves), I see nothing in that requiring a mechanical interpretation or differentiating Harvey's account from that of Aristotle in any essential matter. There is a clearer mechanical analogy in *De Motu Cordis* Chapter, where Harvey likens the heart to a musket, but only in so far as both act too swiftly for the human eye to analyse their motions at normal speed.[81]

So Harvey used analogies that we might consider to be mechanical and indeed, some historians, seeking to make Harvey more modern have thought them mechanical. On closer examination these analogies turn out to be less mechanical and it is clear that Harvey, an arch anti-mechanist, did not consider them to be mechanical at all. Returning to the Hippocratics, they did use analogies that we consider to be mechanical. Did the Hippocratics consider them to be mechanical? Given that, like Harvey, the dominant analogies in their works are non-mechanical, one must have serious doubts about that. It is true that the Hippocratics did not give any clear anti-mechanical statement in the way that Harvey did, but that may well be because a mechanical account of the body was simply not an issue for them.

## Conclusion

The Hippocratic authors used *kubernan* and *kratein* in interesting ways. This is important as it broadens the range of early Greek thinkers using these terms. They also made prolific use of the terms *kata phusin* and *para phusin* in interesting ways. That at least some of the Hippocratics considered diseases, and indeed the whole of nature to be divine is unproblematic. It is likely that they held some form of pantheism, which allowed them to explain certain aspects of cosmogony, cosmology and disease without recourse to the gods. It is clear that for the Hippocratics the cosmos behaved in an orderly manner. The Hippocratics did not justify their writings by any reference to divine revelation or to the Muses. While that may seem straightforward, it is significant and their attitude to the origins of medical knowledge and their optimism to the future acquisition of greater medical knowledge are starkly different from Homer and Hesiod. The Hippocratics had an eclectic approach to the analogies they used for the human body and its processes. Some of those were taken from the technology of the time. As we might consider some of these analogies to be mechanical, it has been argued that the Hippocratics used at least some mechanical analogies. It is unlikely that the Hippocratics considered these analogies to be mechanical, and it is clear that they did not give them any privileged position relative to other analogies. There is an interesting comparison with William Harvey, an avowed anti-mechanist, who used what we might consider to be mechanical analogies, but clearly did not see these analogies as mechanical or in any way threatening to his anti-mechanical stance.

# Conclusion

Among the early Greeks we can find a variety of views on nature. It is important in investigating these to take into account evidence from the poets, historians, medical writers and playwrights of the time as well as the 'presocratic philosophers'. It is possible to find a time in early Greek thought where there was no real conception of *phusis*, with Homer and Hesiod using the term only once and having no conception of the unnatural, the beyond the natural, or that which is contrary to nature. So too they had no real conception of enquiry. The terms *historia* and *skopein* are absent from Homer and Hesiod. If humans wished to learn anything significant, they had to do so from the gods, not from any enquiry of their own. It is important to recognize that when we talk of *peri phuseōs historia* that not only was the idea of *phusis* generated by the early Greeks, the notion of enquiry was as well.

There was a significant tradition in early Greek thought that investigated *phusis* and used the verbs *kubernan* to steer and *kratein* to control. It is worth stating again a list of these thinkers as they make up a significant proportion of early Greek thought on *phusis*: Anaximander, Anaximenes, Xenophanes, Heraclitus, some of the Hippocratics, the Derveni author, Parmenides, Diogenes, Empedocles and Anaxagoras. So too we can find interesting uses of these verbs in Pindar, Bacchylides and Euripides, indicating that gods could steer or control. These verbs were used in critical cosmogonical and cosmological passages. The cosmos acquired its order, maintained its order and behaved in a lawlike manner through steering or control. It is critical to understand here that for at least a significant number of early Greek thinkers intelligence, rather than any *mēchanē* available to them, was the paradigm of regularity, an interesting reversal of modern suppositions. It is significant that Plato has an ideal intelligence generating absolute regularities, but there is no discussion of what an ideal machine or *mēchanē* would be able to generate in early Greek thought. This tradition has been marginalized by scholars, who have sought to find mechanism wherever they could and valued only direct affinities with modern science.

We can trace this tradition back to Homer and Hesiod. We find the phrases *moira krataiē* 'controlling *moira*' and phenomena occur *kata moiran*, 'according to *moira*'. The gods did not specifically steer for Homer and Hesiod, but there are other interesting verbs of guidance and the gods did lead like to like. The gods, in particular Zeus, were implicated in spinning *moira*. The Derveni papyrus is very interesting in saying that air controls all things but has also been called Zeus and Moira. It is possible to extend Jaeger's thesis that the attributes of the gods in Homer and Hesiod, such as being ungenerated, incorruptible, undying and indestructible were transferred to the *archai* of the early enquirers into *phusis*. We can do this by adding that ideas of divine control of the affairs of gods and humans and the cosmos more generally were also transferred and to some extent transformed. So some of the *archai* are capable of steering, or controlling or both. The *archai* do this in an invariant manner. The background of that invariance is either inescapable *moira*, or very strong *moira* that has been transformed into invariance. We can trace the key *kata phusin* phrase, and its contrary *para phusin*, back to Homer and Hesiod on *kata* and *para moira*, with interesting intermediaries in Anaximander with *kata to chreōn*, 'according to what is proper' and *kata tēn tou chronou taxin*, 'according to the ordering of time' and Heraclitus with *kat' erin kai chreōn* 'according to strife and what is proper' and *kata logon* 'according to the logos'. Recognizing that *chreōn* here means 'what is proper' and not 'what is necessary' is an important shift here.

The Phaeacian ships may be an important model for steering *archai*. They did not have helmsmen, and so steered themselves. They did have minds, could discern the thoughts and minds of men, had considerable (synoptic?) geographical knowledge and were always able to reach their destination even in adverse weather. Some *archai* had clearly considerable knowledge, such as those in the Derveni papyrus and Anaxagoras' *nous*, others may well have done too. It is also important to recognize that a *kubernētēs* was not simply the *pedialiouchos*, the person who held the steering oar, but was effectively the captain of the vessel. So too the *kubernētēs* had the ultimate responsibility for the safety of the ship. So if *archai* did steer, they may have been able to do so intelligently, with knowledge and with a mind to the safety of their cosmos.

The historical claim here is that we have a plausible context and origin for early Greek thought about *phusis* and in particular the order of the cosmos. We can understand the early enquirers into nature as developing and reacting to Homer, Hesiod and other poets. We have a context for the fragments and in many cases can understand why the fragments have been phrased in a certain manner. There is no need to suppose any 'Greek Miracle' here with philosophy springing into existence *ex nihilo*. There was no 'Ionian Enlightenment' if we mean by that a spread of mechanical and secular thinking, as the Enlightenment of the eighteenth century has often been characterized. Nor will a simple *muthos* to *logos*, myth to reason account capture the complexity of the relation of the early natural philosophers and the poets, or their debt to them.

It is important that we recognize an intellectual space where we can discuss and recognize the merits of the ideas of *kubernan* and *kratein*. We need to move away from the idea that only that which has affinity to modern science has merit, and the binary division of affinity to modern science or primitive. There were ideas that in their context were rational, plausible, sophisticated and interesting, even if those ideas have now been superseded and rejected. Similarly it is important to reject a binary dichotomy of science and religion and its attendant conflict narrative in favour of more modern ideas about their relation. It is also important to get away from the false dichotomy of teleology or mechanism for the early Greek thinkers, as there were many other fascinating views that they held. This gives us an interestingly broader conception of the early enquiry concerning nature, one which fits with Plato's account in the *Phaedo* and elsewhere, if we read those accounts sensitively and in a non-stereotypical manner.

A radical conclusion of this book is that under any meaningful definition of mechanist, there were no mechanists in early Greek thought. None made a mathematical application of the science of mechanics to bodies in motion, indeed there was no such science to apply. None made machine analogies, indeed there were no machines of the relevant type to make analogies to. There is no single, ahistorical definition of mechanism or mechanist, no Platonic form of either. I make these points because often the question has been why early Greek thinkers failed to be mechanists, as if being a mechanist was ahistorically obvious or natural. Instead it is interesting to ask why anyone in early Greece would have been a mechanist. Their *mēchanē* would not have suggested themselves as a good model for *phusis*. No philosophical question requires or even suggests mechanism rather than atomism for an answer. One point I have stressed throughout is that people used the analogies that were to hand. There were many of these, and like the thinkers using *kubernan* and *kratein*, it is worth listing them to emphasize their extent. There were architectural, biological, craft, maritime, agricultural, human, meteorological, botanical, culinary, pyrotechnical, commercial and parenting analogies as well as the macrocosm/microcosm analogy. These were not weak analogies. I have argued throughout that these analogies did real and important work and were not mechanical analogies in another guise. In the context of early Greek thought, where machines were prone to rapid wear and failure, machine analogies would have been weak analogies for the regularities of nature. The early Greeks were well aware of this. Even in the imaginary context of Parmenides' poem, the axles of his chariot were wearing rapidly. The mechanical philosophy could only come about when machines were sophisticated and reliable enough to act as a model for natural phenomena. If fully-fledged mechanical analogies had been used in early Greek thought, that would have been a miracle. They were not, the early Greeks used the analogies they had to hand and their work, while brilliant and seminal, was no miracle. It is important that we ask why an idea would have come about in a specific context, and not assume the idea is obvious or atemporal and restrict ourselves to asking why it did not come about. We must rid ourselves of the idea that mechanical analogies are always primary and strong, whatever the historical context, and that other analogies are therefore always alternative or weaker.

Leucippus and Democritus are clearly a critical case. The key issue is their use of *ou mallon* consideration, crucial in their reply to Parmenides. The size, shape, distribution and velocities of atoms in the void were *ou mallon*, so too were vortex and cosmos formation with respect to time and place. It is difficult to see how any mathematical mechanics could apply here even if they existed at the time and indeed there is no record of any such application. This is important as it means we cannot 'retrofit' a mechanics, that is, assume all the requisites for a mechanical treatment are there and impose a later mechanics. A second important consequence flows from the use of *ou mallon* considerations, which is that Leucippus and Democritus' atomism does not accord with Laplace's demon. There cannot be knowledge of the positions and velocities of the atoms, and the time and place of cosmos formation is *ou mallon*. So they turn out be neither mechanists, nor in this sense determinists. If we look at the analogies that Leucippus and Democritus used, then we find biological, maritime, agricultural, human and meteorological analogies. We also find use of the macrocosm/microcosm analogy, and I find it historiographically interesting that this is not mentioned in some studies. It is difficult to tell if in some situations Leucippus and Democritus believed in the generation or diminution of motion contrary to mechanist principles, largely, I would suggest, because this was not an issue for them. Their motivation was to reply to Parmenides, not to try to deal with issues that were important to Descartes or Hobbes. They were indeed atomists but not mechanists or determinists. Like to like was not an attractive force for Leucippus and Democritus (a further modern imposition) but was a sorting principle that operated only in vortices. So too Love and Strife were not forces for Empedocles, but were principles of association and dissociation. We need a more nuanced account of like to like, as there is considerable variety in what is like what and how subsequent effects are mediated.

We need to recognize the limitations if using seventeenth-century mechanical philosophy as a reference point for the study of the early Greeks. Of course there are certain similarities, not least because these mechanical philosophers based some of their views on those of Leucippus and Democritus. However, there are also major differences, based not least on the fact that the mechanical philosophers were all Christians working in a strongly Christian environment and they made use of their Christian god rather than *ou mallon* principles. A further key point is this. The mechanical philosophy, though an excellent idea and research programme in the seventeenth and eighteenth centuries, has long been superseded and rejected. Science simply does not have this world picture or explain in this way anymore and has not done so for many years.

There has also been debate over whether Anaximander was a mechanist or not. I have put the case that he was not. There is no evidence he believed in vortices and it is almost certainly anachronistic to suppose that Anaximander, or indeed anyone before Parmenides, thought in terms of particles. Anaximander did liken his celestial rings to wheels, but it is an interesting question how far that goes. Not as far as being wood, or having a hub or having spokes. Not even as far as being rigid, as the rings were composed of fire and air. So perhaps all that comes from this is that the rings rotate like wheels do.

Some scholars have sought to find mechanical analogies in the Hippocratics. There are, not surprisingly, some technological and physical analogies in the Hippocratics, the question then being whether they considered these analogies to be mechanical or not. That we in the modern world consider some of these technological and physical analogies to be mechanical does not mean that the Hippocratics did. Here parallels with the arch anti-mechanist William Harvey are important. Harvey used analogies that we, in the modern world might think mechanical, but clearly he did not. Again, if we look at the other analogies that the Hippocratics used, the dominant analogies are botanical, with culinary and other analogies. The macrocosm/microcosm analogy is more widespread in the corpus and does more work than is commonly assumed.

I would like to have gone into more depth with some of the figures in this book, Heraclitus, Empedocles and Anaxagoras in particular, but such are the confines of modern academic book lengths. I hope to have established that there was an important tradition based around *kubernan* and *kratein* and that this will stimulate further debate about the nature of the early Greek enquiry into nature. I hope too to at least have started a debate about how we think about and value supposed mechanistic analogies in the early Greek world. That in turn may lead us to reconsider whether we overestimate the number of successive *cosmoi* and coexistent *cosmoi* theories.

In closing this book, I would emphasize again that it is not my intention to denigrate the early Greek thinkers by arguing that there were no early mechanists. My attack is on historiographies that give undue importance to superficial affinities between ancient and modern science and seek to see mechanism wherever they can in ancient science. It also attacks the (in my view bizarre) historiography of seeking affinities between the early Greeks and seventeenth-century mechanical philosophy, when that mechanistic view has long been rejected by science as inadequate and unsophisticated. Anaximander becomes a more interesting, coherent and original thinker if we stop trying to see him as a mechanist; so too with Anaximenes, Empedocles and some of the Hippocratics. Leucippus and Democritus have a fascinating and original reply to Parmenides if we stop trying to see their views as precursors to the seventeenth-century mechanical philosophy. Anaxagoras is more coherent and interesting if we allow *nous* its full role in controlling the vortex and stop trying to read multiple worlds into him. All these thinkers are more coherent and stronger for allowing their original analogies for natural processes to come through rather than forcing mechanical analogues on them, all the more so given what I have argued about the weakness of mechanical analogues in an early Greek context. This approach also improves the history of early Greek cosmogony/cosmology. Thinkers who went in for co-existent or successive multiple worlds (Leucippus, Democritus, Empedocles) did so with a clear account of why they were doing so, what that would explain and with a well thought out philosophical and cosmological infrastructure to support that idea. There is a very sharp distinction with those who did not, who had equally coherent but opposed positions. There are no confused positions in the middle. Plato's account of early Greek natural philosophy is also more interesting, more sophisticated and more informative if we recognize there was more to his view than a supposed binary split between the mechanical and teleological.

The development of early Greek thought on nature becomes interesting and explicable and we have no need of a 'Greek Miracle' to explain the *ex nihilo* arrival of a mechanistic view of the world. The treatment of William Harvey is an important historiographical parallel. It used to be thought that Harvey was a mechanist by historians who valued such things, but this has been shown to be conclusively untrue. A much richer account of Harvey has emerged, one that treats him as no less of an innovator, no less of an interesting and radical thinker, but one that embeds him much more firmly and plausibly in the thought of his time. Ultimately this book has been about what we value and why with the early Greek enquiry into nature and how we do history and philosophy of this period.

# Notes

## Introduction

1 Cf. Laks (2006), (2018).
2 Naddaf (2005), *The Greek Concept of Nature* is an admirable book and I agree with much of it, but I see greater diversity in early thinking about nature.
3 See Chapter 3 herein for further discussion and specific references.
4 Starting with Homer (!) and including virtually every thinker in the investigation of nature tradition.

## Chapter 1 Methodological Issues

1 Personally I find 'primitive' too pejorative and disparaging, but this is the term that has been used in the debates.
2 Cf. Berryman (2009) p. 3.
3 Agreeing here with recent work by Tybjerg 2003, 2005, Schiefsky 2008, Berryman 2009.
4 Von Staden (1992), cf. Pingree (1992).
5 Gregory (2016).
6 Gomperz (1911–12) p. 196. Eastman (1905) p. 702, cf. Zeller and Nestle (1881) vol. I. p. 255, Burnet (1930) p. 71, de Rademaker (1953) p. 35.
7 Whitteridge (1971) is the fullest statement of the older view. See Pagel (1976), Frank (1980), Cunningham (1987), Wear (1990), French (1994), McMullen (1998), Gregory (2000b), (2001), (2014a) for the modern view.
8 See Gregory (2000b), (2001), (2014a).
9 It is important not to stereotype Aristotle's views on quantification here. See Gregory (2000), (2001).
10 On analogies in Harvey, see Gregory (2000b) and (2001).
11 There are also similar re-appraisals of the work of Johannes Kepler (1571–1630) and Isaac Newton (1642–1727).
12 Unguru (1975). The view he opposes is expressed by Van der Waerden: 'Theatetus and Apollonius were at bottom algebraists, they thought algebraically even though they put their reasoning in geometric dress', B. L. van der Waerden, Science

Awakening (New York: John Wiley & Sons, Inc., 1963) p. 265–66. See Unguru (1975) p. 71 for further examples.
13 Unguru (1975) p. 71.
14 See Gregory (2000a), (2001), (2014b).
15 Hankinson (1998), Barnes (1979), Burnet (1930).
16 Hesse (1961) p. 39.
17 Burkert (1972) p. 335, Cf. Pedersen (1974) p. 26: 'In many ways, the Timaios (sic) reflects an animistic and anthropomorphic philosophy foreign to the Ionian philosophers' fundamental attitude, although there are a few similar ideas.'
18 See Tor (2017) pp. 14–15 for the most recent discussion.
19 Keynes (1921) p. 247: 'The common sense of the race has been impressed by weak analogies', quoted by Lloyd (1966) pp. 179, 357.
20 Berryman (2009) p. 6.
21 Cf. Berryman (2009) pp. 55–6, Micheli (1995) pp. 9–11.
22 Lonie (1981) p. 123. Lonie also has 'mutual contact and pressures of bodies, both solid and fluid' as mechanistic explanation.
23 Lonie (1981) p. 123.
24 So even if we reduce to the chemistry of the brain, modern chemistry is not mechanical – atoms are no longer solid particles bumping into each other, nor are sub-atomic particles, and the relevant quantum mechanics are highly unmechanical.
25 Such as inertial motion, perfectly elastic collisions, first law of thermodynamics (energy conversation). Leucippus and Democritus also fail the 'Laplace's Demon' test for mechanical and deterministic systems in an interesting way.
26 See here Berryman (2009) pp. 10/11.
27 Pyle (1995) p. 142 ff.
28 Glennan and Illari (2018) p. 2.
29 As Berryman (2009) p. 10 has commented: 'Some confusion might easily be avoided if we were to describe the opposition here as between teleological and materialist approaches.'
30 Cf. Owen (1986), Hussey (1991), Bodnar (2004), Berryman (2009), De Groot (2014), Johnson (2017) on mechanics in Aristotle and the pseudo-Aristotle *Mechanica*.
31 Cf. Berryman (2009) p. 19, Garber and Roux (2013) p. xi, Glennan and Illari (2018) p. 2.
32 Pneumatic analogies were also an important part of the mechanical philosophy. The technology for generating a vacuum and experimenting in it, critical for many of these analogies, was only generated in the seventeenth century.
33 Heidel (1910) p. 95.
34 Heidel (1910) p. 128.

35  Dijksterhuis (1961) p. 3.
36  Berryman (2009) p. 1.
37  So too it failed to account for magnetism.
38  The discovery of the cell, a biological entity, as the basic unit of organisms, and not something mechanical was a serious blow to mechanical biology.
39  Garber and Roux (2013) p. xii.
40  Salmon (1984) p. 241.
41  Glennan and Illari (2018) p. 1.
42  Glennan and Illari (2018) p. 2.
43  Mourelatos (2018), cf. Naddaf (2005) pp. 3, 11 ff., Heidel (1910) p. 97 ff.
44  Homer, *Odyssey* X/ 302 ff. See Naddaf (2005) pp. 13–14 for *phusis* in Homer. I disagree here with both Naddaf and Lloyd (1991) p. 148 who consider the Moly to be magical.
45  Lloyd (1991) p. 418, (2003) p. 48.
46  Grant (2007) p. 1.
47  Lloyd (1991) pp. 418, 431–32.
48  The early Greeks also discovered the idea of invariance for nature – informally expressed, that in the same circumstances the same things happen. Cf. Lloyd (1991) p. 419.
49  Burnet's 'natural history' has too many resonances with the nineteenth-century discipline and overly restricts the sense of *historia*. There is not much to be gleaned from Plato's other uses of *historia* and its cognates (*Phaedrus* 244c9, *Cratylus* 437b1, *Sophist* 267e2) other than he is generally positive about it.
50  See e.g. Menn (2010).
51  See French (1994) p. 6 and note his use of italics.
52  Homer uses *phusis* (*Odyssey* X, 303), while Xenophanes explains using a god.
53  Grant (2007) p. 1. Cf. Lloyd (1991) 'a domain of nature encompassing all natural phenomena'.
54  In my view Plato takes natural philosophy seriously and addresses issues of cosmogony, cosmology, astronomy, zoogony, the origin of the elements, the nature of the human body and disease, etc. in interesting and constructive ways, sometimes rejecting, sometimes building on or transforming earlier ideas.
55  Plato, *Philebus* 28d.
56  So, *contra* Hirsch (1990), I do think the early atomists were anti-teleological, being opposed to the *kubernan* and *kratein* tradition.
57  I would reject this even in Socrates' autobiography, which is more nuanced in its critique of predecessors than many stereotypical accounts of it allow.
58  Plato, *Philebus* 17e5, cf. *Philebus* 64e and *Theaetetus* 183b. Is this one reason why Plato does not name some of his predecessors?

59 Here I disagree with Heidel (1910) p. 96: 'Henceforth the world is definitively divided into two spheres, one subject to mechanical, the other to final causes.' Cf. Heidel (1910) pp. 126, 128.
60 What is this method? First it must be considered whether what we are investigating is simple or multiform (*haploun hē polueides*), then if it is simple we must consider what ability it has to act or be acted upon, and if it is diverse then we must number its forms and then proceed for each as with something simple.
61 It is very interesting here that it is possible for there to be *ho alēthēs logos*, however we wish to translate that (the true account?), about the enquiry/contemplation concerning nature. There are several echoes of or allusions to the *Phaedo* here. Socrates says that we should see if what Hippocrates says agrees (*sumphōnei*) with our investigation, echoing the famous use of *sumphōnein* in relation to hypotheses at *Phaedo* 100a5. As with *Phaedo* 99de, at *Phaedrus* 270de there is an association of the wrong method with blindness.
62 See *Ancient Medicine* XX for a Hippocratic view on this.
63 The verb *skopein* is very common in Plato, interlocutors often beginning speeches with *skopei*, 'consider'. There follows: 'it is necessary taking in mind the nature of anything' (*dei dianoeisthai peri hotououn phuseōs*). Here *dianoeisthai* standardly means to have in mind or to intend.

## Chapter 2  Order in Homer and Hesiod

1 Jaeger, (1939) pp. 204 ff.
2 Rochberg (2016).
3 Rochberg (2016) 1. Cf. Lloyd (2007) 131–2, 'There are ... societies where there is no explicit concept of "nature" as such at all though that should not be confused with a denial that they have an implicit grasp of it.'
4 See Chapter 8 herein for further discussion on this point.
5 Ideas of what we would understand as contagion were also similar. In Babylonia, if one person had offended the gods, their immediate family, their entire family or even their whole village could be affected by the punishment. In Homer the whole Greek army at Troy suffers for Atreides dishonouring Chryses, in Hesiod, at *Theogony* 238 ff., Zeus punishes the whole city of one bad man, sending famine and plague.
6 Rochberg (2016) p. 282.
7 Rochberg (2016) pp. 182, 283.
8 Hesse (1961) p. 39.
9 I take the same view on definitions of magic and the supernatural and how we approach these in an ancient context. See Ogden (2008) p. 5 ff., Dickie (2001) Chapters 1 and 2, Collins (2008) Chapter 1.

10 Nor would I deny this for the Babylonians, whose achievements in healing and astronomy are well known. They also had catalogues of flora and fauna, see Rochberg (2016) p. 19.
11 Grant (2007) p. 1, Cf. Lloyd (1991) p. 419.
12 Heubeck and Hoekstra (1989) p. 60.
13 Naddaf (2005) pp. 13–14.
14 On the theme of the Greek term *mēchanē* and its cognates, *polumēchanos* in relation to Odysseus does not mean he has many machines, rather that he has many ruses.
15 Gregory (forthcoming), 'Was Homer's Circe a Witch?' *Other than the Binary*. A word of caution to Greekless readers here – many English translations (including the Loeb and the Penguin) assume that Circe was a witch and translate some terms in line with that assumption. My paper deals with this in some detail and argues that there are better alternative translations.
16 Terms such as *strix* and *pharmakis* for witch are not in Homer (or Hesiod), nor are terms such as *magos* or *goēs* for magic.
17 So if we define magic as: 'Magic may be said to be the exercise of preternatural control over nature by human beings, with the assistance of forces more powerful than they' (Flint (1991)), then Circe is not a magic user. So too there are no demonic forces and no devil for Circe to ally herself too.
18 Circe is immortal, *athanatē* (*Odyssey* XII, 302), is the daughter of Helios the sun god (X, 138) and Perse who is the daughter of Okeanos (*Odyssey* X, 139), is she is a *dia thaeōn*, divine goddess (*Odyssey* XII, 155), her handiwork, *hoia theaōn*, that of a goddess (*Odyssey* X, 222), she is *potnia*, 'revered' or 'queenly' (*Odyssey* X, 394, 549). Circe's house is a 'sacred dwelling,' *hiera domata* (*Odyssey* X, 426, 44), and is within a 'sacred grove' *hieras bēssas* (*Odyssey* X, 275) and she has four handmaidens (*Odyssey* X, 348), who are children of the springs and groves and of the sacred river (*hierōn potamōn*). Beware that many of the negative descriptions of Circe in English translations are also applied to other goddesses. So *deinē theos* is awesome goddess applied to other goddesses, but because of the assumption that Circe is a witch becomes 'dread goddess' when applied to her.
19 Twice when Odysseus leaves Aiaia, Circe gives him a favourable northerly wind. Weather working, by gods such as Zeus or Poseidon, or goddesses such as Athena and Aphrodite, is commonplace among Homeric divinities.
20 Circe gets to the ship before Odysseus, as 'Against the will of a god who could see them with eyes as they go to and fro?' (*Odyssey* X, 574), which I take to be a capacity of all Homeric gods.
21 Athena works various transformations on Odysseus, *Odyssey* VI, 229, VIII, 20 and XIII, 429 XVI, 172 XVIII, 70 XXIII, 156 XXIV, 520 gives him great strength. She is also able to transform herself (XIII, 221).

22 Divine foresight is standard in Homer; for example, Hermes tells Odysseus what Circe will do (*Odyssey* X, 281 ff.) and Circe says that Hermes prophesied to her that she would meet with Odysseus (*Odyssey* X, 331 ff.). Athena prophesies the death of the suitors (*Odyssey* I, 252).
23 Aphrodite has power over all animals, *Homeric Hymn to Aphrodite* I, 3–5. Fierce grey wolves, lions, bears and leopards fawn on her, *Homeric Hymn to Aphrodite* I, 69–72, cf. Circe and her pet lions and wolves.
24 Athena and Hermes both have similar groups of powers to Circe.
25 Circe turns them back again, and is very generous to Odysseus and his crew. She bathes, anoints, clothes and feeds them for a year, gives good advice, the materials Odysseus will require to meet the ghosts and a favourable wind to take him away. When Odysseus returns there is more food, advice and another favourable wind.
26 *Odyssey* XI for Odysseus, Hermes leading the ghosts of the suitors (*Odyssey* XXIV, 1 ff.), Persephone sending ghosts to Odysseus and his mother (*Odyssey* XI, 226 ff.) and scattering ghosts (*Odyssey* XI, 385ff.).
27 Dickie (2001) p. 23.
28 Circe is said to *thelgein*, (*Odyssey* X, 214, 291, 318, 326) and I take that to mean 'beguile' rather than 'bewitch'. There is considerable use of this verb elsewhere in Homer where it clearly means 'to beguile'. If it does mean bewitch, then there will be many more witches and warlocks in Homer.
29 By simple preparation here I am thinking of a mixing with water or wine.
30 Some translations attribute a herb to Hermes/Odysseus and drugs to Circe with no justification – they are all *pharmaka*.
31 It may be hard for mortals to pick, but it does grow in the ground – Hermes has not brought this with him.
32 At *Iliad* XX, 94 the snake is described as *bebrōkōs kaka pharmak'*, 'having eaten *kaka pharmaka*', presumably plants. The Egyptian *pharmaka* may also be *esthla* or *lugra*, *Odyssey* IV, 230.
33 Cf. Homer *Iliad* XI, 624, 641.
34 Circe gives, *edōken*, the *pharmaka* that transformed the wild animals (X, 213), at X, 235 she mixes up *pharmaka* with food, *anamisgō*, and at X, 317 she simply throws, *hēke*, the *pharmakon* into Odysseus' drink.
35 See Page (1973) p. 55, 57.
36 Cf. the bag of winds.
37 Cf. Ogden (2008) p. 20.
38 See Page (1973) p. 55, 69.
39 Someone who is *polupharmakos* is then not necessarily a witch. Note that Odysseus is *polumēchanos, polutropos, polutlas and polumētis*.
40 A healer and not a magical practitioner.
41 See Chapter 3 herein for more on this.

42 Jaeger (1939) p. 204 ff.
43 See Chapter 7 herein on like to like in Leucippus and Demcritus.
44 Terpander lived in the first half of the seventh century BCE and was important in the development of Greek music and lyric poetry.
45 See e.g. *Odyssey* V, 245, XVII, 342, XXI, 44, XXI, 121.
46 Cf. Iliad, XXIV, 362 – guiding a horse.
47 Aiming an arrow, see e.g., *Iliad* XXIII, 871, *Odyssey* XXII, 8.
48 It is interesting to note that *krataiē* does not occur anywhere else in Homer or Hesiod other than in this phrase.
49 *Iliad* XVIII, esp. XVIII, 414 ff.
50 See Berryman (2009) p. 24.
51 Asimov, Bladerunner, Star Trek TNG for serious sci-fi; Hitch Hikers' Guide to the Galaxy and Red Dwarf for a more humorous take.
52 *Iliad* XVIII, 410–20.
53 *Iliad* XVIII, 375–6 and 468.
54 Cf. Bosak-Schroeder (2015) p. 123 ff.
55 Cf. Berryman (2009) p. 25.
56 Some uses of *kata cosmon or* ou *kata cosmon,* to speak well (*Odyssey* VIII, 489), speak improperly or without manners (*Odyssey* VIII, 179, XIV, 363), disorderly words (*Iliad* II, 214), improper behaviour (*Odyssey* XX, 181), attend assembly in poor order (*Odyssey* III, 138), battle kit in good order (*Iliad* X, 472), horses in good order (*Iliad* XI, 48, XII, 85), improper armour stripping (*Iliad* XVII, 205), cooking preparations in good order (*Iliad* XXIV, 623).
57 For *moira*, e.g. not well said (*Odyssey* II, 251), not well done (*Odyssey* IX, 352), for *aisa* see *Iliad* III, 59, VI, 333, X, 445 and XVII, 716.
58 So e.g. ships all in good order (*Odyssey* IV 783, VIII, 54), ewes and goats in turn (*Odyssey* IX, 245, 342), retreat in good order (*Iliad* XVI, 367).
59 The adjective *krataiē* does not occur in Homer or Hesiod outside this phrase and *moira krataiē* only occurs outside of Homer and Hesiod as a quotation.
60 The instance at Hesiod Frag. 212b1 is without any context.
61 Gods, *Iliad* XXIV, 525, *Odyssey* I, 17, III, 208, XI, 139 XX, 195, VIII, 579, Zeus, *Odyssey* IV, 208, a daemon XVI, 64.
62 Cf. *Iliad* XXII, 178.
63 Zeus saves others as well, e.g. *Iliad* XIII, 784.
64 See Tsagarakis (2000) p. 47 n.163, Allan (2006) p. 16 n.73.
65 The idea of a day of death/fate/lot is common in Homer, e.g. *Iliad* XV, 613, *Odyssey* X, 175, *morsimon hēmar* and Odyssey XVI, 280, Iliad VIII, 72, XXI, 100, XXII, 212 for *aisimon hēmar.*
66 One important point that comes out of this passage is that *kēra* clearly does mean *moira* rather than simply death. This opens up another set of passages where we find constructions such as *phuge kēra, ekphuge kēra* and *hupekphuge kēra.*

67 This is not a criticism of Homer, more a recognition of his historical situation, and I would also cite some twentieth century epic literature as having ideas about fate/destiny that do not stand up to much philosophical probing, e.g. Tolkien's *Silmarillion* and *Lord of the Rings*, Le Guin's *Earthsea Trilogy* and Bradley's *Mists of Avalon*. This does not mean these works are not interesting as literature.

68 In Hesiod *aisa* is used twice, both meaning portion (*Theogony* 422 and 578), while *kēra* and *moros* only appears as personified goddesses (*Theogony* 211 and 221, *Moros kai Kēra, Moira kai Kēra*). Nor is *morsimos* used at all.

69 *Tuchē* is used once in Hesiod, at *Theogony* 360 as a name for a goddess but luck as such plays no part in his description of the world.

70 Cf. *Iliad* I, 132 where Agamemnon does not wish to be cheated with mind and will not be deluded or persuaded by Achilles.

71 Cf. *Works and Days* 122 ff.

72 Rochberg (2016), cf. Lloyd (2007) p. 131–2.

## Chapter 3   Early Ideas on Knowledge and Enquiry

1  In the Babylonian culture, all diseases were thought to be caused by the gods.
2  Homer, *Iliad*, I, 1 ff. Trans. W. Leaf, A. Lang, E. Myers.
3  Cf. Homer *Odyssey* V, 394 ff., *Odyssey* XI, 409 ff.
4  Hesiod, *Theogony* 238 ff., Trans. West. A more famous passage in Hesiod would be *Works and Days* 85 ff., the tale of Pandora's jar carrying diseases, sent by Zeus as a punishment. For more on Homer and Hesiod, see Longrigg (1993) p. 8 ff.
5  Homer, *Iliad* XIX, 86 ff., see Dodds (1951) pp. 2–3, cf. Vlastos (1975) p. 13 for a discussion of Dodds on *atē*.
6  A further interesting instance of 'lots' is Poseidon's speech at *Iliad* XV, 185 ff. When Zeus, Poseidon and Hades are allotted their shares of the world, is that by chance or is there something guiding that?
7  At *Iliad* V, 209 *kakē aisē* is best translated as ill lot rather than bad luck.
8  Martin (2004) p. 15 has commented that 'It has rightly been questioned whether the notion of intervention in nature is a modern one and is inappropriate for the ancient Greeks.'
9  Hankinson (1998) p. 8.
10 Hankinson (1998) p. 8.
11 See e.g. *Iliad* VIII, 133, IX, 236, XXI, 198, *Odyssey* XXIV, 539.
12 I am avoiding the phrase 'divine revelation' or even just 'revelation' here as the Christian connotations of that are a trustworthy, veridical revelation, which we do not get in Homer. This point also important in relation to Parmenides' poem. Is

what the goddess tells the *kouros* a 'divine revelation'? If so, in the Christian sense or the early Greek pagan sense?
13 Guthrie, *HGP* I, p. 398.
14 Most (2006), 23 n7.
15 For further god/human contrasts, see Lesher (2008) p. 476 n.1.
16 Hussey (1990) 11.
17 See *Iliad* I, 526.
18 That Zeus does not hear or does not pay attention (*Iliad* XII, 173) to this address is not relevant – the point is that a human can have such a concern about a god.
19 Cf. Hussey (1990) p. 11, n.2.
20 Agamemnon's dream is in *Iliad* II, his apology *Iliad* XIX, 87.
21 Xenophanes Fr. 11, the gods steal, commit adultery and deceive each other.
22 So too Solon, as in the Hymn to the Muses *moira* is unpredictable and capricious, see Noussia-Fantuzzi (2010) p. 133.
23 Clay (1972). Clay cites Plato *Cratylus* 391e on divine names here.
24 Clay (1972) p. 129.
25 Zellner (1994).
26 Zellner (1994) p. 313.
27 Cf. Zellner (1994) p. 314. The Muses are daughters of Zeus so cannot have been present at all times.
28 Mortals are attributed with knowledge of events they were not present at, either past or future, Zellner (1994) p. 309. See also Lesher (1981) on knowledge terms in Homer and how they are used in relation to humans.
29 This is an attempt to get this passage as literally as possible into English.
30 Cf. Zellner (1994) p. 308.
31 Clay (2003) makes the interesting point that Homer only ever uses 'we' to refer to himself twice, both in relation to the Muses, both making Homer human but allowing him a privileged account among humans.
32 Hussey (1990) p. 17.
33 Hussey (1990) p. 13.
34 Hussey (1990) p. 13, Zellner (1994) p. 308–9.
35 Jouanna (1999) p. 237 ff.
36 See e.g. *Iliad* VII, 238 ff.
37 Lesher (2008) p. 462.
38 See Lesher (2008) p. 461. This test was often a military or athletic competition.
39 Cf. Herodotus 2, 142.
40 See here the Hippocratic *Prognostic* I, *Prorrhetic* II, 2, *On Regimen* I, 11–12, *On Regimen in Acute Diseases*, III.
41 See *Theogony* 1, 25, 36, 52, 93, 94, 96, 100, 114, 916, 966, 1022.

42 Agreeing with Tor (2017) p. 96 that the optative with *ke* should be rendered 'I should like to speak' rather than 'I will speak'.
43 Most (2006) p. 87.
44 Clay (2003) pp. 80, 175.
45 Clay (2003) pp. 75–80.
46 It is not the only event that is beyond human experience in *Works and Days* (e.g. 42 ff. and 106 ff.) but its proximity to the invocation makes it important.
47 As noted earlier, that the Muses in Hesiod are untiring may be an interesting allusion to the ship's catalogue passage in Homer.
48 Cf. Pindar Fragment 150: 'Give me an oracle, Muse, and I will be your prophet.'
49 Here *eumachanian* could serve as an excellent warning for taking *mēchanē* and its cognates as 'machine' in early Greek thought.
50 Solon too invoked the Muses, children of Memory and Zeus, but why he did so is complex and contested, see Noussia-Fantuzzi (2010) pp. 213 ff. See also Theognis 769 ff.
51 One might add here Fr. 34 on no man knowing about the gods and Fr. 35 on things being opined resembling the truth.
52 Lesher (1992) p. 143. The prime example is that of the rainbow.
53 Cf. Fr. 12.
54 Xenophanes Fr. 1, 21–3.
55 Or possibly secret, uncertain or doubtful things.
56 Lesher (2008) pp. 481 n.44.
57 Of course, much here depends on how one sees Parmenides, so some brief comments where I cannot go into this in full. I take Parmenides to be a philosopher of challenge rather than a philosopher of dogma. I believe he intends to make his reader/listener think philosophically and try to meet the issues raised in the poem, rather than give a set position of his own. So the divine revelation by the goddess is not something that the boy or we have to accept as dogma but something we have to use our judgement on whether to accept or not. I also see more continuity between the three parts of the poem than most, and see the third part as setting interesting challenges to any putative account of nature rather than a demonstration of why any such account should be dismissed out of hand. I see the kouros' journey as a *katabasis* rather than an *anabasis*. See Gregory (2014a), Primavesi (2005).
58 See Gregory (2014a). There is a large literature on these issues so here I only state rather than defend my view.

## Chapter 4  Anaximander and the *Kubernan* Tradition

1 Conche (1991) p. 139 ff. Cf. Babut (1972) p. 2, that Anaximander 'Substitue un processus de séparation purement mécanique des éléments constitutifs du monde à la generation.'

2  Babut (1972) p. 6.
3  This is Kahn's view as well (1960) p. 44. He also cites the frequency of use in other early sources.
4  Plato, *Philebus* 28d, cf. *Philebus* 30d. Plato also uses *diakubernan* for the relation of the demiurge to the cosmos at *Timaeus* 42e and for the relation of god to all that is at *Laws* 709b.
5  *Gorgias* 508a1–5, quoted in Chapter 1, is also important in showing that Plato recognized traditions in cosmological explanation other than the purely physical.
6  See KRS (1983) for textual variations here.
7  There are no other early Greek uses of *oiakizein*.
8  Hippocratic author, *On Regimen* I/10.
9  Heraclitus Fr. 41.
10 Taking *ton auton hapantōn* as genuine with Guthrie, Vlastos and Kahn but against Kirk and KRS.
11 Heraclitus Fr. 30.
12 Hippocratic author, *On Regimen* I/10.
13 Plato, *Politicus* 272d.
14 Plato, *Politicus* 273b ff.
15 In the *Timaeus*, the demiurge would not do anything to endanger the cosmos, but then the *Timaeus* cosmos has been made inherently deathless and ageless.
16 Kirk (1955), p. 35 n.1. 'How does the Boundless "govern" or "steer" all things? By virtue, obviously, of surrounding or containing them; but what actual control can it exercise within the cosmos, if the idea of innumerable destructions and re-creations is rejected? The question is difficult to answer on any hypothesis.'
17 Plato, *Philebus* 28d.
18 Cf. Drozdek (2008) p. 12.
19 Here I would emphasize that I do not subscribe to modern Intelligent Design myself, so this is not an attempt to read such a view back into the ancients.
20 Cf. *Iliad* XIII, 558 for a similar construction showing consciousness and intent.
21 *Odyssey* VIII, 555.
22 See Chapter 8 for a fuller discussion of this passage.
23 Derveni papyrus, Col. 19.
24 Anaxagoras Fr. 12.
25 Pseudo-Plutarch v, 19, 4, this passage is discussed more fully in Chapter 5.
26 Theophrastus. HP 1. 11. 1.
27 Cf. Sophocles, *Oedipus Tyrannus* 923, we are all afraid as with those who see fear in the helmsman (*kubernētēn*) of a ship.
28 Herodotus quite rightly has his own doubts, VIII, 119.
29 Herodotus VIII, 118 and 119.
30 Cf. Plato *Laws* 945c4 for the state as a ship and *hupozōmata*.

31  See Gregory (2007), (2013a) and (2016).
32  There is an alternative reconstruction of some missing text here, *kubernatai*, in the Loeb, I am following the TLG text.
33  Bacchylides Ode 5, 47 has a horse's jockey as a *kubernētan*.
34  Aristotle, *Physics*, I/ 4, 187a 20, DK12A9.
35  See Aristotle *History of Animals* 578a11, 572b22.
36  See Aristotle *Generation of Animals* 765b10.
37  Pseudo-Plutarch, *Stromateis* 2.
38  Cornford (1957) p. 163.
39  Damascius, *De Principiis* 123 (DK1B12) gives Kronos, Aether and Chaos as the usual precursors, later on he gives a more exotic version.
40  Aristotle, *On the Heavens*, II/13, 295a7 ff.
41  Does Aristotle include Thales here? Aristotle recognized that for Thales the earth floats on water (*On the Heavens*, II/13, 294a28 ff.) and for Aristotle, floating on water does involve forces (*On the Heavens*, IV). For Thales the heavens are generated. I have argued elsewhere (Gregory (2007) Chapter 2) that Thales did not believe in vortices. West (1963) p. 172 ff., cf. (1971) pp. 212–13 gives the case that he did.
42  See Aristotle, *On the Heavens*, II, 13, 295b10 ff.
43  West (1963) p. 173.
44  Simplicius, *Commentary on Aristotle's Physics*, 1121, 5, Anaximander: 'Produces coming to be not through alteration of the element, but through the separating off of opposites through the eternal motion.' Hippolytus, *Refutation of All Heresies*, I, 6, 1–7, Anaximander: 'Says that the *archē* and element of all existing things is the unlimited, being the first to call it by the name *archē*. Further, there is eternal motion in this and subsequently the heavens are generated.'
45  West (1963) p. 174.
46  Vlastos (1947) p. 171 note 140.
47  Vlastos (1947) p. 173.
48  Stokes (1963) p. 11 note 1.
49  Simplicius *Physics* 327, 24. See also Simplicius *Physics* 327, 330, 14, Themistius *Physics* 49, 13, Cicero *De Natura Deorum* I, 24, 66.
50  As Vlastos (1947) p. 168. Says, we must 'Guard against reading into Anaximander atomic physics or Parmenidean logic', cf. Vlastos (1947) p. 171.
51  See Gregory (2016).
52  Hippolytus *Ref.* 1, 13, 2. Cf. Aristotle *Physics* B4, 196a24 ff.
53  I do not see the state of complete dissociation of the elements as one might as the result of one of Aristotle's thorough experiments – that is a sphere of earth in the middle followed by concentric shells of water, air and fire. Rather I see it more like a 1960's lava lamp, where there are four immiscible fluids taking up a variety of shapes and motions. So there is not a singular end point to an Empedoclean cycle where the next cycle can repeat a previous one from. See Gregory (2007).

54 Stobaeus I, 22, 3 says: 'Of those who claimed the *cosmoi* to be unlimited, Anaximander held that they were equally far away from each another.' However, there are questions of reliability and plausibility here. We only find this in Stobaeus and not any earlier source and this looks like a rather desperate attempt to save a multiple co-existent *cosmoi* view for Anaximander in conjunction with his account of the stability of the earth.
55 One can argue for a conception of the *apeiron* as more conducive for infinite co-existent *cosmoi* but one would also have to be very aware of the motivation for doing so.
56 See Gregory (2007).
57 Diogenes Laertius may not be our best witness (earth spherical, moon lit by sun) but he does get some things right as well.
58 The context here (the next lines describe earth, moon and sun) would indicate that the whole here is the *cosmos*.
59 Aristotle, *On the Heavens*, III, 1, 298b29.
60 Aristotle, *On the Heavens*, I, 9, 278b8ff.
61 This is so for Homer, Hesiod and the Babylonian cosmology.
62 See Kahn (1960) p. 32 ff.
63 Simplicius, *Commentary on Aristotle's Physics*, 24, 13. Hippolytus, *Refutation of All Heresies*, I, 6, 1 has 'the heavens and the *cosmos* (singular) within them'. Some scholars take Simplicius to be the more reliable source but Hippolytus is a very plausible reading, a single *cosmos* within the wheels of the stars, moon and sun.
64 If Anaximander believed in a cycle of human civilisations he might refer to each civilisation as a *cosmos*, there being many civilisations over time, but no successive worlds. See Kahn (1960) p. 51, Kirk (1955) pp. 29–30, 32. Cf. Hippolytus, *Refutation of all Heresies* I, 14, 5 on Xenophanes.
65 If this is early (*c*. C5 BCE? there are dating issues with *On Sevens*), then we have an early use of *cosmoi* relating to organized areas, so Anaximander may have used *cosmoi* similarly, while if it is later, then *cosmoi* in Theophrastus need not immediately be taken as infinite worlds. See Kahn (1960) pp. 84–5. The key study is Mansfeld (1971), though see too West (1971). Craik (2015) has recently suggested that a fifth century BCE date is possible.
66 Kahn's translation, (1960) p. 85.
67 Aristotle, *Meteorology* 355a22–3 talks of *tēs gēs, kai tou kosmou tou peri tēn gēn*, 'the earth and the *cosmos* around the earth'.
68 Why some of the doxography after Theophrastus explicitly attributes multiple *cosmoi* to Anaximander is complex, but one can see how that came about through a combination of assimilation to early atomists ideas, confusion on the nature of the *apeiron*, running a multiple worlds interpretation of Theophrastus' 'all the heavens (*ouranoi*) and the *cosmoi* within them' and the influence of Aristotle's modal argument that what is generated must decay.
69 Aristotle, *Meteorology* II, 1, 353b6 ff.

70 Aristotle, *Meteorology* II, 1 356b.
71 Aristotle, *Meteorology* II, 1 352a25 ff.
72 Apollonius of Rhodes, iv, 269 *scholium*.
73 One issue for diachronic change is what happens to the *apeiron* – if for the cosmos to become drier it becomes wetter, does that then improperly characterize the *apeiron* as moist?
74 See Gregory (2016) for a more detailed discussion of this possibility – if time is equated with the motion of the heavens (common in early Greek thought) then day on one side of Anaximander's earth will be night on the other side and this will change under the ordering of time/the sun.
75 Mansfeld (2011) p. 15.
76 Kirk (1955), p. 29.
77 I disagree with Hankinson (1998) p. 17 that referring to the change of the four elements/*apeiron* explains structure for Anaximander – there is more structure in his cosmos than this will explain.
78 Stobaeus I, 25, 1c, Stobaeus I, 26, 1a, Pseudo-Plutarch, II, 21, 1, Pseudo-Plutarch II, 25, 1, Stobaeus I, 26, 1a, Hippolytus, *Refutation of All Heresies* I, 6, 1–7.
79 Pseudo-Plutarch II, 20, 1.
80 Berryman (2009) p. 31.
81 If the rings are fluid, Anaximander had better not have a like to like principle as like to like between the rings will quickly deform them out of shape.
82 If some motion in celestial latitude were possible, this would be useful in modelling the daily motions of moon and sun, and Anaximander might be able to account for the motions of the planets relative to the fixed stars.
83 Couprie (1995), (2009a), (2009b), (2011).
84 Gregory (2016).
85 Gregory (2001), (2016).
86 Tannery (1895) pp. 91–2.
87 Pseudo-Plutarch II, 20, 1, II, 21, 1, II, 25, 1, Stobaeus I, 25, 1c, Stobaeus I, 26, 1a, Hippolytus *Refutation of All Heresies* I, 6.
88 See Gregory (2016) Chapter 9 on alternative sequences.
89 West (1971), Diels (1897), Heath (1913) p. 38.
90 See here Couprie (2011) p. 119, Hahn (2003) p. 85 ff.
91 See Gregory (2016) Chapter 9.

## Chapter 5  New Explanations, New Philosophies of Nature

1 Graham's paper at the London ancient Science Conference 2020 has persuaded me that a more precise translation for *prēstērōn* is fire whirl (there are such things!) and

for *tuphōnōn* tornado, rather than the standard hurricane and typhoon, which are meteorologically inappropriate for Greece.

2. Pseudo-Plutarch, III, 3, 1 = Aetius, III, 3, 1 = DK12A23. We have two versions of this report on Anaximander, Stobaeus, 1, 29, 1 and Pseudo-Plutarch, III, 3, 1, identical except Pseudo-Plutarch has *panta* instead of *eipe* in line 2. The first line is a heading so should be differentiated from the rest of the passage. Is 'thunder, lightning, thunderbolts, fire whirls and tornados' a category generated by the doxographers, into which they fit disparate views of Anaximander, or a category generated by Anaximander himself? I discuss this fully in Gregory (2016) p. 55 ff. but these are the key points. The first known grouping of these five phenomena is Aristotle *Meteorology* II, 9. This does not seem a natural group for Aristotle, so it is likely he is picking up on an earlier grouping. The doxographers give no priority to Aristotle's views here. Stobaeus I, 29, 1 tells us that: 'Anaximenes, the same (as Anaximander), adding what happens with the sea, which flashes when broken by oars.' This very strongly suggests that these five phenomena are a group for Anaximander and that Anaximenes treats them as a group as well, adding something extra in terms of explanation.
3. Homer, *Iliad* VIII, 133, IX, 236, XXI, 198, *Odyssey* XXIV, 539. In the *Odyssey* there is a recurring motif of a ship being hit by the thunderbolt of Zeus, *Odyssey* V, 128, VII, 249, XII, 415, XIV, 305, XXIII, 330.
4. See Hesiod *Theogony* 687 ff.
5. Hesiod, *Theogony* 845–6.
6. See Gregory (2013a). This list is not meant to be exhaustive but does contain the key examples from that book.
7. See Gregory (2013a) Chapters 1 and 3.
8. Kahn (1960) p. 99 ff. finds little development in Greek meteorology once Anaximander gives naturalistic explanations; Taub (2003) p. 10 finds rather more. I tend to side with Taub, though I would locate the development to producing explanations of more meteorological phenomena (rainbows, St, Elmo's fire etc.) and to giving more detailed explanations consistent with the philosophical developments.
9. Xenophanes Fr. 32.
10. Pseudo-Plutarch, 5, 1, 1: 'Xenophanes and Epicurus did away completely with divination.'
11. See Gregory (2013a) Chapter 6.
12. See Gregory (2013a) Chapters 4 and 5.
13. See Gregory (2013a) Chapter 6.
14. See Gregory (2013a) Chapter 10.
15. Empedocles is an interesting case as he too clearly alludes to Homer and Hesiod, but seems to do so for different reasons, often emphasizing that humans can do, or aspire to do what in Homer and Hesiod is reserved for the gods.

16 Heraclitus Fr. 64.
17 I take the *Timaeus* to be at last in part a running commentary on early Greek natural philosophy.
18 Or perhaps, to be more precise, Aristotle's version of his views.
19 Empedocles Fr. 17, 26. cf. Fr. 35, 1–2: 'I shall turn back once more to the path of song recounted previously, as I draw off account upon account, in that way', which may be an allusion to Parmenides Fr. 6, where mortals wander on a backwards turning path; see also Guthrie II pp. 138–9. The opening of Fr. 17 may also recall Parmenides – see here KRS p. 287. I believe that Empedocles makes the same sorts of allusions to Heraclitus' work as well and that Heraclitus does with Anaximander.
20 Xenophanes Fr. 1, 21–3.
21 Xenophanes Fr. 32.
22 Lesher (1992) p. 143.
23 Lloyd (1991) p. 420.
24 Lloyd (1991) p. 420.
25 Lloyd (1991) p. 422.
26 Lloyd (1991) p. 423.
27 Pseudo-Plutarch's passage is perhaps a touch more emphatic in this respect with its *panta*, but it is clear in the Stobaeus passage as well that all of the five phenomena mentioned are to be explained in terms of wind.
28 Pseudo-Plutarch III, 7.
29 Hippolytus, *The Refutation of all Heresies* 1, 6, 7.
30 Hesiod, *Works and Days* 53 for Zeus as cloud-gatherer and *Works and Days* 416 for Zeus as rain bringer.
31 See e.g. Homer, *Iliad* XII, 25 ff. where he rains continually to submerge a strategically important wall; Homer, *Iliad* XI, 385 ff. to punish unjust men.
32 See e.g. Homer, *Iliad* XV, 3789 ff. to aid the Achaeans in battle; Homer, *Iliad* XI, 385 ff. to punish unjust men; Homer, *Odyssey* IX, 67 ff. one of many storms at sea.
33 For winds in Hesiod, see *Theogony* 253, 706 and the battle between Zeus and the Titans beginning at 821 and especially the comments on Typhoeus at 869. For winds in Homer, see e.g. the first part of Homer, *Odyssey* X. Circe generates winds at *Odyssey* XI, 6, XII, 146, Calypso does at Odyssey V, 167, 268 and Athena at *Odyssey* II, 420, V, 108 XV, 292.
34 Stobaeus I, 29, 1.
35 This is the only occurrence we are aware of for *metabiōnai*. LSJ give 'live after, survive'. Kahn (1960) says that: 'A verbal compound in *meta-* normally indicates a change from one condition to another, and *metabiōnai* should mean "to live a different life" or "to survive in a different form." Either sense is applicable to Anaximander's view.' I opt for the second alternative here, with a sense of metamorphosis to survive in a different form. See Gregory (2016) Chapter 2.

36 I preserve the comparative *zēroteron* (some translations use dry rather than drier, Graham (2006a) has 'moved onto land'), as there is a difference between moving onto the (absolutely) dry and moving onto something relatively drier, which may still be significantly moist, such as a submerged stone or log.
37 I would disagree with Barnes when he says that 'There is no suggestion that this mode of reproduction occurred more than once' (Barnes (1979) p. 22). Caddisflies do this every year.
38 See Zeller (1881) vol. I. p. 255, Gomperz (1911–12), p. 196, Eastman (1905) p. 702, Heath (1913) p. 39, Burnet (1930) p. 71, F. de Rademaker (1953), p 35.
39 I do not attribute a modern understanding of metamorphosis to Anaximander here, just an observation of a natural process generating a more complex organism.
40 E.g. Kahn (1960) p. 109, Guthrie (1965) pp. 90–1, KRS (1983) pp. 141–2, Freudenthal (1986) pp. 216–17, cf. Kleisner and Kocandrle (2013) p. 116: 'Here we find once again reference to a "prickly bark" that broke on the dry land. We can suppose it had a protective function since it was an organ of creatures living in a moist environment. It could have been seen as analogical to the above-mentioned shells or scales. The breaking of the bark would in a way describe the appearance of life on the dry land.'
41 We do have different verbs though for the *cosmos* and the first animals, *apoppageisēs*, meaning 'to be broken off or severed from' and *perirrēgnumenou*, 'shedding for themselves'. We might also compare *periechomena*, with *periphuēnai*, 'to have formed around'. The first creatures create their own cases, the earth has its sphere of flame formed for it. Perhaps we should give Anaximander some greater credit here in differentiating between what passively happens to the *cosmos* and what living things are capable of doing for themselves.
42 KRS (1983) p. 142 ff.
43 KRS (1983) p. 142.
44 KRS (1983) p. 142.
45 Barnes (1979) p. 22.
46 Simplicius, *Physics* 24, 13.
47 See KRS (1983) pp. 105 f., 117 ff. This is disputed as well though, especially the words preceding *kata to chreōn* – see below. Mansfeld (2011) takes the whole first sentence from *ex hōn* as part of the fragment.
48 Though as Mansfeld (2011) p. 15 has suggested, it can also mean death.
49 Mourelatos (1970), (2008) p. 277 ff.
50 Some commentators use 'fate' here, as 'selon le destin' or 'selon ce qui doit être', Rivaud (1906) p .93, Conche (1991) p. 157, though I would expect other terms if that was what Anaximander intended. Kahn believes that *chreōn* 'combines the ideas of right and necessity'.
51 Redard (1953).

52 It is worth noting here that in Plato's *Timaeus* there is a strong moral sense to all the actions of the demiurge.
53 See *Odyssey* I, 296, II, 369, IV, 492, X, 380, XV, 393, XVIII, 17, XIX, 500, *Iliad* VII, 109, IX, 146, IX, 613, X, 479, XVI, 721, XIX, 420, XX, 133, XXIII, 478. I agree with Redard and Mourelatos that *Odyssey* XIX, 500 is not exceptional and the phrase here means 'it is not proper' in the sense of 'it is not your role'.
54 Or perhaps 'you ought to know'.
55 Heraclitus Fr. 80, agreeing with the usual emendation of *chreōn* for *chrōmena*, see KRS (1983) p. 193.
56 See here KRS (1983) p. 194 and Vlastos (1955) p. 356 for slightly different views on this.
57 KRS (1983) p. 194 comment that: 'This must be a deliberate amendment of Anaximander's dictum that things pay retribution to each other for the *injustice* of their alternate encroachments in the process of natural change.'
58 For criticism of this view, see Havelock (1978) p. 264.
59 KRS (1983) p. 121 back this with a reference to Solon Fr. 24, 1–7:

> Why did I cease before I gained the objects for whose sake I brought together the people? The great mother of the Olympian deities would be my best supporting witness for this in the court of Time (*Chronou*) – black Earth, whose boundary-stones, fixed in many places, I once removed; formerly was she enslaved, now is she free.

60 Graham (2006) p. 35.
61 Hesiod, *Theogony* 74–5, trans. West.
62 Hesiod, *Works and Days* 277, trans. West
63 Theognis lived in the sixth century BCE and is one of the earliest poets whose work survives in any substantial quantity. One of his topics was anxiety over the current political situation; he was also a moralizer. He was concerned with the possible deterioration of the city, so: 'Wealth has mixed up blood. And so, Polypaides, do not be surprised that the townsman's stock is becoming enfeebled, since what is noble is mixing with what is base.' Theognis 190–2, Gerber's translation.
64 Theognis 677–8, trans. Vlastos.
65 Vlastos (1947) p. 174.
66 Cf. Furley (1987) p. 13.
67 Gregory (2000), (2001), (2003).
68 Plato, *Timaeus* 34a. The six motions are up, down, left, right, backwards and forwards.
69 Plato, *Timaeus* 40a.
70 'Wandering' is an issue here as Burkert comments that in the *Republic*, Plato: 'Was still of the opinion that real exactitude was impossible in the physical world, so that

the true astronomer should not depend on sense perception but busy himself with purely ideal magnitudes and movements. In the *Timaeus*, too, Plato speaks without hesitation of the "wandering" of the planets'. Burkert (1972) p. 324, cf. Heath (1913) p. 171, Mittelstrass (1962) pp. 130 ff., Owen (1953) p. 325 ff.

71 Thought of in terms of a compromise between reason and necessity, the compromise is that the heavens move, not that they move irregularly.

72 One might also contrast the regular flow of time in the cosmos with the irregularity of the pre-cosmos chaos.

73 Plato, *Laws* 967b.

74 Though there is in seventeenth-century thought, in particular with Leibniz and his god generating a perfect clockwork world which that god would not need to attend to. See the Leibniz–Clarke correspondence for interesting debate here.

75 See e.g. Plato, *Gorgias* 506b5. The *Laws* is also adamant that prayer or other offerings will be of no avail in trying to change the minds of the gods.

76 Is the comment that follows, *Gorgias* 511d6-7, that 'geometrical equality has great power among gods and men' an allusion to Anaximander whose cosmology is set out with considerable geometrical equality – an earth that does not move because there is no reason for it to do so, rings of stars moon and sun that do not move because there is no reason for them to do so?

77 See Seaford (2004) p. 194.

78 So the *apeiron* and the steering principle are both natural in the sense of being part of *phusis* and behaving in an invariant manner. See Gregory (2013a) Chapter 1 for discussion and definitions of natural/supernatural and what is and is not part of *phusis* for the ancients.

79 See Vlastos (1947) p. 173, Freudenthal (1986) pp. 197, 227, Naddaf (2005) p. 15, Drozdek (2008) pp. 10–11.

80 Burnet (1930) p. 13, cf. Matson (1953).

81 Jaeger (1947) p. 36, cf. Burch (1949–50).

82 Draper (1874) and White (1896) are the classic statements of the conflict thesis. See Brooke (1991) and Dixon (2008) for comment and the new complexity theory. Babut (1972) is considered the best piece on the divine in Anaximander, but even he speaks of 'Le conflit entre l'explication rationnelle des phénomènes, tentée par la science ionienne.' Babut (1972) p. 2. Cornford (1957), v, is an interesting statement of older views, including the idea of successive phases.

83 See Brooke (1991), Dixon (2008).

84 In relation to this, I would disagree with Drozdek who says: 'Physics for Anaximander is secondary to theology – it is used to substantiate theology; physics becomes an afterthought of sorts that is used to make his physics less otherworldly.' Drozdek (2008) p. 11, cf. Seligman (1962) p. 60. I agree with Babut that: 'Anaximandre transforme profondément le concept du divin, détaché d'un seul coup

de toute référence humaine', Babut (1972) p. 22. cf. p. 1, 'Face à la religion populaire, son attitude est plutôt celle du détachement et de l'objectivité.'
85  See e.g. Vlastos (1952) p. 119. Cf. Lloyd (1979) p. 11, Jaeger (1947), Hussey (1972), Gregory (2007) Chapter 2, Sedley (2007) Chapter 1, Trepanier (2010).
86  See Spinoza (1677). The term was first made popular by Toland in 1705, although it was first used in 1697. Toland (1705) *Socinianism Truly Stated, by a Pantheist*. Raphson (1697) *De Spatio Reali*.
87  In distinction to the nineteenth-century German tradition of pantheism, which was idealist.
88  Aristotle, *On Animals* I, 2, 405a19, and *On Animals* I, 2, 411a7.
89  See Stobaeus I, 10, 12, cf. Pseudo-Plutarch I, 3, 4. Cf. Stobaeus I, 1, 29b, Cf. Cicero, *De Natura Deorum*, 1, 10, 26.
90  Plato, *Philebus* 28d '*nous* and a marvellous organizing intelligence steer the cosmos' might indicate panpsychism but we cannot be sure this applies to Anaximander and even if it does Plato may have his own agenda for supposing that there is some form of soul behind the steering. The self-steering Phaeacian ships might support the idea of soul.
91  Cornford (1912) p. viii.
92  Xenophanes, Fr. 11, cf. Fr. 12.
93  So in an ancient context, I disagree with Dawkins' notorious comment that 'Pantheism is sexed-up Atheism', Dawkins (2007), 40.
94  See Gregory (2007).
95  Plato, Laws 889b ff.
96  See Gregory (2007).
97  West (1971) p. 77.
98  Barnes (1982) p. 20.
99  Draper (1874) History of the Conflict Between Religion and Science and White (1896) History of the Warfare of Science with Theology in Christendom. The book titles may give some indication of their orientation. Lindberg and Numbers (1992) and Brooke (1991) are seminal for the modern complexity view.

# Chapter 6  Anaximenes and the *Kratein* Tradition

1  The Hippocratic authors will be dealt with in the next chapter.
2  See Stobaeus I, 10, 12 =Aetius I, 3, 4, DK13B2), cf. Pseudo-Plutarch I, 3, 4, Diogenes of Apollonia Fr. 5 and Derveni papyrus Col. 19, Anaxagoras Fr. 12.
3  Aetius 1, 3, 4.
4  *Cosmos* need not have the precise technical sense it had later, and while *pneuma* may look like a typical Stoic accretion, the term was in use at this stage.

5   KRS (1983) p. 159 ff.
6   KRS (1983) p. 159.
7   Cf. the discussions in Longrigg (1964) and KRS (1983).
8   KRS (1983) p. 160.
9   KRS (1983) p. 160.
10  KRS (1983) p. 161.
11  As I argued in my *Presocratics and the Supernatural*, there are relations such as sympathy, harmony, correspondence and indeed macrocosm/microcosm that may be (and often were) natural in many circumstances, on a reasonable definition of natural. Such relations could also be mystical or supernatural in some circumstances.
12  See Plato, *Timaeus* 88de.
13  See Plato, *Timaeus* 81ab.
14  In Aristotle's somewhat terse and elliptical Greek 'large' in this context would readily be understood to mean 'large world'.
15  Aristotle, *On Generation and Corruption* II, 10. This passage was much referred to as an example of the macrocosm/microcosm analogy in Aristotle.
16  *DMC* Chapter 8. See Aristotle *De Generatione et Corruptione* II, 10, *De Anima* 415b3–8, *De Mundo* 399a20–35 for the Aristotelian background here. For Aristotle it is the sun that is the cause of the weather cycle – this is in the very strong Aristotelian sense of being both efficient and final cause – see *Meteorologica* 346b20 ff.
17  Longrigg (1964).
18  KRS (1983) pp. 158–60, cf. the KRS quote above on rationality.
19  Aristotle, *On the Heavens*, II, 13, 295a7 ff.
20  Aristotle, *On the Heavens*, II, 13, 294b13.
21  Hippolytus *Refutation of all Heresies* 1, 7, 6.
22  Hippolytus, *Refutation of all Heresies* 1, 7, 4.
23  See Aetius II, 14, 3 and II, 22, 1.
24  Aetius II, 23, 1.
25  Pseudo-Plutarch, *Stromateis* 3. Cf. Aristotle Metaphysics I, 3 984a, Hippolytus *Refutation of all Heresies* 1, 7, 1, Simplicius, *Physics* 24, 26.
26  Stobaeus I, 29, 1.
27  Xenophanes Fr. 25.
28  Xenophanes Fr. 26.
29  I am happy to translate an understood 'divine law' here though Heraclitus' Greek just has *tou theiou* (following *hoi anthrōpeioi nomoi*, the human laws). However, cf. Kahn (1979) p. 118. My thanks to Chiara d'Agostino who pointed out to me that the presence of the article here makes this read 'all human laws are nourished by THE one divine.'

30 KRS (1983) p. 212.
31 Though investigation for Heraclitus is not always on its own a good thing – Fr. 129 has Pythagoras as the best human investigator, but his great learning brings only *kakotechniēn*.
32 Taking *ton auton hapantōn* as genuine with Guthrie, Vlastos and Kahn but against Kirk and KRS.
33 Heraclitus Fr. 30.
34 Heraclitus Fr. 31.
35 So, e.g. all Euclidean triangles have internal angles adding up to 180 degrees.
36 'Father of all' may be an allusion to Homer, where Zeus is frequently referred to in this way.
37 Cf. *Timaeus* 91a ff., where we find that the male indeed supplies the seed (like the fruit from a tree, *apo dendrōn karpon*, 91d) while the woman supplies the place in which it grows (it is sown as in a tilled field, *arouran* 91d2).
38 Graham (2003).
39 One might object here that as the 'truth' part of the poem is so different from the 'opinion' part such a comparison is not compelling, but I take the view that the poem is more of a whole and that all three parts of the poem (proem, truth, opinion) pose important and interrelated philosophical issues. See Gregory (2014).
40 See Mourelatos (1970), (2008), p. 8 ff. especially but otherwise *passim*.
41 The grammar here is not entirely clear and the pronoun may refer to several people, but most likely to Aegisthus.
42 Derveni papyrus Col 19, 1–15.
43 Anaxagoras Fr. 12.
44 Col. 4 also rejects a role for chance in explaining why the cosmos has order. It is worth noting that chance plays no role in Heraclitus' cosmology either.
45 Derveni papyrus, Col. 4, 5–6.
46 Cf. Heraclitus, Fr. 3.
47 Cf. Heraclitus, Fr. 94.
48 Derveni papyrus. Col. 9, 5–8.
49 Derveni papyrus, Col. 25 lines 9–12. Cf. Col. 15: 'Colliding them with each other, he made the sun separate, the things that are standing apart from each other. For as the sun became separated and encircled, he coagulated and held fast both the things that are above and those that are below the sun.'
50 See Derveni papyrus, Col. 10, 11–13, quoted above.
51 Betegh (2004) p. 355.
52 See especially Derveni papyrus, Col. 20.
53 Simplicius *Physics* 157. 25, line 19.
54 See *Odyssey* I, 16 and XI, 248 for similar constructions with the seasons and the years moving round.

55 So Wright (1981) p. 181.
56 So Inwood (2001) p. 231 'in the turns assigned by destiny'.
57 See Wright (1981) p. 223. If Wright is correct, and the language here is that of a potter and clay, then I would shift to claiming an important and interesting craft analogy here.
58 Taking the TLG text of *diassēthentos* here, rather than *diatmēthentos* as I think this makes a little more sense.
59 Tor (2017) p. 327.
60 Empedocles, Fr. 111.
61 See Gregory (2013a) Chapter 9.
62 Kingsley (1995) pp. 225–6 argues for the later and compares it to the work of a shaman. Cf. Dodds (1951).
63 There may be lost medical writings of Empedocles. There are two definite references to Empedocles' medical writings, Diogenes Laertius, *Lives of the Philosophers* VIII, 77, and *Suda* (DK31A2). Two possible references are Aristotle Poetics 1447b16 and Pliny, *Natural History*, XXXVI, 69, 202. Galen, *On the Method of Healing* I, 1 also seems to consider Empedocles to have been a doctor.
64 Curd (2005) p. 13 comments that 'In B111 Empedocles holds forth the promise of remarkable and seemingly supernatural skills, yet embeds this promise in the naturalistic account of the roots of all things, of the forces that combine and separate these roots and the consequent formation of the *kosmos* and living things.' Cf. Longrigg (1993) p. 27: 'Nowhere can there be found any recourse to supernatural agency to account for the origin of the world or the operation of cause and effect within it.'
65 Empedocles Fr. 112 generates a similar debate. See see Dodds (1951), Guthrie II, Kingsley (1995) and Gregory (2013a) Chapter 9.
66 Furley (1987) p. 79 praises Empedocles for 'The postulation of two physical forces, qualitatively different from each other.'
67 Cf. Guthrie II pp. 156–7 and Dodds (1951) pp. 145–6.
68 Lamb (1961) p. 43.
69 Taking the verbs here as middles rather than passives (it is not dispersed ... is not set together).
70 The Loeb translation of 'birds of a feather flock together' is not entirely helpful here!
71 Plato also says at *Republic* 329a that: 'Many times there is a coming together of those of us with the same age, thus proving the old proverb.' He is not specific as to what the old proverb is (some translations add 'of like to like' at the end of this sentence, but it is not there in the Greek).
72 See Sedley (1992).
73 Anaxagoras Fr. 12.
74 Broadie (1999) p. 206.

75 Theophrastus *On Plants* 3, 1, 4, Anaxagoras held that the air holds the seeds of all things and these, carried down by rain form plants.
76 Plato, *Phaedo* 97d ff.
77 See Cornford (1933), Guthrie (1965), Vlastos (1947).
78 See Gregory (2007) Chapter 6., cf. Curd (2005).
79 Democritus Fr. 34.

## Chapter 7  Leucippus and Democritus

1 Later in antiquity, *ou mallon* arguments were used to generate skeptical conclusions, but here I argue they are a fundamental part of the early atomists reply to Parmenides. See Gregory (2014).
2 Taylor (1999) p. 5.
3 This sieving does work and was agricultural practice. The contents of the sieve are separated out by density.
4 For a more extended discussion, see Gregory (2014).
5 Plato is critical of cosmogony based on this alone, as for him the cosmos is a harmonious blend of opposites, something highly unlikely to be produced from a like to like principle alone, see *Laws* 889b.
6 Attraction, *holkē*, *Timaeus* 80c3.
7 The verb here, *perikleklasmenein* has a primary meaning of to twist or bend.
8 Pseudo-Plutarch, I, 4.
9 Simplicius *Physics* 327, 24. See also Simplicius *Physics* 327, 330, 14, Themistius *Physics* 49, 13, Cicero *De Natura Deorum* I, 24, 66.
10 Cf. Aristotle, *Physics* II, 4, 196a24 ff.
11 Cf. Stobaeus I, 16, 1.
12 It is also significant that Democritus takes a reductive line on mind/soul, believing it to be constituted from spherical atoms – see Aristotle *de Anima* 403b30.
13 Pyle (1995) p. 142 ff.
14 See here Dijksterhuis (1961) p. 12, Hirsch (1990), Berryman (2009) p. 18 for discussion.
15 Hesse (1961) p. 51.
16 Salmon (1984) p. 241.
17 See Gregory (2007) Chapters 5, 9 and 10.
18 Taylor (1999) p. 194.
19 Philoponus *Commentary on Aristotle's Physics* 494, 198 ff., *Commentary on Aristotle's On Generation and Corruption* 158, 26 ff. and 160, 7 ff.
20 Bodnar (1998).
21 Aristotle Fr. 208, Stobaeus I, 10, 14 and I, 14, 1 and I, 16, 1, Simplicius *De Caelo Commentary* 295, 5, Philo Judaeus *De Plantatione* 7, 3 all use *nastos*.

22 Aristotle *On the Heavens* III, 4, 303a7.
23 Simplicius, *De Caelo Commentary*, 295, 11.
24 Simplicius, *De Caelo Commentary*, 242, 21.
25 See below for a further discussion of this passage.
26 Reading *epekrusin* here with the MSS tradition (the alternative being *epekkrisin*).
27 Berryman (2009) p. 7
28 Furley (1987) p. 13.
29 See here Berryman (2009) p. 19.
30 Dijksterhuis (1961) p. 12.
31 Is there an assumption here that once we have knowledge it is not lost? One might argue that for knowledge as justified true belief (though I am not convinced historically that holds) but one might also question that if the early atomists did assume something like Newton's first law it was not backed by any significant justification.
32 Simplicius, *Physics*, 28, 8.
33 Sedley (1982).
34 See Parmenides Fr. 8 29–30, Sedley (1982).
35 See e.g. Drabkin (1938) and Owen (1986), pp. 315–34. Note the parallels here to how we ought to approach the early atomists and the question of whether they were mechanists.
36 See Wardy (1990), cf. Carteron (1975) and de Gandt (1982).
37 See Lloyd (1987).
38 See Gregory (2001).
39 Lloyd, (1987) p. 219.
40 Wardy (1990) p. 303.
41 I take it as uncontroversial that the *Mechanics* is by a later Aristotelian.
42 Aristotle *De Caelo* I, 8, 277a27–30. Cf. *Physics* 230b23–5, 265b12–16 and *De Caelo* 277b5–9, and see Hussey (1983) pp. 199–200.
43 See Drabkin (1938) pp. 72–3, Owen (1986) p. 156. I will leave these terms untranslated as the English renditions of *ischus* as 'strength', *dunamis* as 'force' or 'power' and *rhope* as 'impulse' or 'momentum' are apt to be misleading if taken in any technical sense.
44 *Metaphysics* IV, 12 and VIII, 1 do discuss *dunamis*, but in the broader sense of capacity or power.
45 See e.g. *Physics* IV, 8, 215a14–18.
46 Aristotle, *Physics* VIII, 10 266a26–8. Cf. *Physics* 250a28 ff. and *De Caelo* 275 a32 ff.
47 It makes a difference in accounting for the orbits of the planets (how much their perihelia advance), most notably for Mercury.
48 Gregory, forthcoming.
49 Myself included, see Gregory (2014), which accepts determinism in the early atomists.

50 Pierre Simon Laplace, *A Philosophical Essay on Probabilities*.
51 Simplicius *Physics* 28, 8.
52 Simplicius *De Caelo* 295, 5, reporting Aristotle *On Democritus*, see below.
53 Parmenides, Fr. 8, 42–5.
54 Gregory (2013).
55 Parmenides Fr. 8, 5–10.
56 See Gregory (2013).
57 Simplicius *Physics* 327, 24.
58 Pseudo-Plutarch, I, 4.
59 Plutarch, *Adversus Colotem* 1109a.
60 Barnes (1982) p. 405.
61 Taking the verbs here as middles rather than passives (it is not dispersed ... is not set together).
62 Pierre Simon Laplace, *A Philosophical Essay on Probabilities*.
63 LSJ give 'at random, without reason' for *matēn*.
64 Stobaeus I, 4.
65 Diogenes Laertius, IX, 45.
66 Aristotle, *Physics* II, 4, 196a25 ff., cf. *Parts of Animals* 641b20 ff.
67 Simplicius, *Physics Commentary* 330, 14–20. There is also a debate about whether modern notions of determinism and free will are appropriate or anachronistic for Aristotle.
68 Aristotle's view that chance events occur in the absence of teleology (even when there is necessity) and its influence is another factor here.
69 See e.g. Themistius, *Commentary on Aristotle's Physics*, 49, 13–16. Eusebius *Preparatio Evangelica* XIV, 22, 3. See also Furley (1989) p. 77 ff.
70 Aristotle, Physics, 203b28
71 Gregory (2014) p. 463.
72 Specifically, Fr. 8, lines 31, 42, 49 but also see Mourelatos (1970) p. 28 on the idea of limit pervading Fr. 8.
73 Boyle, *A Disquisition about the Final Causes of Natural Things*, Works vol. 5, p. 409.
74 Newton, *Optics* IV 260.
75 Cf. Hirsch (1990).
76 Keynes (1921) p. 247, Lloyd (1966) pp. 179, 357.

# Chapter 8 The Hippocratic Authors

1 Gomperz (1922) is the classic statement for naturalist traditions, see van der Eijk (2011) for opinions on why this view has persisted, cf. Longrigg (1993) pp. 1, 8, 26 and Porter (1999) p. 53. Edelstein (1967) is the classic statement of the non-natural view.

2  The first line of Tablet BM 47753, 25th or 26th tablet in a series known as *Sakikiu*, 'all diseases', reads 'If epilepsy falls once upon a person or falls many times, it is as the result of possession by a demon or a departed spirit.' This dates to the middle of the first millennium BC, trans. Wilson and Reynolds (1990).
3  See *New Testament* Mark Mark 9:14–29.
4  The only remedy being to assuage the anger of the gods. Cf. Homer *Odyssey* V, 394 ff., *Odyssey* XI, 409 ff.
5  Hesiod, *Theogony* 238 ff., quoted in full Chapter 3.
6  Temkin (1971) p. 3
7  Cf. Plato *Republic* 364b ff., *Laws* 909a ff. on itinerant charm and incantation sellers.
8  Hippocratic author, *On the Sacred Disease* XVI, 42–6.
9  Again, this use of *amēchanon* should make us consider very carefully what *mēchanē* would have meant for the early Greeks.
10  Hippocratic author, *On the Sacred Disease* XXI, 1–26.
11  I am inclined to believe this experiment was done (that the goat brain was foul smelling I would say comes from experience rather than invention) though see Lloyd (1979) pp. 23–4.
12  It is worth noting that there are healing songs in Homer, though the attack on incantations is quite general. See Homer, *Odyssey* XIX, 455 ff. for healing songs.
13  Hippocratic author, *On the Sacred Disease* IV, 21–35.
14  Lloyd, 1979 pp. 19 ff.
15  Hippocratic author, *On the Sacred Disease* IV, 10–16, Cf. IV, *On the Sacred Disease* 1–4: 'For is they can bring down the moon, to eclipse the sun, make storm and good weather, rain and drought, the sea impassable and the earth barren, and all the other such things.'
16  Hippocratic author, *On the Sacred Disease* IV, 16–21.
17  Hippocratic author, *On Airs, Waters and Places* Chapter XXII, 8–14.
18  Hippocratic author, *On the Art*, VI 14–20.
19  Jouanna (1999) pp. 254–5.
20  Calls for prayer are rare in the Hippocratic corpus, see Hankinson (1998a) p. 30.
21  'The function of prayer is not to influence God, but rather to change the nature of the one who prays.' Kierkegaard. See Gregory (2013).
22  Xenophanes Fr. 1, 15–16.
23  Plutarch, *On the Cessation of Oracles* 17, 419a, cf. Democritus Fr. 37 and Fr. 112. So too Aristotle, in the *Nicomachean Ethics* says that 'Humans should pray that what is absolutely good is good for them, and choose the things that are good for them.' Aristotle, *Nicomachean Ethics* V, 1, 1129 b3.
24  Hippocratic author, *On Regimen* IV, 87.
25  Though cf. Hankinson (1998) p. 33, n. 57.
26  Hankinson (1998) p. 11.

27 Hankinson (1998) p. 12. Hankinson continues in parentheses: Although it is another question whether the Hippocratics could have realized this, and hence that any such talk of the divine was mere linguistic window-dressing.
28 Hankinson (1998) p. 13.
29 Contrast Draper (1874) and White (1896) with Brooke (1991), Lindberg and Numbers (1992), Dixon (2008).
30 We should not be misled by Aristotle's theologoi/physiologoi distinction into following conflict theory.
31 LSJ give to divide and marshal, muster, array with usages drawn from Homer and Thucydides. Cf. Mourelatos (1970) p. 230 on a similar use in Parmenides.
32 Hippocratic author, *On Regimen* I,10.
33 See also *On Regimen* IV, 89.
34 Hippocratic author, *On Regimen* IV, 89.
35 Dodds (1951) p. 119 sees these dreams as symbolic, in line with his Freudian views, but I think that is anachronistic and would remove the need for any macrocosm/microcosm analogy.
36 In comments on Hankinson's paper, Hankinson (1998) p. 31, n. 56.
37 In comments on Hankinson's paper, Hankinson (1998) p. 31, n. 56.
38 See Gregory (2013) Chapter 1 for discussion on natural and beyond the natural on an ancient context.
39 Hankinson (1998) p. 31, n. 56.
40 Cf. *Timaeus* 82a, *Symposium* 186, *Laws* 906c.
41 Cf. the optimism of *On the Sacred Disease* XXI, no disease is intractable or untreatable, someone who can produce hot, cold, wet or dry in humans can cure any disease etc.
42 See my earlier discussion in Chapter 3 and Lesher (2008) p. 461.
43 This is a better translation of *peri parthenion* for our times than the more traditional 'On Girls'.
44 On this see Jouanna (1992) pp. 237 ff.
45 Hippocratic author, *Prognostic* I. Trans Adams.
46 Homer, *Iliad* I, 62, I, 106, I, 384, *Odyssey* X, 493, XII, 267, XV, 252, XVII, 384.
47 Homer, *Iliad* I, 62, I, 106, I, 384, *Odyssey*, XVII, 384.
48 Hesiod, *Theogony* 25 ff.
49 Hesiod, *Theogony* 31-2.
50 See e.g. *Iliad* I, 69 and 343, III, 109, XVIII, 250, *Odyssey* XXIV, 452.
51 Contra the Loeb, there is no 'force of blowing' here, just blowing.
52 Sextus Empiricus *Against the Mathematicians* VII 116-18
53 Lonie (1981) pp. 129-30.
54 Compare the discussion in the previous chapter about like to like in the absence of moiton.

55 Sextus Empiricus *Against the Mathematicians* VII, 116–21.
56 Lonie (1981).
57 Lonie (1981) p. 123.
58 Lonie (1981) p. 125.
59 Lonie (1981) p. 128.
60 Lonie (1981) p. 123.
61 The Loeb's 'unbolts the mouth' goes with the other sense of *mochlos*, a bar placed across gates to lock them shut.
62 Aetius 1, 3, 4.
63 There are textual variations of *kinēsin* and *sustasin* here, if we accept *sustasin* then 'the natural composition of the blood'. I believe *kinēsin* makes slightly more sense, but I do not associate 'the things in the body make a rapid circulation' with the circulation of the blood.
64 Lonie (1981) p. 125.
65 Lonie (1981) p. 124.
66 Lloyd (1973) p. 47.
67 Lonie (1981) p. 124.
68 See Lloyd (1966) pp. 347–8 for further examples here.
69 Lonie (1981) p. 127.
70 Wright (1981) pp. 83–4, Inwood (2002) p. 258.
71 Sedley (1998) p. 20, cf. Campbell (2003) p. 3.
72 See Gregory (2007) Chapter 5 for further discussion on this issue.
73 Lonie (1981) p. 127 comments in relation to a broader mechanistic view that: 'It is doubtful whether we should want to characterize Empedocles' physical philosophy in this way, despite the extensive use which he makes of the concept of effluences and pores into which they fit.'
74 Harvey, *On the Generation of Animals*, Exercise 11.
75 See Gregory (2001) p. 133 ff.
76 See Basalla (1962), Webster 1965, Pagel (1967) p. 213.
77 The Anatomical Lectures of William Harvey (ed. G. Whitteridge 1964) p. 272.
78 'A Clack is a peece of Leather nailed over any hole having a peece of lead to make it lie close, so that Ayer or Water in any Vessel may thereby be kept from going out.' John Bates, *The Mysteries of Art and Nature*, p. 13, quoted from Basalla (1962) p. 469. The aortic and pulmonary valves of the heart are also flexible.
79 Aristotle, *De Respiratione*, 480a20–3, cf. 478a10. Galen also frequently likens the heart to a forge bellows.
80 For Aristotle on the heart especially as a source of motion, see e.g. *De Anima* 405 b14, *On the Soul* 408b38, 432b31, 456a4, 469a10.
81 Harvey is concerned with distinguishing systole and diastole here.

# Bibliography

Adkins, A. W. H. 1997. 'Homeric Ethics'. In I. Morris and B. Powell (eds), *A New Companion to Homer* (*Mnemosyne* Suppl. 163, Leiden), pp. 694–713.

Alexander, H. G. 1970. *The Leibniz-Clarke Correspondence, together with extracts from Newton's Principia and Opticks, edited with introd. and notes by H. G. Alexander*. Manchester: Manchester University Press.

Allan, W. 2006. 'Divine Justice and Cosmic Order in Early Greek Epic'. *Journal of Hellenic Studies* 126, 1–35.

Babut, D. 1972. 'Le divin et les dieux dans la pensée d'Anaximandre'. *Revue des Études Grecques* 85, 1–32.

Bailey, C. 1928. *The Greek Atomists and Epicurus*. New York: Russell & Russell.

Baldry, H. 1932. 'Embryological Analogies in Presocratic Cosmogony'. *Classical Quarterly* 26, 27–34.

Balme, D. 1939. 'Greek Science and Mechanism I. Aristotle on Nature and Chance'. *Classical Quarterly*, 33, 123–38.

Balme, D. 1941. 'Greek Science and Mechanism II. The Atomists'. *Classical Quarterly*, 35, 23–8.

Barnes, J. 1982. *The Presocratic Philosophers*. 2nd edition. London and New York: Routledge and Kegan Paul.

Barnes, J. 1987. *Early Greek Philosophy*. London: Penguin.

Barratt, W. S. 1964. *Euripides: Hippolytus*. Oxford: Oxford University Press.

Basalla, G. 1962. 'William Harvey and the Heart as a Pump'. *Bulletin of the History of Medicine* 36, 467–70.

Beardslee, J. 1918. *The Use of phusis in Fifth Century Greek Literature*. Chicago, IL: University of Chicago Press.

Bensuade-Vincent, B. and Newman, W. (eds) 2017. *The Artificial and the Natural: An Evolving Polarity*, Cambridge, MA: Harvard University Press.

Bernadete, S. 1965. '*Chré* and *Dei* in Plato and Others'. *Glotta* 43, 285–98.

Berryman, S. 2009. *The Mechanical Philosophy in Ancient Greek Natural Philosophy*. Cambridge: Cambridge University Press.

Betegh, G. 2004. *The Derveni Papyrus*. Cambridge: Cambridge University Press.

Betegh, G. 2006. 'Greek Philosophy and Religion'. In M. Gill and P. Pellegrin (eds) *A Companion to Ancient Philosophy*. Oxford: Blackwell.

Bicknell, P. 1966. 'Anaximenes' Simile'. *Apeiron* 1, 17–18.

Bodnar, I. M. 1998. 'Atomic Independence and Indivisibility'. *Oxford Studies in Ancient Philosophy* 16, 35–61.

Bodnar, I. M. 2004. 'The Mechanical Principle of Animal Motion'. In A. Laks and M. Rashed (eds) *Aristote et le movement des animaux: dix etudes sur le De Motu animalium*. Villeneuve d'Ascq: Presses universitaires du septentrion, pp. 137–47.

Bosak-Schroeder, C. 2015. 'The Religious Life of Greek Automata'. *Archiv fur Religionsgeschichte* 17, 123–36.

Bottéro, J. 1992. *Mesopotamia: Writing Reasoning and the Gods*. Chicago, IL: University of Chicago Press.

Bremmer, R. N. and Erskine, A. *The Gods of Ancient Greece: Identities and Transformations*. Cambridge: Cambridge University Press.

Broadie, S. 1999. 'Rational Theology'. In A. A. Long (ed.) *The Cambridge Companion to Early Greek Philosophy*. Cambridge: Cambridge University Press, pp. 205–24.

Brooke, J. 1991. *Science and Religion: Some Historical Perspectives*. Cambridge: Cambridge University Press.

Burch, G. B. 1949–50. 'Anaximander, the First Metaphysician'. *Review of Metaphysics*, 137–60.

Burkert, W. 1963. 'Iranisches bei Anaximander'. *Rheinisches Museum für Philologie* 106: 97–134.

Burkert, W. 1972. *Lore and Science in Ancient Pythagoreanism*. Cambridge, MA: Harvard University Press.

Burkert, W. 1992. *The Orientalizing Revolution: Near Eastern Influence on Greek Culture in Early Archaic Age*. Trans. M. Pindar and W. Burkert. Cambridge, MA: Harvard University Press.

Burnet, J. 1930. *Early Greek Philosophy*. 4th edition. London: Adam and Charles Black.

Campbell, G. 2003. *Lucretius on Creation and Evolution*. Oxford: Oxford University Press.

Carteron, H. 1975. 'Does Aristotle Have a Mechanics?' *Articles on Aristotle, 1, Science*. J. Barnes, M. Schofield and R. Sorabji (eds.) London: Duckworth.

Casson, L. 1971. *Ships and Seamanship in the Ancient World*. 2nd edition. New Jersey: Princeton University Press.

Cherniss, H. F. 1935. *Aristotle's Criticism of Presocratic Philosophy*. Baltimore, MD: John Hopkins Press.

Cherniss, H. F. 1944. *Aristotle's Criticism of Plato and the Academy*. Baltimore, MD: John Hopkins Press.

Cherniss, H. F. 1951. 'The Characteristics and Effects of Presocratic Philosophy'. *Journal of the History of Ideas* 12, 319–45.

Clagett M. (ed.) 1957. *Critical Problems in the History of Science*. Madison, NJ: Wisconsin University Press.

Clay, J. S. 1972. 'The Planktai and Moly: Divine Naming and Knowing in Homer'. *Hermes* 100, 127–31.

Clay, J. S. 1983. *The Wrath of Athena. Gods and Men in the* Odyssey. Princeton, NJ, Princeton University Press.

Clay, J. S. 2003. *Hesiod's Cosmos*. Cambridge: Cambridge University Press.
Cohen M. R. and Drabkin I. E. 1948. *A Source Book in Greek Science*. Cambridge, MA: Harvard University Press.
Collingwood, R. 1945. *The Idea of Nature*. Oxford: Oxford University Press.
Collins, D. 2001. 'Theories of Lemnos and the Criminalization of Magic in Fourth Century Athens'. *Classical Quarterly* NS 51, 477–93.
Collins, D. 2003. 'Nature, Cause and Agency in Greek Magic'. *Transactions of the American Philological Association* 133, 17–49.
Collins, D. 2008. *Magic in the Ancient Greek World*. London: Blackwell.
Conche, M. 1991. *Anaximandre. Fragments et Témoignages*. Paris: Presses Universitaires de France.
Cornford, F. M. 1931. *The Laws of Motion in Ancient Thought*. Cambridge: Cambridge University Press.
Cornford, F. M. 1933. 'Innumerable Worlds in Presocratic Philosophy'. *Classical Quarterly* 28, 1–16.
Cornford, F. M. 1950. *Before and After Socrates*. Cambridge: Cambridge University Press.
Cornford, F. M. 1952. *Princium Sapientae*. Cambridge: Cambridge University Press.
Cornford, F. M. 1957. *From Religion to Philosophy*. New York: Harper and Row.
Couprie, D. L. 1995. 'The Visualisation of Anaximander's Astronomy'. *Apeiron* 23, 159–81.
Couprie, D. L. 2001. 'Anaximander's Discovery of Space'. *Essays in Ancient Greek Philosophy VI*. A. Preuss (ed.). Albany, NY: Suny, pp. 23–48.
Couprie, D. L. 2002. 'Imagining the Universe'. *Apeiron* 35, 47–59.
Couprie, D. L. 2003. 'The Discovery of Space: Anaximander's Astronomy'. In D. L. Couprie, R. Hahn and G. Naddaf (eds), *Anaximander in Context*. Albany, NY: Suny, pp. 165–254.
Couprie, D. L. 2004. 'Anaximander und die Geschichte des Griechische Weltmodells. Eine Auseinandersetzung mit Detlev Fehling'. *Prima Philosophia* 17, 127–43.
Couprie, D. L. 2009a. 'Anaximander's Legacy and the Stability of the Earth' (review of Carlo Rovelli, Anaximandre de Milet ou la naissance de la pensée scientifique. Paris: Dunod). *Hyperboreus* 15, 1–10.
Couprie, D. L. 2009b. 'Anaxagoras and the Size of the Sun'. In Elizabeth Close a.o. (eds), Greek Research in Australia. *Proceedings of the Seventh International Conference of Greek Studies*. Flinders University, June 2007. Adelaide: Flinders University.
Couprie, D. L. 2009c. 'Problems with Anaximander's Numbers'. *Apeiron* 42, 167–84.
Couprie, D. L. 2010. Review of Robert Hahn, 'Archaeology and the Origins of Philosophy'. *Aestimatio* 7(25), 78–96.
Couprie, D. L. 2011. *Heaven and Earth in Ancient Greek Cosmology: From Thales to Heraclides Ponticus*. New York: Springer.
Couprie, D. L., Hahn, R. and Naddaf, G. 2003. *Anaximander in Context: New Studies in the Origins of Greek Philosophy*. Albany, NY: State University Press.

Couprie, D. L. and Kočandrle, R. 2013. 'Anaximander's "Boundless Nature"'. *Peitho/ Examina Anitiqua* 1, 63–91.
Craik, E. 2015. *The Hippocratic Corpus*. London: Routledge.
Cunningham, A. 1987. 'Harvey'. In R. Porter (ed.), *Man Masters Nature*. London: BBC.
Curd, P. 2005. 'On the Question of Religion and Natural Philosophy in Empedocles'. *Pierris*, 137–62.
Curd, P. and Graham, D. 2008. *The Oxford Handbook of Presocratic Philosophy*. Oxford: Oxford University Press.
Danek, G. 1998. *Epos und Zitat. Studien zu den Quellen der Odyssee* (Wiener Studien Beiheft 22). Vienna.
Dawkins, R. 2007. *The God Delusion*. London: Black Swan.
de Gandt, F. 1982. 'Force et Science des Machines'. In J. Barnes, J. Brunschwig, M.Burnyeat, M. Schofield and I. E. Drabkin (eds). *Science and Speculation*. Cambridge: Cambridge University Press.
De Groot, J. 2014. *Aristotle's Empiricism: Experience and Mechanics in the 4th Century BC*. Parmenides: Las Vegas.
de Raedmaeker, F. C. 1953. *De Philosophie de Voorsokratici*. Antwerpen: Amsterdam.
De Santillana, G. 1961. *The Origins of Scientific Thought, Vol. I, From Anaximander to Proclus – 600 BC to 300 AD*. London: Weidenfeld and Nicholson.
Debus, A. 1970. 'Harvey and Fludd: The Irrational Factor in the Rational Science of the Seventeenth Century'. *Journal of the History of Biology* 3, 81–105.
Deichgräber, K. 1938. 'Xenophanes *peri phuseos*'. *Rheinisches Museum* 87, 1–31.
Dickie, M. 2001. *Magic and Magicians in the Greco-Roman World*. Abingdon: Routledge.
Diels, H. 1879. *Doxographi Graeci*. Berlin: de Gruyter.
Diels, H. 1897. 'Uber Anaximander's Kosmos'. *Archiv für Geschichte der Philosophie* 10, 228–37.
Diels, H. and Kranz, W. 1951–52 (6th edition). *Die Fragmente der Vorsokratiker*. Zürich and Hildesheim: Weidmann.
Dietrich, B. C. 1965. *Death, Fate and the Gods*. London: University of London.
Dijksterhuis, E. J. 1961. *The Mechanisation of the World Picture*. Trans. C. Dikshoorn. Oxford: Oxford University Press.
Dixon, T. 2008. *Science and Religion: A Very Short Introduction*. Oxford: Oxford University Press.
Dodds, E. R. 1951. *The Greeks and the Irrational*. Berkeley, CA: University of California.
Dodds, E. R. 1965. *Pagan and Christian in an Age of Anxiety*. Cambridge: Cambridge University Press.
Dodds, E. R. 1973. *The Ancient Concept of Progress*. Oxford: Oxford University Press.
Doyle, R. E. 1984. *ATH, Its Use and Meaning*. New York: New York University Press.
Drabkin, I. E. 1938. 'Notes on the Laws of Motion in Aristotle'. *The American Journal of Philology* 59, 60–84.
Draper, J. 1874. *History of the Conflict between Religion and Science*. Project Gutenberg: NetLibrary.

Drozdek, A. 2001. 'Anaximander: Theological Provenance of the *apeiron*'. *Giornale di Metafisica* 23, 103–18.
Drozdek, A. 2008. *In the Beginning was the* Apeiron: *Infinity in Greek Philosophy*. Stuttgart: Franz Steiner Verlag.
Ducatillon, J. 1990. 'Le facteur divin dans les maladies d'apris le *Pronostic*'. In P. Potter et al. (eds). *La maladie et lesmaladies dans la collection hippocratique*, Actes du Vie Colloque International Hippocrarique, pp. 61–73.
Eastman, C. R. 1905. 'Anaximander, Earliest Precursor of Darwin'. *Popular Science* 67, 701–6.
Edelstein, L. 1967. *Ancient Medicine*. C. Lilian Temkin (trans). Owsei Temkin and C. Lilian Temkin (eds). Baltimore: The Johns Hopkins Press.
Edmunds, L. 1972. 'Necessity, Chance and Freedom in the Early Atomists'. *Phoenix* 26, 342–57.
Edwards, M. W. 1987. *Homer: Poet of the* Iliad. Baltimore and London: Johns Hopkins University Press.
Engemann, J. 1991. 'Cosmic Justice in Anaximander'. *Phronesis* 36, 1–25.
Erbse, H. 1986. *Untersuchungen zur Funktion der Gotter im Homerischen Epos*. Berlin: de Gruyter.
Fenik, B. 1974. *Studies in the* Odyssey (Hermes Einzelschrift 30). Finley, MI: Wiesbaden.
Fenik, B. 1977. *The World of Odysseus* 2nd ed. London: Routledge.
Finkelberg, A. 1993. 'Anaximander's Conception of the *Apeiron*'. *Phronesis* 38, 229–56.
Finkelberg, A. 1994. 'Plural Worlds in Anaximander'. *American Journal of Philology* 115, 485–506.
Finkelberg, A. 1997. 'Xenophanes' Physics, Parmenides' Doxa and Empedocles' Theory of Cosmological Mixture'. *Hermes* 125, 1–16.
Flint, V. I. J. 1991. *The Rise of Magic in Early Medieval Europe*. Oxford: Oxford University Press.
Ford, A. 1992. *Homer. The Poetry of the Past*. Ithaca, NY: Cornell University Press.
Fowler, R. (ed.) 2004. *The Cambridge Companion to Homer*. Cambridge: Cambridge University Press.
Frank, R. 1980. *Harvey and the Oxford Physiologists*. Berkeley, CA: California University Press.
Fränkel, H. 1955. *Wege und Fromen fruhgreiechischen Denkens*. Munich: Beck.
Fränkel, H. 1973. *Early Greek Poetry and Philosophy*. Hadas and Willis (trans). New York and London: Harcourt Brace & Jonovich.
Fränkel, H. 1974. Xenophanes' Empiricism and His Critique of Knowledge B34'. In A. P. D. Mourelatos (ed.), *The Presocratics, A Collection of Critical Essays*, pp. 118–31. Berlin: de Gruyter.
French, R. 1994. *William Harvey's Natural Philosophy*. Cambridge: Cambridge University Press.
Freudenthal, G. 1986. 'The Theory of the Opposites and an Ordered Universe: Physics and Metaphysics of Anaximander'. *Phronesis* 31, 197–228.

Fuchs, T. 2001. *The Mechanization of the Heart: Harvey and Descartes*. Rochester, NY: University of Rochester Press.
Furley, D. J. 1967. *Two Studies in the Greek Atomists*. Princeton, NJ: Princeton University Press.
Furley, D. J. 1987. *The Greek Cosmologists*. Cambridge: Cambridge University Press.
Furley, D. J. 1989. *Cosmic Problems*. Cambridge: Cambridge University Press.
Furley, D. J. and Allen, R. E. (eds). 1975. *Studies in Presocratic Philosophy*. 2 Vols. London: Routledge and Kegan Paul.
Gagarin, M. 1986. *Early Greek Law*. Berkeley, CA: University of California Press.
Garber, D. and Roux, S. 2013. *The Mechanisation of Natural Philosophy*. Dordrecht, Heidelberg, New York and London: Springer.
Gerson, L. 1990. *God and Greek Philosophy: Studies in the Early History of Natural Theology*. London: Routledge.
Gill, C. et al. (eds). 1998. *Reciprocity in Ancient Greece*. Oxford: Oxford University Press.
Gill, M. and Pellegrin, P. (eds). *A Companion to Ancient Philosophy*. Oxford: Blackwell.
Glennan, S and Illari, P. 2018. *The Routledge Handbook of Mechanisms and Mechanical Philosophy*. London: Routledge.
Gomperz, H. 1911–12. *Greek Thinkers – A History of Greek Philosophy*. Cornell University Press.
Gomperz, H. 1943. 'Problems and Method in Early Greek Science'. *Journal of the History of Ideas* 4, 161–76.
Gomperz, T. 1922. *Greek Thinkers, Vol. 1*. London: Murray.
Graf, F. 1997. *Magic in the Ancient World*. Cambridge, MA: Harvard University Press.
Graham, D. W. 1990. 'Socrates, the Craft Analogy and Science'. *Apeiron* 23, 1–24.
Graham, D. W. 2003. 'Does Nature Love to Hide? Heraclitus B123'. *Classical Philology* 98, 175–9.
Graham, D. W. 2006. *Explaining the Cosmos: The Ionian Tradition of Scientific Philosophy*. Princeton and Oxford: Princeton University Press.
Graham, D. W. 2006a. *The Texts of the Early Greek Philosophers*. Cambridge: Cambridge University Press.
Grant, E. 2007. *A History of Natural Philosophy*. Cambridge: Cambridge University Press.
Greene, W. C. 1944. *Moira. Fate, Good and Evil in Greek Thought*. Cambridge, MA: Harvard University Press.
Gregory, A. D. 2000. *Plato's Philosophy of Science*. London: Duckworth.
Gregory, A. D. 2000a. 'Plato and Aristotle on Eclipses'. *Journal for the History of Astronomy* xxxi, 245–59.
Gregory, A. D. 2000b. *Harvey's Heart: The Discovery of Blood Circulation*. London: Icon.
Gregory, A. D. 2001. 'Harvey, Aristotle and the Weather Cycle'. *Studies in History and Philosophy of Science Part C: Studies in History and Philosophy of Biological and Biomedical Sciences* 32(1), 153–68.

Gregory, A. D. 2003. 'Eudoxus, Callippus and the Astronomy of the Timaeus'. In R. W. Sharples and A. Sheppard (eds). *Ancient Approaches to Plato's Timaeus*. London: Institute of Classical Studies, pp. 5–28.

Gregory, A. D. 2007. *Ancient Greek Cosmogony*. London: Duckworth.

Gregory, A. D. 2011. 'Anaximander's Zoogony'. In M. Rosetto, M. Tsianikas, G. Couvalis and M. Palaktsoglou (eds). *Greek Research in Australia: Proceedings of the Eighth Biennial International Conference of Greek Studies*, Flinders University June 2009. Adelaide: Flinders University Department of Language – Modern Greek, pp. 44–53.

Gregory, A. D. 2013a. *The Presocratics and the Supernatural*. London: Bloomsbury.

Gregory, A. D. 2013b. 'Leucippus and Democritus on Like to Like and *ou mallon*'. *Apeiron* 46, 446–68.

Gregory, A. D. 2014a. 'Parmenides, Cosmology and Sufficient Reason'. *Apeiron* 47, 16–47.

Gregory, A. D. 2014b. 'William Harvey, Aristotle and Astrology'. *British Journal for the History of Science* 47, 1–17.

Gregory, A. D. 2016. *Anaximander: A Re-Assessment*. London: Bloomsbury.

Guthrie, W. K. C. 1950. *The Greek Philosophers from Thales to Aristotle*. London: Methuen.

Guthrie, W. K. C. 1957. *In the Beginning: Some Greek Views on the Origins of Life and the Early State of Man*. London: Methuen.

Guthrie, W. K. C. 1962. *A History of Greek Philosophy. Vol. 1. The Earlier Presocratics and the Pythagoreans*. Cambridge: Cambridge University Press.

Guthrie, W. K. C. 1965. *A History of Greek Philosophy. Vol. 2. The Presocratic Tradition from Parmenides to Democritus*. Cambridge: Cambridge University Press.

Hahn, R. 2001. *Anaximander and the Architects*. Albany, NY: State University of New York Press.

Hankinson, R. 1998. *Cause and Explanation in Ancient Greek Thought*. Oxford: Oxford University Press.

Hankinson, R. 1998a. 'Magic, Religion and Science: Divine and Human in the Hippocratic Corpus'. *Apeiron* 31, 1–34.

Hankinson, R. 2008. 'Reason, Cause and Explanation in Presocratic Thought'. In P. Curd and D. Graham, *The Oxford Handbook of Presocratic Philosophy*. Oxford: Oxford University Press, pp. 434–57.

Havelock, E. A. 1978. *The Greek Concept of Justice. From Its Shadow in Homer to Its Substance in Plato*. Cambridge, MA: Cambridge University Press.

Havelock, E. A. 1982. *The Literate Revolution in Greek and its Cultural Consequences*. Princeton, NJ: Princeton University Press.

Heath, T. L. 1913. *Aristarchus of Samos: The Ancient Copernicus*. Oxford: Clarendon Press.

Heidel, W. A. 1906. 'The Dinh in Anaximenes and Anaximander'. *Classical Philology* 1, 279–82.

Heidel, W. A. 1910. '*Peri Phuseos*'. *Proceedings of the American Academy of Arts and Sciences* 45, 77–133.

Hesse, M. B. 1961. *Forces and Fields*. London and New York: Nelson.
Heubeck, A. and Hoekstra, A. 1989. *A Commentary on Homer's Odyssey*. Oxford: Oxford University Press.
Hirsch, U. 1990. 'Was Demokrits Weldbilt Mechanistisch und Antiteleologisch?' *Phronesis* 35, 225–34.
Horster, M. and Reitz, C. (eds). 2005. *Wissensvermittlung in Dichterischer Gestalt*. Stuttgart: Franz Steiner.
Huffman, C. A. 2014. *A History of Pythagoreanism*. Cambridge: Cambridge University Press.
Hussey, E. 1972. *The Presocratics*. London: Duckworth.
Hussey, E. 1990. 'The Beginnings of Epistemology: from Homer to Philolaus'. In E. Hussey, *Epistemology, Companions to Ancient Thought*: Vol. 1. Cambridge: Cambridge University Press, pp. 11–38.
Hussey, E. 1991. 'Aristotles Mathematical Physics: A Reconstruction'. In L. Judson (ed.), *Aristotle's Physics, A Collection of Essays*. Oxford: Oxford University Press, pp. 213–42.
Inwood, B. 2001 (1992). *The Poem of Empedocles*. Revised edition. Toronto: Toronto University Press.
Jackson, M. (ed.). 2011. *The Oxford Handbook of the History of Medicine*. Oxford: Oxford University Press.
Jaeger, W. 1939. *Paideia: The Ideals of Greek Culture*. 3 vols. G. Highet (trans). Oxford: Blackwell.
Jaeger, W. 1947. *The Theology of the Early Greek Philosophers*. Oxford: Clarendon Press.
Janko, R. (ed.). 1992. *The Iliad: A Commentary, Vol. 4: Books 13–16*. Cambridge: Cambridge University Press.
Johnson, M. R. 2017. 'Aristotelian Mechanistic Explanation'. In J. Rocca (ed.), *Teleology in the Ancient World: Philosophical and Medical Approaches*. Cambridge: Cambridge University Press, pp. 107–24.
Jouanna, J. 1989. 'Hippocrate de Cos et le Sacre'. *Journal des Savants*, Janvier-Juin, 3–22.
Jouanna, J. 1990. *De l'ancienne medecine*. Paris: Les Belles Lettres.
Jouanna, J. 1999. *Hippocrates*. M. B. DeBevoise (trans). London: Johns Hopkins University Press.
Kahn, C. 1960. *Anaximander and the Origins of Greek Cosmology*. Indianapolis, IN: Hackett.
Kahn, C. 1979. *The Art and Thought of Heraclitus*. Cambridge: Cambridge University Press.
Karsai, G. 2000. 'La Magie dans l'Odyssey: Circe'. In A. Moreau and J-C. Turpin (eds). *La actes du colloque international de Montpellier, 25–27 mars 1999. T.2 La magie dans l'antiquité grecque tardive; les myths*, vol. 2, pp. 185–98. Montpellier: Université Paul Valéry.
Keynes, J. M. 1921. *A Treatise on Probability*. MacMillan: London.
Kingsley, P. 1995. *Ancient Philosophy, Mystery and Magic: Empedocles and the Pythagorean Tradition*. Oxford: Oxford University Press.

Kirk, G. S. 1955. 'Some Problems in Anaximander'. *Classical Quarterly* 49, 21–38.

Kirk, G. S., Raven, J. E. and Schofield, M. 1983. *The Presocratic Philosophers*. Cambridge: Cambridge University Press.

Kleisner, R. and Kocandrle, R. 2013. 'Evolution Born of Moisture: Analogies and Parallels Between Anaximander's Ideas on Origin of Life and Man and Later Pre-Darwinian and Darwinian Evolutionary Concepts'. *Journal of the History of Biology* 46, 103–24.

Kullmann, W. 1985. 'Gods and men in the *Iliad* and the *Odyssey*'. *HSCP* 89, 1–23.

Laks, A. 2006. *Introduction à la philosophie présocratique*. Paris: Presses universitaires de France.

Laks, A. 2018. *The Concept of Presocratic Philosophy*. G. Most (trans). Princeton, NJ: Princeton University Press.

Laks, A. and Louguet, C. 2002. *Qu'est-ce que la philosophie présocratique?* Villeneuve-d'Ascq: Presses universitaires du septentrion.

Laks, A. and Most, G. 1997. *Studies on the Derveni Papyrus*. Oxford: Oxford University Press.

Laks, A, and Most, G. 2016. *Early Greek Philosophy*. 9 Vols. Cambridge, MA: Harvard University Press.

Lamb, W. R. M. 1961. *Plato: Lysis, Symposium, Gorgias*. Cambridge, MA: Loeb.

Lesher, J. 1978. Xenophanes' Scepticism. *Phronesis* 23, 1–15.

Lesher, J. 1981. Perceiving and Knowing in the *Iliad* and *Odyssey*. *Phronesis* 26, 2–24.

Lesher, J. 1992. *Xenophanes of Colophon: Fragments*. Toronto: University of Toronto Press.

Lesher, J. 1995. 'Mind's Knowledge and Powers of Control in Anaxagoras DKB12'. *Phronesis* 40, 125–42.

Lesher, J. 2008. 'The Humanizing of Knowledge in Presocratic Thought'. In P. Curd and D. Graham, *The Oxford Handbook of Presocratic Philosophy*. Oxford: Oxford University Press, pp. 458–84.

Lindberg, D. C. and Numbers, R. L. 1992. *God and Nature*. Berkeley, CA: University of California Press.

Lloyd, G. E. R. 1966. *Polarity and Analogy*. Cambridge: Cambridge University Press.

Lloyd, G. E. R. 1968. 'Plato as a Natural Scientist'. *Journal of Hellenic Studies* 28, 78–92.

Lloyd, G. E. R. 1970. *Early Greek Science to Aristotle*. London: Chatto and Windus.

Lloyd, G. E. R. 1975. 'Aspects of the Interrelations of Medicine, Magic and Philosophy in Ancient Greece'. *Apeiron* IX, 1–16.

Lloyd, G. E. R. 1978. 'Saving the Appearances'. *Classical Quarterly* 88, 202–22.

Lloyd, G. E. R. 1979. *Magic, Reason and Experience*. Cambridge: Cambridge University Press.

Lloyd, G. E. R. 1983. *Science, Folklore and Ideology: Studies in the Life Sciences in Ancient Greece*. Cambridge: Cambridge University Press.

Lloyd, G. E. R. 1986. *Hippocratic Writings*. Harmondsworth: Penguin.

Lloyd, G. E. R. 1987. *The Revolutions of Wisdom*. Berkeley, CA: California University Press.

Lloyd, G. E. R. 1990. *Demystifying Mentalities*. Cambridge: Cambridge University Press.
Lloyd, G. E. R. 1991. *Methods and Problems in Greek Science*. Cambridge: Cambridge University Press.
Lloyd, G. E. R. 2003. *In the Grip of Disease*. Oxford: Oxford University Press.
Lloyd, G. E. R. 2004. *Ancient Worlds, Modern Reflections*. Oxford: Oxford University Press.
Lloyd, G. E. R. 2007. *Cognitive Variations: Reflections on the Unity and Diversity of the Human*. Oxford: Oxford University Press.
Lloyd-Jones, H. 1971 (1983). *The Justice of Zeus*. Berkeley, CA and London: University of California Press.
Loenen, J. H. M. M. 1954. 'Was Anaximander an Evolutionist?' *Mnemosyne* 7, 215–32.
Long, A. A. 1999. *The Cambridge Companion to Early Greek Philosophy*. Cambridge: Cambridge University Press.
Longrigg, J. 1964. 'A Note on Anaximenes' Fragment 2'. *Phronesis* 9, 1–4.
Longrigg, J. 1989. 'Presocratic Philosophy and Hippocratic Medicine'. *History of Science* xxvii.
Longrigg, J. 1993. *Greek Rational Medicine*. London: Routledge.
Lonie, I. M. 1981. 'Hippocrates the Iatromechanist'. *Medical History* 25, 113–50.
Loraux, N. 1991. 'Origins of Mankind in Greek Myths: Born to Die'. In *Dictionary of Mythologies*, 2 vols., V. Bonnefoy and W. Doniger (eds). Chicago, IL: University of Chicago Press. 390–5.
Lovejoy, 1909. 'The Meaning of *phusis* in the Greek Physiologers'. *The Philosophical Review* XVIII, 369–83.
Mansfeld, J. 1971. *The Pseudo-Hippocratic Tract Peri Hebdomaden. Ch. I-II and Greek Philosophy*. Assen: Vangorcum
Mansfeld, J. 1980. 'Plato and the Method of Hippocrates'. *Greek, Roman and Byzantine Studies* 21, 341–62.
Mansfeld, J. 1995. 'Empedocles and his Interpreters'. *Phronesis* 40, 109–15.
Mansfeld, J. 2002. 'Theophrastus and Simplicius on Anaximander'. *Philosophia* 32, 25–46.
Mansfeld, J. 2011. 'Anaximander's Fragment: Another Attempt'. *Phronesis* 56, 1–32.
Martin, M. 2005. *Magie et Magicienes dans le Monde Greco-Romain*. Paris: Errance.
Martin, D. B. 2004. *Inventing Superstition*. Cambridge MA, Harvard University Press.
Matson, W. I. 1953. 'The Naturalism of Anaximander'. *The Review of Metaphysics* 8, 387–96.
McMullen, E. 1998. *William Harvey and the Use of Purpose in the Scientific Revolution*. Lanham, MD: University Press of America.
Menn, S. 2010. 'On Socrates' First Objection to the Physicists'. *Oxford Studies in Ancient Philosophy* 38, 37–63.
Micheli, G. 1995. Le Origini del Concetto de Macchina. Firenze: Olschki.
Miller, H. W. 1953. 'The Concept of the Divine in *De Morbo Sacro*'. *Transactions and Proceedings of the Amercian Philological Society* 84, 1–15.

Mittlestrass, J. 1962. *Die Rettung der Phanomene.* Berlin: De Gruyter.

Morris, I. and Powel, I. B. (eds). 1997. *A New Companion to Homer. Mnemosyne Suppl.* 163, Leiden: Brill.

Moreau, A. and Turpin, J-C. 2000. *La magie: actes du colloque international de Montpellier, 25–27 mars 1999. T.2 La magie dans l'antiquité grecque tardive; les myths vol. 2.* Montpellier: Université Paul Valéry.

Most, G. W. 2006. *Hesiod: Theogony and Works and Days.* Cambridge, MA: Loeb.

Moulton, C. 1977. 'Similes in the Homeric Poems'. *Hypomnemata* 49, Gottingen: Vandenhoeck und Ruprecht.

Mourelatos, A. P. D. 1970. *The Route of Parmenides.* New Haven: Yale University Press.

Mourelatos, A. P. D, (ed.). 1974. *The Presocratics, A Collection of Critical Essays.* Berlin: de Gruyter.

Mourelatos, A. P. D. 1993. *The Presocratics: A Collection of Critical Essays.* Princeton, NJ: Princeton University Press.

Mourelatos, A. P. D. 2002. 'La terre et les etoiles dans la cosmologie de Xenophane'. In A. Laks and C. Louguet, *Qu'est-ce que la philosophie présocratique?* Villeneuve-d'Ascq: Presses universitaires du septentrion.

Mourelatos, A. P. D. 2008. The Cloud-Astrophysics of Xenophanes and Ionian Materil Monism. In P. Curd and D. Graham (eds). *The Oxford Handbook of Presocratic Philosophy.* Oxford: Oxford University Press.

Mourelatos, A. P. D. 2018. Review of Laks and Most, Early Greek Philosophy, *Bryn Mawr Classical Review.*

Naddaf, G. 1998. 'On the Origin of Anaximander's Cosmological Model'. *Journal of the History of Ideas* 59, 1–28.

Naddaf, G. 2005. *The Greek Concept of Nature.* Albany, NY: SUNY.

Netz, R. 1999 *The Shaping of Deduction in Greek Mathematics: A Study in Cognitive History.* Cambridge: Cambridge University Press.

Netz, R. 2014. 'The Problem of Pythagorean Mathematics'. In C. A. Huffman (ed.). *A History of Pythagoreanism.* Cambridge: Cambridge University Press, pp. 167–84.

Noussia-Fantazzi, M. 2010. *Solon the Athenian, the Poetic Fragments* (Mnemosyne Supplement 326). Leiden: Brill.

Ogden, D. 2001. *Greek and Roman Necromancy.* Princeton, NJ: Princeton University Press.

Ogden, D. 2002. *Magic, Witchcraft and Ghosts in the Greek and Roman Worlds: A Sourcebook.* Lanham, MD: Oxford University Press.

Ogden, D. 2008. *Nights Black Agents.* Hambledon: Continuum.

Owen, G. E. L. 1953. 'The Place of the Timaeus in Plato's Dialogues'. Reprinted in R. E. Allen (ed.). *Studies in Plato's Metaphysics.* London: Routledge and Kegan Paul, pp. 313–39.

Owen, G. E. L. 1986. 'Aristotelian Mechanics'. In G. E. L. Owen (ed.). *Logic, Science, Dialectic.* London: Duckworth, pp. 315–33.

Page, D. L. 1973. *Folktakes in Homer's Odyssey.* Cambridge, MA: Harvard University Press.

Pagel, W. 1967. *William Harvey's Biological Ideas*. Basel: New York: Karger.
Pagel, W. 1976. *New Light on William Harvey*. Basel: New York: Karger.
Panchenko, D. 1994. 'ΟΜΟΙΟΣ and ΟΜΟΙΟΤΗΣ in Thales and Anaximander'. *Hyperboreus* 1, 28–55.
Pedersen, O. 1974. *Early Physics and Astronomy*, 2nd edition. Cambridge: Cambridge University Press.
Penrose, R. and Schrodinger, E. 1996. *Nature and the Greeks*. Cambridge: Cambridge University Press.
Pingree, D. 1992. 'Hellenophilia vs. the History of Science'. *Isis* 83, 554–63.
Porter, R. 1999. *The Greatest Benefit to Mankind*. London: Fontana Press.
Primavesi, O. 2005. 'Theologische Allegorie: zur philosophischen Funktion einer poetischen Form bei Parmenides und Empedokles', in M. Horster and C. Reitz (eds). *Wissensvermittlung in dichterischer Gestalt*, pp. 69–93.
Prioreschi, P. 1991. *A History of Medicine: Primitive and Ancient Medicine*. Lewiston: The Edwin Mellen Press.
Prioreschi, P. 1992. 'Supernatural Elements in Hippocratic Medicine'. *Journal of the History of Medicine* 47, 389–404.
Pyle, A. 1995. *Atomism and Its Critics: From Democritus to Newton*. Bristol: Thoemmes Press.
Ramnoux, C. 1954. 'Sur quelques interprétations modernes d'Anaximandre'. *Revue de métaphysique et de morale* 59, 233–52.
Redard, G. 1953. *Recherhes sur Chré, Chrésthai*. Paris: Etude Semantique.
Rivaud, A. 1906. *Le Probleme Du Devenir Et La Notion de La Matiere Dans La Philosophie Grecque Depuis Les Origines Jusqu'a Theophraste*. Kesinger Legacy Reprints.
Rochberg, F. 2016. *Before Nature*. Chicago, IL: Chicago University Press.
Rovelli, C. 2009a. 'Anaximander's Legacy'. *Collapse. Philosophical Research and Development* V, 50–71.
Rovelli, C. 2009. *Anaximandre de Milet ou la naissance de la pensée scientifque*. Paris: Dunod.
Rovelli, C. 2011. *The First Scientist. Anaximander and His Legacy*. Yardley: Westholme.
Rudberg, G. 1921–22. 'Anaximandros Biologi'. *Eranos* 20, 51–7.
Rudberg, G. 1940. 'Biologie und Urgeschichte im ionischen Denken'. *Symbolae Osloensis* 20, 1–20.
Salmon, W. 1984. *Scientific Explanation and the Causal Structure of the World*. Princeton, NJ: Princeton University Press.
Sambursky, S. 1956. *The Physical World of the Greeks*. London: Routledge and Kegan Paul.
Sambursky, S. 1959. *The Physics of the Stoics*. London: Routledge and Kegan Paul.
Schiefsky, M. J. 2008. 'Art and Nature in Ancient Mechanics'. In B. Bensuade-Vincent and W. Newman (eds), *The Artificial and the Natural: An Evolving Polarity*. Cambridge, MA: Harvard University Press, pp. 67–108.

Schurman, A. (ed.). 2005. *Geschicte der Mathematik und der Naturwissenschaften in der Antike*, vol. 3. Franz Steiner: Stuttgart.
Scodel, R. 1982. 'The Achaean Wall and the Myth of Destruction'. *HSCP* 86, 33–50.
Seaford, R. A. S. 2004. *Money and the Early Greek Mind: Homer, Philosophy, Tragedy*. Cambridge: Cambridge University Press.
Segal, C. 1971. *The Theme of the Mutilation of the Corpse in the Iliad* (Mnemosyne Suppl. 17). Leiden: Brill.
Segal, C. 1992. 'Divine Justice in the *Odyssey:* Poseidon, Cyclops, and Helios'. *AJP* 113, 489–518.
Sedley, D. 1989. 'Teleology and Myth in the Phaedo'. *Proceedings of the Boston Colloquium on Ancient Philosophy* 5, 359–83.
Sedley, D. 1992. 'Empedocles' Theory of Vision and Theophrastus' De Sensibus'. In W. W. Fortenbaugh and D. Gustas (eds), *Theophrastus*. Leiden: Brill, pp. 21–31.
Sedley, D. 1998. 'Platonic Causes'. *Phronesis* 43, 1–21.
Sedley, D. 1998a. *Lucretius and the Transformation of Greek Wisdom*. Cambridge: Cambridge University Press.
Sedley, D. 2007. *Creationism and Its Critics in Antiquity*. Berkeley, CA: University of California.
Seligman, P. 1962. *The Apeiron of Anaximander, A Study in the Origin and Function of a Metaphysical Idea*. London: Athlone Press.
Sider, D. 1981. *The Fragments of Anaxagoras*. Meisenheim am Glan: Verlag Anton Hein.
Sider, D. 1997. 'Heraclitus in the Derveni Papyrus'. In A. Laks and G. Most, *Studies on the Derveni Papyrus*. Oxford: Oxford University Press, pp. 129–48.
Solmsen, F. 1975. *Intellectual Experiments of the Greek Enlightenment*. Princeton, NJ: Princeton University Press.
Staden, H. von. 1992. 'Affinities and Elisions'. *Isis* 83, 578–95.
Staden, H von. 2007. 'Phusis and Techne in Greek Medicine'. In B. Bensuade-Vincent and W. Newman (eds), *The Artificial and the Natural: An Evolving Polarity*. Cambridge, MA: Harvard University Press, 67–108.
Stanford, W. B. 1945. 'That Circe's *rhabdos* Was Not a Magic Wand'. *Hermathena* 66, 69–71.
Stratton, K. B. 2006. *Naming the Witch: Magic, Ideology, and Stereotype in the Ancient World*. Columbia, NY: Columbia University Press.
Stokes, M. 1962. 'Hesiodic and Milesian Cosmogonies I'. *Phronesis* 7, 1–37.
Stokes, M. 1963. 'Hesiodic and Milesian Cosmogonies II'. *Phronesis* 8, 1–34.
Tannery, A. 1882a. 'Anaximandre de Milet, l'infini, l'évolution et l'entropie'. *Revue Philosophique de la France et de l'Étranger* 13, 500–29.
Tannery, A. 1882b. 'Histoire du concept de l'infini au VIe siècle avant J. C'. *Revue Philosophique de la France et de l'Étranger* 14, 618–36.
Tannery, A. 1895. 'Une nouvelle hypothèse sur Anaximandre'. *Archiv für Geschichte der Philosophie* 8: 443–8. Also in *Mémoires scientifiques* VII, 1925, 187–92.
Tannery, A. 1904. 'Pour l'histoire du mot 'apeiron''. *Revue de philosophie* 5, 703–7.

Taub, L. 2003. *Ancient Meteorology*. London: Routledge.
Taylor, C. C. W. 1997. *From the Beginning to Plato: Routledge History of Philosophy*, vol. 1. London: Routledge.
Taylor, C. C. W. 1999. The Atomists: Leucippus and Democritus. Toronto: Toronto University Press.
Temkin, O. 1971. *The Falling Sickness: A History of Epilepsy from the Greeks to the Beginnings of Modern Neurology*. 2nd edition. Baltimore MD: Johns Hopkins Press.
Thivel, A. 1975. 'Le Divin dans la Collection Hippocratique'. In *La Collection Hippocratique, Colloque de Strasburg organist par le Centre de Recherches sur la Grece Antique*. Leiden: Brill, pp. 57–76.
Tsagarakis, O. 2000. *Studies in Odyssey 11*. Stuttgart: Franz Steiner.
Tor, S. 2017. *Mortal and Divine in Early Greek Epistemology*. Cambridge: Cambridge University Press.
Trepanier, S. 2010. 'Early Greek Theology: God as Nature and Natural Gods'. In R. N. Bremmer and A. Erskine (eds), *The Gods of Ancient Greece: Identities and Transformations*. Cambridge: Cambridge University Press.
Tybjerg, K. 2003. 'Wonder-making and the Philosophical Wonder in Hero of Alexandria'. *Studies in History and Philosophy of Science* 34, 443–66.
Tybjerg, K. 2005. 'Hero of Alexandria's Mechanical Treatises: Between Theory and Practice'. In A. Schurman (ed.) *Geschicte der Mathematik und der Naturwissenschaften in der Antike*. Franz Steiner: Stuttgart, pp. 204–26.
Unguru, S. 1975. 'On the Need to Rewrite the History of Greek Mathematics'. *Archive for the History of the Exact Sciences*, 15, 67–114.
van der Eijk, P. 1991. 'The "Theology" of the Hippocratic Treatise on the Sacred Disease'. *Apeiron* 23(2), 87–119.
van der Eijk, P. 2008. 'The Role of Medicine on the Formation of Early Greek Thought'. In P. Curd and D. Graham (eds), *The Oxford Handbook of Presocratic Philosophy*. Oxford: Oxford University Press.
van der Eijk, P. 2011. 'Medicine and Health in the Graeco-Roman World'. In M. Jackson (ed.), *The Oxford Handbook of the History of Medicine*. Oxford: Oxford University Press.
van der Waerden, B. L. *Science Awakening*. New York: John Wiley & Sons, Inc.
Vlastos, G. L. 1947. 'Equality and Justice in Early Greek Cosmologies'. In D. J. Furley and R. E. Allen (eds), *Studies in Presocratic Philosophy*, vol. I. London: Routledge and Kegan Paul, pp. 56–91.
Vlastos, G. L. 1950. 'The Physical Theory of Anaxagoras'. *Philosophical Review* 59, 31–57.
Vlastos, G. L. 1952. 'Theology and Philosophy in Early Greek Thought'. *The Philosophical Quarterly* 2, 97–123.
Vlastos, G. L. 1955. 'On Heraclitus'. *The American Journal of Philology* 6, 337–68.
Vlastos, G. L. 1975. *Plato's Universe*. Oxford: Clarendon.
Wachsmann, S. 1997. *Seagoing Ships in the Bronze Age*. Chatham: London.

Wardy, R. B. B. 1990. *The Chain of Change: A Study of Aristotle Physics VII*, Cambridge: Cambridge University Press.
Wasserstein, A. 1962. 'Greek Scientific Thought'. *Proceedings of the Cambridge Philological Society*, n.s. 8, 51–63.
Waterlow, S. 1982. *Passage and Possibility*. Oxford: Oxford University Press.
Wear, A. 1990. 'The Heart and the Blood from Vesalius to Harvey'. In Olby et al. (eds) *Companion to the History of Modern Science*. London: Routledge.
Webster, C. 1965. 'Harvey's Conception of the Heart as a Pump', *Bulletin of the History of Medicine* 39, 508–17.
Webster, C. 1967. 'Harvey's De Generatione: Its Origin and Relevance to the Theory of Circulation'. *British Journal for the History of Science* 3, 262–74.
West, M. L. 1963. 'Three Presocratic Cosmologies'. *Classical Quarterly*, n.s. 13(2), 154–76.
West, M. L. 1966. *Hesiod: Theogony*. Oxford: Oxford University Press.
West, M. L. 1971. *Early Greek Philosophy and the Orient*. Oxford: Oxford University Press.
West, M. L. 1983. *The Orphic Poems*. Oxford: Oxford University Press.
White, A. 1896 (1960). *A History of the Warfare of Science with Theology in Christendom*. New York: Dover Publications.
Whitteridge, G. 1964. *The Anatomical Lectures of William Harvey*. Edinburgh: Livingstone.
Whitteridge, G. 1971. *William Harvey and the Circulation of the Blood*. London: McDonald.
Whitteridge, G. 1976. *An Anatomical Disputation Concerning the Movement of the Heart and Blood*. Oxford: Blackwell.
Wilford, F. 1968. 'Embryological analogies in Empedocles' Cosmogony'. *Phronesis* 13, 108–18.
Willis, R. T. 1847. *The Works of William Harvey*. Sydenham Society.
Wöhrle, G. 1992. 'Zur Prosa der Milesischen Philosophen'. *Würzburger Jahrbücher für die Altertumswissenschaft* 18, 33–47.
Wöhrle, G. 2012. *Die Milesier: Anaximander und Anaximenes*. Berlin and Boston: Walter de Gruyter.
Wright, M. R. 1981. *Empedocles: The Extant Fragments*. New Haven: Concordance.
Wright, M. R. 1995. *Cosmology in Antiquity*. London: Routledge.
Zeller, E. 1892. *Outlines of the History of Greek Philosophy*. London, Longmans Green.
Zeller, E. and Nestle, W. 1881. *Die Philosophie der Griechen in ihrer geschichtlichen Entwicklung dargestellt. Erster Teil. Ie Abteilung, Algemeine Einleitung. Vorsokratische Philosophie, Ie Hälfte*. Leipzig: Reisland.
Zellner, H. M. 1994. 'Scepticism in Homer?' *Classical Quarterly* 44, 308–15.
Zhmud, L. 1994. 'Die Beziehungen Zwischen Philosophie und Wissenschaft in der Antike'. *Sudhoffs Archiv* 78, 1–13.

# Index

Achilles 35–6, 38, 41, 46–8, 54, 59, 198
Aeneas 38
Aeolus 97
Aeschylus 1, 75
affinities 3–6, 13, 115, 118, 165, 185, 190
Agamede 30–1
Agamemnon 36, 47, 52–3, 67, 198–9
*aisa* 34–5, 36, 44, 47, 54, 128, 197, 198
Alexander, 86, 221
analogies 1, 4, 7–8, 12–13, 15–17, 89–90, 93, 113, 115–16, 118, 121–3, 125, 128, 133, 135–7, 142, 143–6, 160, 169–70, 175, 179–84, 187–92, 211, 213, 218, 235
Anaxagoras 9, 14, 17, 21, 74, 78–80, 94–5, 113, 117, 119, 126, 132–6, 185–6, 189–90, 201, 210, 212–14, 223, 229, 233–4
Anaximander 5–6, 9–10, 12–13, 17, 25, 31–2, 35, 37, 64, 69, 70–1, 73–105, 107–11, 114, 117, 118–19, 123, 133–4, 136, 152, 185–6, 189–90, 200, 202–10, 222–5, 227–33, 235
*apeiron* 9, 25, 32, 70, 734, 76, 78–80, 823, 86–7, 100–3, 108–10, 118, 133, 152, 157, 168, 203–4, 209, 225, 233
Aphrodite 28, 39, 41, 47–8, 181, 195, 196
*archai* 10, 25, 31–2, 38, 44, 112, 186
Archelaus 95
Ares 54
Aristophanes 1, 75
Aristotle 7, 14, 16, 20, 69–76, 78–81, 84–8, 91, 95, 102, 114, 116–17, 119–21, 128–9, 135, 139–42, 144, 148–50, 152, 156–8, 182–3, 191–2, 202–6, 210–11, 213–19, 221–22, 224, 226–29, 235
astronomy 26, 69, 90–1, 123, 193, 195
*atē* 49, 52–3, 66, 198
Athena 1, 29, 33–4, 37, 39, 41, 46–8, 77, 195–6, 206, 222
atomists 4, 13, 15, 117, 137, 140–3, 146, 148, 149, 151–2, 155, 160, 188

atoms 4, 15, 19, 80, 115, 130, 132, 136–7, 139–44, 146–49, 151–5, 157–60, 176, 181–2, 188, 192, 214
Aubrey, J. 182

Babylonia 26, 194
Babylonian 26–7, 145, 161, 198, 203
Bacchylides 1, 44, 63, 76–8, 185, 202
Bailey, C. 135, 221
Baratt, W. S. 101
Barnes, J. 9, 49–50, 99, 111, 153, 192, 207, 210, 216, 221–2, 224
Benardete, S. 101
Berryman, S. 14, 18, 89, 144, 191–3, 197, 204, 214–15, 221
Betegh, G. 127–8, 212, 221
Boyle, R. 159, 216
Broadie, S. 133, 213, 222
Burkert, W. 11
Burnet, J. 9, 109, 191–3, 207, 209, 222

Calypso 38–9, 46, 54, 206
chance 22–3, 25, 43, 47–8, 70, 80–3, 92, 110, 139, 146, 153, 155–6, 158, 198, 212, 216
Cheiron 59
Christian 76, 146, 155, 159–61, 189, 198–9, 224
Chrysippus 95
Circe 5, 28–31, 39, 43, 46–7, 49, 52, 55, 195–6, 206, 228, 233
Clay, J. S. 55, 61, 199–200, 222–3
clockwork 12, 19, 105, 160, 180, 209
Conche, M. 69, 200, 207, 223
conflict model 109, 167
control 2–3, 9, 22, 31–2, 36–8, 40, 44, 72–3, 96–7, 102, 107, 113–14, 120–1, 126, 128–30, 134–5, 169, 171–2, 175, 177–8, 185–6, 195, 201
Cornford, F. M. 78, 109, 134, 202, 209–10, 214, 223

cosmogony 69, 71–3, 81, 84, 88, 99, 100, 110, 118, 126, 133–4, 142, 154, 167, 184, 190, 193, 214
*cosmoi*, 69, 81–6, 100, 110, 134–6, 140, 142–3, 146, 155–7, 167, 189, 203
cosmology 10, 21–2, 69, 73, 82, 90–1, 102, 127, 130, 142, 168, 170, 178, 184, 190, 193, 203, 209, 212
cosmos 1–2, 9–12, 14, 21–2, 24, 26, 32, 35, 38, 61, 71–2, 74, 76, 78–89, 91–2, 103–4, 107–8, 110–11, 115–18, 121–3, 127, 129, 135–6, 138–9, 141, 143, 146, 151–3, 155–8, 160, 166–7, 172, 175, 180, 184–6, 188, 201–4, 207, 209–10, 212, 214

demiurge 11, 82, 87, 104, 107, 151, 159, 201, 208
Democritus 2, 4, 15–17, 21, 24, 80–1, 83, 86, 94–5, 111, 113, 117, 119, 130, 132, 134–7, 139–43, 145, 147–60, 166, 175, 182, 188–90, 192, 214, 216–17, 227, 232, 234
Demodocus 57
Derveni papyrus 1, 9, 37, 113, 125–8, 185–6, 201, 210, 212, 221, 229, 233
determinism 34, 41, 137, 154–6, 158, 160, 165, 170, 215–16
deterministic 137, 151, 154, 156, 160, 165–6, 170, 192
Diels, H. 91, 135, 204, 224
Dijksterhuis, E. J. 17–18, 146, 193, 214–15, 224
Diogenes 9, 70–1, 76, 84, 86–7, 91, 95, 113–14, 142, 154, 156, 185, 203, 210, 213, 216
divine 9, 12–13, 31–2, 55–6, 61, 69, 73, 82, 101–2, 108–10, 121, 133, 162–5, 167–8, 174, 181–2, 184, 186, 195, 198–9, 200, 209, 211, 218
doxography 78–80, 82, 84–5, 102, 114, 135, 139, 153, 156, 203
Draper, J. E. 111, 167, 209–10, 218, 224

early atomists 2, 4, 13–15, 83, 100, 132, 137, 139–43, 145–8, 150–5, 160, 193, 203, 214–15
Empedocles 9, 13, 17, 78–81, 83–4, 95, 109, 113, 128–30, 132, 134–5, 140, 167, 180–2, 185, 188–90, 205–6, 213, 219, 224–5, 228, 230, 233, 235

Enlightenment 13–14, 25, 186–7, 233
epistemology 5–6, 16, 21, 33, 45, 53, 56, 58, 66, 108, 154
Erinyes 47, 122–3, 127
Euripides 1, 32, 37, 102, 185, 221
explanation 4, 13–14, 16, 20–2, 64, 83, 87–8, 94, 96–7, 99, 109–12, 116, 128, 134, 140, 161, 165, 167, 170–1, 192, 201, 205

Freeman, K. 135

geocentrism 10
gods 1, 5–6, 10–11, 13–14, 21–2, 25–6, 29–34, 36–42, 44–59, 61–7, 70–1, 76–9, 94–8, 100–5, 107–8, 110–12, 121–2, 125–6, 129, 131, 161–2, 164, 166–7, 169, 171–4, 184–6, 194–5, 198–200, 205, 209, 217
Graham, D. 102, 123–4, 135, 204, 207–8, 212, 224, 226–7, 229, 231, 234
Grant, E. 21–2, 27, 193, 195, 226
Greek Enlightenment 25
Greek Miracle 2, 6, 13, 25, 38, 111, 186, 190
Guthrie, W. K. C. 51, 134, 199, 201, 206–7, 212–14, 227

Hankinson, R. 9, 49–50, 167, 170, 192, 198, 204, 217–18, 227
Harvey, W. 7–8, 116, 181–4, 189–91, 219, 221, 224–7, 230, 232, 235
heavens 1, 7, 11, 22, 26–7, 46, 76, 79–80, 85–6, 88, 90–1, 100, 106–7, 115–19, 170, 202–4, 209
Hecabe 35, 54–5, 67
Hector 35–6, 47–9, 54–5, 67, 125
Heidel, W. A. 17, 192–4, 227
Helen 30–1
helmsmen 10, 32, 73, 186
Hephaestus 6, 26, 34, 54
Hera 35, 37, 39, 42, 46, 48, 51–3, 55
Heraclitus 9–10, 12, 32, 37, 65–6, 70–1, 76, 84, 91, 93–5, 102, 113, 121–3, 127–8, 136, 152, 169, 185–6, 189, 201, 206, 208, 211–12, 226, 228, 233–4
Hermes 20, 28–31, 34, 52, 55, 59, 196, 222, 225
Herodotus 1, 59, 75, 199, 201

Hesiod 1–2, 5–6, 9–10, 13–14, 20, 24–7, 29, 31–5, 37–9, 41–51, 53–7, 59–67, 84, 87, 91–5, 97–8, 100, 103–4, 108, 110–13, 124–5, 136, 152, 161, 169, 172–4, 184–6, 194–5, 197–8, 200, 203, 205–6, 208, 217–18, 223, 231, 235
Hesse, M. 11, 27, 140, 192, 194, 214, 228
Hippocrates 23, 176, 194, 228, 230
Hippocratic 1, 9, 26, 60, 70–1, 75–6, 85, 91, 94, 113–14, 128, 161–9, 171–84, 194, 199, 201, 210, 216–18, 224, 227, 229–30, 232, 234
Hippocratic corpus 1, 60, 128, 166, 172, 176, 180, 217
Hippolytus 88, 97–8, 119, 202–4, 206, 211, 221
*historia* 6, 21–3, 26, 44–5, 59, 67, 172, 185, 193
historiography 2–3, 12, 17, 82, 109, 111, 144, 148, 150, 158, 160, 167, 180, 190
Hobbes T. 15, 140, 188
Homer 1–2, 5–6, 9–10, 13–14, 20, 24–60, 62–7, 70, 75–6, 91–5, 97–8, 100–2, 104–5, 108, 110–13, 120, 124–5, 128, 131, 136, 152, 161, 166, 169, 171–4, 184–6, 191, 193–200, 203, 205–6, 212, 217–18, 221–2, 225, 227–8, 231, 233, 235
*hupozōmata* 76, 201
Hussey, E. 52, 57, 192, 199, 210, 215, 228

*Iliad*,6, 9, 26, 28–31, 33, 35–42, 45–8, 51–7, 59–60, 75, 98, 120, 124–5, 161, 174, 196–9, 201, 205–6, 208, 218, 225, 228–9, 233
intelligence 11–12, 22, 70–1, 73, 104–5, 107, 113, 121, 135, 160, 185, 210
invariance 93, 97, 108, 111–12, 122, 150, 170, 186, 193, 209

Jaeger, W. 31–2, 109, 186, 194, 197, 209–10, 228
justice 22, 43, 50, 61–2, 78, 102, 104, 107–8, 122–3, 127, 155

*kat' aisan* 35
*kata chreōn* 32
*kata erin*,32

*kata kosmon* 35, 57
*kata moiran*,10, 26, 33, 35, 37, 43–4, 101, 186
*kata phusin* 10, 12, 26, 32–3, 35, 37, 44, 65, 70, 93, 102, 104, 106, 113–14, 123, 127, 161, 165–6, 169–72, 178, 184, 186
*kata to chreōn*,32, 37, 100–2, 104, 186, 207
*kata ton logon* 32, 65, 123
*kata tou chronou taxin* 32
Kierkegaard, S. 166, 217
Kirk, G. S. 87, 99, 102, 135, 201, 203–4, 212, 229
Kirk, G. S., Raven J. E., and Schofield, M. 99, 102, 114–15, 117, 121, 135, 201, 206–8, 211–12
*kratein* 2–3, 9, 23–6, 31–3, 37–8, 43–4, 71, 102, 113–14, 117–18, 120–6, 128–9, 132–6, 160–1, 171–2, 177–8, 184–5, 187, 189, 193
Kronos 39, 46, 52, 79, 103, 202
*kubernan* 2–3, 9, 22–5, 32, 38, 44, 69–78, 91, 113–14, 118, 120, 122–5, 132–3, 136, 160–1, 171, 178, 184–5, 187, 189, 193
*kubernētēs* 9, 33, 72, 74–6, 81–2, 104, 186

Laplace's Demon 137, 152–4, 160, 165, 192
Lavoisier, A. 19
law 9, 11–12, 43, 45, 93, 98, 101–2, 104–5, 108–9, 121–3, 127, 132, 147, 192, 211, 215
laws 1, 4, 11, 38, 45, 49–51, 67, 98, 104–5, 121, 128, 146–8, 150, 156, 176, 211
Lesher, J. 59, 64, 66, 95, 199–200, 206, 218, 229
Leucippus 2, 4, 15–17, 21, 24, 80–1, 83, 94–5, 110, 130, 132, 134–5, 137, 139–43, 145, 147–60, 175, 188–90, 192, 197, 214, 227, 234
like to like 10, 13, 22, 32–3, 70, 80, 88, 92, 110, 124, 130–2, 137–40, 143, 147, 153, 155, 157–8, 161, 174–6, 179, 186, 188, 197, 204, 213–14, 218
Lloyd, G. E. R. 21, 95–6, 148, 178, 192–5, 198, 206, 210, 215–17, 219, 229–30
Lonie, I. M. 14, 175–80, 182, 192, 218–19, 230
Love and Strife 9, 13, 128–30, 140, 181, 188

machine 4, 11, 14–17, 19, 105, 107, 123, 128, 136–7, 142–6, 160, 176, 185, 187, 200
macrocosm 7–8, 13, 15, 113, 115–17, 135–6, 143, 161, 169–70, 177, 183, 187–9, 211, 218
magic 20, 28–30, 34, 43, 115, 129, 163–4, 166, 174, 194–5
Mansfeld, J. 87, 203–4, 207, 230
materialism 4, 15–16, 21, 27
mathematics 8, 11, 14–16, 105, 111, 123, 127–8, 137, 143, 147, 149–52, 154, 160, 176, 179, 181, 187–8
*mechanē* 105, 107, 143–5, 147
*mēchanē* 14, 185, 187, 195, 200, 217
mechanical 2–4, 6–8, 11–20, 22–3, 34, 69, 78, 81, 88–90, 92–3, 99–100, 105, 111–12, 118–19, 125, 128, 133–4, 137, 139, 140, 143–6, 149–51, 154, 159–61, 172, 175–84, 187–90, 192–4
mechanical philosophy 3–4, 11–12, 15–20, 105, 139–40, 145, 149, 188–90, 192
mechanics 4, 14–16, 18–19, 137, 146–7, 150–2, 154, 176, 187–8, 192
mechanism 2–3, 6, 12, 15–16, 20, 34, 79, 82, 89, 136, 146, 160, 176, 181, 185, 187, 190
mechanist 2–3, 7–8, 13–15, 24, 78, 150, 181, 184, 187–90
mechanistic 3–6, 14, 16–18, 83, 92, 128, 140, 146, 150–1, 175–6, 178–9, 180–2, 189–90, 192, 219
mechanists 2, 4, 14–15, 22–4, 137, 140, 143, 160, 187–8, 190, 215
mechanization 7, 18
Menelaus 28, 33, 39, 41, 47–8
Meriones 47
meteorology 1, 93, 96–8, 100, 108, 205
Metrodorus 95, 142
microcosm 7–8, 13, 15, 113, 115–17, 135–6, 143, 161, 168–70, 177, 183, 187–9, 211, 218
modelling 4, 16, 19, 89, 101, 204
*moira*, 5–6, 10, 26–7, 33–45, 47–8, 54–5, 66–7, 101–2, 104–5, 108, 113, 123–5, 128, 186, 197, 199
*moira krataiē*, 35
Moly 20, 28, 30–1, 55–6, 59, 193, 222

Muses 5, 33, 36, 42, 45, 56–67, 96, 108, 129, 172, 174, 184, 199–200
*muthos* to *logos* 14, 25, 77, 187

nature 1–7, 10–21, 23–8, 31–3, 38, 41–5, 55–7, 59, 62, 65, 67, 70–1, 74, 76, 80, 82, 84, 93, 97, 100, 102, 104–9, 111–14, 118, 122–4, 126–32, 135–6, 139, 144–5, 150–1, 153, 155–6, 159, 161–9, 171–3, 177, 179, 182, 184–7, 189–1, 193–5, 198, 200, 203, 217
necromancy 29
Nestor 53
Newton, I. 16, 19, 140, 1478, 150, 159, 191, 215–16, 221, 232

Odysseus 14, 20, 28–33, 37–40, 46–7, 50, 52, 54–5, 59, 77, 91, 97, 124, 130, 195–6, 225
*Odyssey* 5–6, 9, 28–40, 46–7, 50–1, 54–5, 57, 60, 74, 82, 97–8, 124–5, 130, 138, 174, 193, 195–8, 201, 205–6, 208, 212, 217–18, 222, 225, 228–9, 231, 233–4
ontologies 4
order 1–2, 6, 9–13, 24–6, 30–3, 35–8, 44–6, 48, 52, 57, 59, 61, 67, 75, 81, 83, 88, 92, 101–2, 104–8, 110, 114–15, 117, 125–6, 131, 136, 142, 146, 150, 154, 159, 162, 166, 170, 173, 177, 185–6, 197, 212
*ou mallon* 15, 23, 83, 137, 142, 151–60, 188–9, 214, 227

Pantheism 165, 167, 210
*para phusin* 161, 172, 184, 186
Paris 28, 39, 41, 47, 223, 228–30, 232
Parmenides 9, 15, 66, 70–2, 83, 91, 95, 100, 113, 118, 124–5, 131, 144–5, 148–9, 152–4, 158, 160, 185, 188–90, 198, 200, 206, 214–16, 218, 224–5, 227, 231–2
Patroclus 36, 39, 48
Persephone 29, 196
Phaeacians 6, 32, 34, 73
*pharmaka* 30–1, 129, 196
*pharmakon* 29–31, 196
Philolaus, 10, 228
*phusis* 3, 6, 12, 14, 20–3, 26, 28, 31, 35, 44–5, 55, 59, 67, 74, 97–8, 108, 123–4, 161–2, 168, 173, 185–7, 193, 209, 221, 230
Pindar 1, 44, 62–4, 75–7, 185, 200, 222

Plato 3, 9, 11–13, 21–3, 70, 72–6, 80–2, 84, 87, 90–1, 95, 105–7, 110, 115–16, 119, 123, 131–5, 138, 140, 151, 159, 171, 181, 185, 187, 190, 193–4, 199, 201, 208–11, 213–14, 217, 221–2, 226–7, 229–31, 234
poets 1–2, 6, 10, 26, 42, 44, 51, 62, 77–8, 92–3, 95–6, 104, 185–7, 208
*polupharmakos* 30–1, 196
Polydamna 30–1
Poseidon 1, 39, 46, 48–9, 50–1, 97, 195, 198, 233
Priam 35, 54–5
Prometheus 42, 53, 62
Pyle, A. 15, 140, 192, 214, 232

Redard, G. 101, 207–8, 232
regularities 1, 12, 46, 93, 103, 105, 107, 160, 185, 187
religion 2, 109–11, 167–8, 187, 210
*rhabdos* 29, 233
Rochberg, F. 26, 43, 194–5, 198, 232

sacred disease 94, 161–5, 217–18, 234
Sarpedon 35–6, 39, 41, 47
science 2–7, 11, 13–14, 16, 18–19, 93, 109, 111, 115, 117, 123, 136, 145–6, 149–52, 154, 160, 165, 167–8, 176, 181, 185, 187, 190, 209
Sedley, D. 148, 156, 181, 210, 213, 215, 219, 233
Seneca 142, 147
ships 9, 33, 51, 55, 59, 73–6, 171, 179, 186, 195, 200–1, 205, 222, 234
*skopein* 22–3, 44–5, 59, 67, 172–3, 185, 194
Snell-Frankel thesis 58
Socrates 3, 21–3, 70, 132, 193–4, 223, 226, 230
Socrates' autobiography 22–3
Solon 1, 50, 103, 199–200, 208, 231
Sophocles 1, 77, 201
steering 2, 6, 9–10, 32, 44, 69–78, 80–3, 87, 89, 91–3, 100–1, 104–5, 107–8, 110–11, 122, 167–70, 185–6, 209–10
Stobaeus 95, 98, 119, 203–6, 210–11, 214, 216
Strato 95

Tannery, A. 90, 204, 233
targeting thesis 94

*taxis* 81, 88, 90–1, 102–4, 110
Taylor, C. C. W. 135, 138, 141, 148, 214, 234
Temkin, O. 161, 217, 225, 234
Terpander 1
Teucer 47
Thamyris 56
Theognis 103, 200, 208
*Theogony*, 42–3, 51, 57, 60–2, 91, 94, 97, 103, 124, 161, 174, 194, 198–9, 205–6, 208, 217–18, 231, 235
Theophrastus 74, 78, 85–7, 201, 203, 214, 230, 233
Thetis 41, 48, 52, 54
Thucydides 1, 59, 66, 218
*tuchē*, 23, 48, 135
Typhoeus 51, 94–5, 97, 206

Unguru, S. 8, 143, 179, 191–2, 234

Vlastos, G. 80, 103, 134, 198, 201–2, 208–10, 212, 214, 234
vortex 13, 19, 79–80, 88, 117–19, 130, 132, 134–5, 138–9, 142–4, 153–8, 160, 188, 190
vortices 69, 79–81, 83, 92, 117–18, 132, 134–5, 139–40, 155–8, 160, 188–9, 202

West, M. L. 79–80, 91, 111, 198, 202–4, 208, 210, 235
wheels 19, 85, 89, 140, 144–5, 189, 203
White, A. 111, 167, 209–10, 218, 235
wind 46, 93, 97–8, 114, 119, 147, 171, 177, 180, 195–6, 206
winds 29, 40, 46, 48, 75, 86, 94–5, 97–8, 119, 129, 142, 163, 196, 206
*Works and Days* 33–4, 42–3, 46, 48, 50–1, 53, 60–2, 97, 103, 161, 198, 200, 206, 208, 231

Xenophanes 9, 54, 64–5, 94–5, 110, 113, 120–1, 152, 166, 185, 193, 199–200, 203, 205–6, 210–11, 217, 224–5, 229, 231

Zeus 1, 28, 33–43, 46–56, 61–2, 69, 74, 77, 87, 94, 97–8, 103, 108, 120, 125–6, 161, 186, 194–5, 197–200, 205–6, 212, 230
zoogony 5, 21, 74, 93, 98–100, 110–11, 193

www.ingramcontent.com/pod-product-compliance
Lightning Source LLC
Chambersburg PA
CBHW072146290426
44111CB00012B/1986